1 PETER
JOY IN SUFFERING

The Proclaim Commentary Series

THE PROCLAIM COMMENTARY SERIES

1 PETER
JOY IN SUFFERING

NEW TESTAMENT
VOLUME 21

MATTHEW STEVEN BLACK

WENATCHEE, WASHINGTON

1 Peter: Joy in Suffering (The Proclaim Commentary Series)
Copyright © 2021 by Matthew Steven Black
ISBN: 978-1-954858-15-2 (Print Book)
978-1-954858-16-9 (eBook)

Proclaim Publishers
PO Box 2082, Wenatchee, WA 98807
proclaimpublishers.com

Cover art: *Taurus Mountain Range, Turkey by Haykirdi*

Unless otherwise quoted, Scripture quotations are from the ESV® Bible (The Holy Bible, English Standard Version®), copyright © 2001, 2016 by Crossway, a publishing ministry of Good News Publishers. Used by permission. All rights reserved.

Scripture quotations marked NASB are taken from the New American Standard Bible®, Copyright© 1960, 1962, 1963, 1968, 1971, 1972, 1973, 1975, 1977, 1995 by The Lockman Foundation. Used by permission.

Scripture quotations marked NKJV are taken from the New King James Version®. Copyright© 1982 by Thomas Nelson. Used by permission. All rights reserved.

Scripture quotations marked NIV are taken from The Holy Bible New International Version®, NIV® Copyright© 1973, 1978, 1984, 2011 by Biblica, Inc.® Used by permission. All rights reserved worldwide.

Scripture quotations marked CSB are taken from the Christian Standard Bible®, Used by permission. All rights reserved. CSB© 2017 Holman Bible Publishers.

Scripture quotations marked NLT are taken from the Holy Bible, New Living Translation, Copyright© 1996, 2004, 2007 by Tyndale House Foundation. Used by permission of Tyndale House Publishers, Inc., Carol Stream, Illinois 60188. All rights reserved.

Scripture quotations marked KJV are taken from the King James Version of the Bible.

All rights reserved. No part of this publication may be reproduced, stored in a retrieval system or transmitted in any form by any means, electronic, mechanical, photocopy, recording or otherwise, without the prior permission of the publisher, except as provided by USA copyright law.

Notes: (1) Ancient quotations have been at times changed to the ESV as well as some archaic language updated, and additional phrases added for clarification. At times verse references (non-existent until recent times) have been interspersed as well to guide the modern reader. (2) We have done our best to be careful in footnoting. Due to the nature of the sermonic material, various items are quoted freely, and may not have proper footnoting. If any great error is noticed, please contact the publisher, and it will be remedied in whatever way is available to us.

First Printing, January 2022
Manufactured in the United States of America

Dedicated to one of my dearest friends on earth: Dr. Ahmed Joktan. You have suffered more than any Christian I know. I esteem how you bear in your body the marks of our Lord Jesus. You are truly an elect exile on this earth.

CONTENTS

INTRODUCTION 21
    Author 21
    Recipients 22
    The Context of 1 Peter 22
    Summary 23

1 | 1 PETER 1:1-2 ELECT EXILES 25
    In Relation to the World, We are Exiles (1:1) 27
        Biblical History of Exile 27
        Examples of Good Exiles 27
        Example of a Bad Exile 27
        What is an "Elect Exile"? 28
        The Place of Exile 29
        Who are the Elect Exiles? 29
            The Jews Only? 29
            More Likely, Christians of all Cultures 29
    In Relation to God, We are Elect (1:1-2) 31
        Chosen by God the Father 31
        Sanctified by the Spirit 33
        Purchased for obedience by the Son 35
            Sprinkling of Blood at Sinai Covenant 35
            Sprinkling of Blood for a Leper 36
            Sprinkling of Blood for the service of Priests 37
    Despite Our Exile, Christians are Blessed (1:2d) 38

2 | 1 PETER 1:3-5 BORN AGAIN 39
    The Source of the New Birth (1:3a) 40
        The Blessing of God the Father 40
        Blessing Despite Suffering 41
    The Motive of the New Birth (1:3b) 41
        Metaphors of God's Mercy 41
        The Recipients of God's Mercy 42
        The Message of God's Mercy 44
        The Blessing of God's Mercy 44
    The Reward of the New Birth (1:4) 45
        God Himself is Our Inheritance 45
        The Holy Spirit is Our Inheritance 46
        The New Creation is Our Inheritance 46

An Imperishable Inheritance 46
An Undefiled Inheritance 47
An Unfading Inheritance 47
The Receiving of the New Birth (1:5) 48
Guarded by Faith 48
Empowered by Faith 49

3 | 1 PETER 1:6-9 GLORIOUS SUFFERING 51

The Promise in Our Suffering (1:6) 52
The Delight of God's Promise 53
The Design of God's Promise 53
The Dependence on God's Promise 53
The Purpose of God's Suffering (1:7) 54
To Be the Prototype of Christ 54
To Bring Praise to Christ at His Coming 55
The Paradox in Our Suffering (1:8-9) 56
We cannot see Christ, but we love him. 56
We cannot see Christ, but we joyfully trust him. 57
We cannot see Christ, but he's still working on us. 57

4 | 1 PETER 1:10-21 BE HOLY 59

Holiness Encountered 60
The Privilege of Holiness (1:10-12) 61
A Privilege Greater than the Prophets 61
A Privilege Greater than the Angels 62
A Privilege to Thank God for 63
The Practice of Holiness (1:13-16) 63
Fight with Preparation 63
Fight with Sobriety 64
Fight with Expectancy 65
Fight with Humility 66
Fight with Identity 67
The Price of Holiness (1:17-21) 68
Conduct Yourselves with Fear 68
Fear the Lord as Father 68
Fear the Lord as Foreigners 69
Fear the Lord as Forgiver 69
Conduct Yourselves with Faith 71
Faith in God's Plan 71
Faith is God's Gift 71

5 | 1 PETER 1:22-25 THE LIVING WORD ... 73

God's Word is Powerful (1:22-23) ... 74
- Power for Purity ... 74
- Power for Obedience ... 76
- Power for Love ... 77

God's Word is Alive (1:23) ... 78
- God's Word is Alive like a Birth ... 78
- God's Word is Alive like a Seed ... 79
- God's Word is Alive like a Roommate ... 80

God's Word is Lasting (1:24-25) ... 80
- What Doesn't Last ... 80
- What Lasts ... 81
- What Love! ... 82

6 | 1 PETER 2:1-3 DESIRING GOD ... 85

What hinders our appetite for God? (2:1) ... 86
- Residing with undetected sin will destroy your appetite. ... 86
  - "Put Away" Illustrated ... 86
  - "Put Away" Practiced ... 87
  - "Put Away" Personalized ... 87
  - "Put Away" Commanded ... 88
- Rationalizing respectable sin will destroy your appetite. ... 88
  - Hurting Others (Malice) ... 89
  - Hiding Your Sin (Deceit) ... 91
  - Impressing Others (Hypocrisy) ... 92
  - High Mindedness (Envy) ... 93
  - Hurtful Speech (Slander) ... 94

What helps our appetite for God? (2:2-3) ... 95
- A New Heart ... 95
- New Desires ... 95
- New Experience ... 96
- A New Family ... 96
  - Applications ... 97

7 | 1 PETER 2:4 JESUS OUR CORNERSTONE ... 99

Jesus is the Living Stone (2:4a) ... 101
- Humanity, Dead Stones ... 102
- Jesus, the Living Stone ... 102
- The Church, a Living Temple ... 103

Jesus is the Rejected Stone (2:4b) ... 104
Jesus is the Chosen Stone (2:4c) ... 106

Jesus is the Precious Stone (2:4d) 107

8 | 1 PETER 2:5-9 GOD'S SPIRITUAL TEMPLE 109

We are God's House (1:5) 110
- A House of Living Stones 110
- A House that is Growing 110
- A House with Priests 112
  - *As Priests, We Have Access* 112
  - *As Priests, We Offer Sacrifices* 112

Jesus is the Cornerstone (1:6) 116
God is the Architect (1:7-9) 116
- Honor the Architect 117
- Fear the Architect 117
  - *Destined to Stumble* 117
  - *Destined to Salvation* 118

9 | 1 PETER 1:9-10 PRAISING OUR CORNERSTONE 119

You are a Chosen Race (1:9a) 120
- We are a Chosen People 121
- We are a Transformed People 122

You are a Royal Priesthood (1:9b) 122
- The Power of the Priesthood 122
- The Power of Praise 123

You are a Holy Nation (1:9c) 124
- A New Nation 124
- A Holy Nation 125

You are a Treasured People (1:9-10) 125
- A People Possessed by God 125
- A People Praising God 126
- A People Adopted by God 127

10 | 1 PETER 2:11-12 WINNING OVER THE FLESH 129

Remember Your Homeland (2:11a) 130
- We are Sojourners and Exiles 130
- We are Exiles 131

Remember Your Victory (2:11b) 133
- Understanding Controlling Desires 133
- Examples of Controlling Desires 133
  - *Fear / Negative Emotions / Depression* 134
  - *Marriage / Relationships* 134
  - *Acceptance / Reputation* 134
  - *Materialism* 135

- *Pleasure* *135*
- *Even "Good" Things* *136*
- Victory Over Controlling Desires 136
- Remember Your Mission (2:12) 138
  - A Mission to Walk Honorably 138
  - A Mission to Walk Eschatologically 138

11 | 1 PETER 1:13-17 HONORING PAGAN GOVERNMENT 141

- Our Master (2:13-14a) 142
  - The Meaning of Submission 143
  - The Motive of Submission 143
  - The Manner of Submission 144
  - The Mystery of Submission 144
- Our Mission (2:15-16) 145
  - The Integrity of Our Mission 145
  - The Tension of Our Mission 146
  - The Order of Our Mission 146
    - *Honor Everyone* *146*
    - *Love Your Forever Family* *147*
    - *Fear God* *147*
    - *Honor Government Leaders* *147*
- Our Message 148
  - Proclaim the Message 148
  - Live Out the Message 149

12 | 1 PETER 2:18-21 SLAVES OF JESUS 153

- A Call to Submit (2:18-19) 155
  - The Instruction to Slaves 155
  - The History of Slavery 155
    - *Modern Slavery* *156*
    - *Slavery in Israel* *156*
    - *Slavery in Rome* *157*
  - The Attitude of a Slave 158
- A Call to Sanctification (2:20-21) 159
  - Growing in Endurance 159
  - Growing in Imitation 159
- A Call to Sonship (2:21b) 160
  - God's Ownership 161
  - Complete Obedience 162
  - Singular Devotion 162
  - Total Dependence 163
  - Simultaneously Slaves and Sons 164

13 | 1 PETER 2:21-25 FOLLOW IN HIS STEPS...165
  The One Way We Cannot Follow Jesus 165
  The Concept of Following Christ (2:21)...167
    The Call to Christlikeness...167
    The Process of Christlikeness 168
    Examples of Christlikeness 169
  The Practice of Following Christ (2:21-23) 170
    Suffering with Christ...170
    Denying Sin with Christ..172
    Gentle with Christ..172
    Trusting with Christ 173
    Obedient with Christ 173
    Application 174
  The Benefits of Following Christ (2:24-25) 174
    New Life in Jesus 174
    Healing in Jesus 175
    Shepherding by Jesus 175

14 | 1 PETER 3:1-6 THE WIFE OF INNER BEAUTY 179
  The Imperishable Beauty of Christ (3:1) 181
    The Beauty of Christ's Submission 181
    The Beauty of Submission in All Realms...181
    Submitted to God's Word..181
  The Wife's Imperishable Beauty Described (3:1-2)................182
    The Power of a Submitted Life 182
      The Preoccupied Husband..183
      The Hobby Husband 184
      The Angry Husband..184
      The Neglectful Husband..184
      The Dangerous Husband...184
      All Husbands Need Christ...185
    The Picture of a Submitted Life 185
      What Submission Means 185
      What Submission Does Not Mean 185
    The Quietness of a Submitted Life 186
      The Natural Inclination of a Wife..187
      The Most Powerful Tool of the Wife 188
  The Wife's Imperishable Beauty Adorned (3:3-4)................... 188
    Our Temptation with External Adorning 189
    Inward Adorning..189
      The Hidden Person of the Heart...189
      A Gentle, Quiet Spirit 190

The Wife's Imperishable Beauty Exemplified (3:5-6) 191
   The Example of the Holy Women 191
   The Example of Sarah 191
   An Example that May Be Frightening 192

15 | 1 PETER 3:7 THE LISTENING HUSBAND 193

Spend Time with Her 194
Study Her 195
   The Intimacy of Listening 196
   The Effort of Listening 196
   The Areas of Listening 198
Honor Her 198
Protect Her 200
   With Patience 200
   With Care 200
   With Gentleness 201
   With Accountability 201
   With a Good Example 201
Open Up to Her 202
Pray with Her 202

16 | 1 PETER 3:8 THE HARD WORK OF CHRISTIAN FELLOWSHIP 205

Work Hard for Unity 208
   Unity Begins with Union with Christ 208
   Unity Requires Hard Work 209
   Unity Requires Death to Self 209
   Unity Requires Love 210
   Unity Requires Tolerance 210
   Unity Requires Forgiveness 211
   Unity is Not Uniformity but Harmony 211
   Unity is a Testimony to the Gospel 212
Work Hard for Sympathy 213
   The Adoption of Sympathy 213
   The Actions of Sympathy 213
Work Hard for Family 214
   The Joy of God's Forever Family 214
   Membership in God's Forever Family 215
Work Hard for Empathy 216
   A Forgiving Heart 216
   A Big Heart 217
   A Gentle Heart 218

Hard for Humility 218
Humility Defined 219
Humility Commanded 219

17 | 1 PETER 3:9-12 BLESSED TO BE A BLESSING 223

Don't Stress (3:9a) 224
The Fact of Stress 224
Don't Focus on Stress 225
Be Sure to Bless (3:9b) 225
The Call to Bless 225
The Choice to Bless 226
The Music of Blessing 226
The Stew of Bitterness 227
The Covering of Blessing 227
Make Sure You Progress (3:10-11) 228
The Pathway to Progress 228
The Hinderance to Progress 229
The Measure of Our Progress 230
You Need to Rest (3:12) 231
Rest in the Lord's Shepherding 231
Rest in the Lord's Sympathy 232
Rest in the Lord's Sovereignty 233

18 | 1 PETER 3:13-22 GIVING AN ANSWER 235

Be Ready to Suffer (3:13-14) 237
Our Foe in Suffering 237
Our Focus in Suffering 238
Our Blessing in Suffering 239
Our Peace in Suffering 239
Be Ready to Speak (3:15-18) 240
Have a Right Heart 240
Have a Ready Answer 241
Have a Radical Evangelism 242
Have a Respectful Attitude 243
Toward the Lost 243
Toward God 244
Have a Restful Conscience 244
The Unrighteous' Shame is Eternal 245
The Righteous' Shame is Only Temporary 245
Have the Right Message 246
Christ's Substitutional Death 246
Christ's Glorious Resurrection 248

Be Ready to Celebrate (3:19-22) 248
- Victory at Christ's Resurrection 248
- Victory in Noah's Day 249
- Victory in Our Day 250
- Christ Victorious Over All! 251

19 | 1 PETER 4:1-11 A SPIRITUALLY GIFTED LIFE 253
- Learning Self-Denial 254

We Live a Crucified Life (4:1-6) 256
- *Definition of Self-Denial* *256*
- The Example of Jesus (4:1-2) 257
  - *Arm Yourself with Christ's Thinking* *257*
  - *Arm Yourself with Christ's Freedom* *258*
  - *Arm Yourself with Christ's Focus* *259*
- The Example of Your Past Life (4:3-5) 260
  - *Once Crazy for the World* *260*
  - *Now Crazy for Jesus* *261*
  - *Now Trusting in Jesus* *261*
- The Example of the Martyrs (4:6) 261

We Live an Abundant Life (4:7-9) 262
- The Abundant Life of Prayer 262
  - *Prayer Requires Self Control* *263*
  - *Prayer Requires Sobermindedness* *263*
- The Abundant Life of Forgiveness 263
- The Abundant Life of Service 264

We Live a Shared Life (4:10-11) 265
- A Spiritual Gift is Given to Every Believer 265
- A Spiritual Gift is a Supernatural Ability 266
- A Spiritual Gift is a Stewardship 266
- Spiritual Gifts Differ 267
- A Spiritual Gift is to be God-Glorifying 267

20 | 1 PETER 4:12-19 WHY SUFFERING? 269

Suffering Brings Refinement (4:12) 271
- Refinement is for the Saints of God 271
- Refinement Should Not be a Surprise 272
- Refinement is for Our Sanctification 272

Suffering Prepares us for Glorification (4:13) 273
- We Share in Christ's Suffering Now 273
  - *Suffering with Christ in Evangelism* *274*
  - *Suffering with Christ in Our Union with Him* *274*
  - *Suffering with Christ in Our Sanctification* *274*
- We Will Rejoice with Christ Soon in Glory 275

Suffering Brings Transformation (4:14) ... 275
   Transformed through Suffering ... 275
   Transformed by the Spirit ... 276

Suffering Brings Evaluation (4:15-18) ... 277
   God Evaluates the Pattern of Our Lives ... 277
   God Evaluates the Passion of Our Heart ... 278
   God Evaluates the People of God ... 278
      It Means Believers are Marked ... 279
      It Means Believers are Pruned ... 280
      It Means Believers are Protected ... 281
      It Means Unbelievers are Judged ... 281

Suffering Brings Mobilization (4:19) ... 282
   Mobilized by God's Will ... 282
   Mobilized To Do Good ... 283

21 | 1 PETER 5:1-4 THE CALLING OF SHEPHERDS ... 285

   Sheep are Dumb ... 287
   Sheep are Distracted ... 287
   Sheep are Dirty ... 288

Shepherds are called to Precede the Flock (5:1) ... 288
   Precede the Flock in Suffering ... 289
   Precede the Flock in Glory ... 290
      The Glory of the Transfiguration ... 290
      The Glory of the Second Coming ... 290

Shepherds are called to Feed the Flock (5:2) ... 291
   Feed with Reverence ... 291
   Feed with Substance ... 292
   Feed with Balance ... 293
   Feed with Gladness ... 293

Shepherds are called to Lead the Flock (5:2-3) ... 295
   Lead with Engagement ... 295
   Lead with Enthusiasm ... 296
   Lead with Effort ... 296
   Lead as an Example ... 297
      An Example, not a Control Freak ... 297

Shepherds Recieve a Crown for the Flock (5:4) ... 298
   The Chief Shepherd's Return ... 298
   The Chief Shepherd's Accounting ... 298
   The Chief Shepherd's Crown ... 298

22 | 1 PETER 5:5-7 GROWING IN SPIRITUAL MATURITY ... 301

Grow in Accountability (5:5a) ... 302

- The Sweat of Accountability 303
- The Scope of Accountability 304
- The Supervisors of Accountability 304

Grow in Humility (5:5b-6) 306
- The Robe of Humility 306
- The Relevance of Humility 307
- The Reward of Humility 307

Grow in Serenity (5:7) 308
- The Damage of Sinful Worry 308
- The Delight of God's Care 309

23 | 1 PETER 5:8-14 GROWING IN SPIRITUAL WARFARE 313

Be Ready for the Fight (5:8-9) 315
- Be Sober-minded 315
- Be Watchful 316
  - *Satan is a Hidden Lion* 316
  - *Satan is a Hungry Lion* 317
  - *Satan is a Hateful Lion* 317
- Be Firm 318
  - *Engage in the Fight* 318
  - *Engage with Faith* 318

Remain Focused (5:9) 319
- Focus on Christ, Not Satan 319
- Focus on Christ, Not Your Suffering 319
- Focus on Christ, not Your Sin 320
- Fight with Christ's Weapons 320
- Fight Side by Side with Christ's Forever Family 321

Rest in God's Favor (5:10-11) 321
- The Lord is with you in Suffering 322
- The Lord is with you in Sanctification 322
- The Lord is with you in His Sovereignty 323

Rejoice in God's Family (5:12-14) 323
- Examples of Spiritual Growth 323
  - *Silas, the Faithful Brother* 323
  - *The Chosen Church at Babylon (Rome)* 324
  - *Peter's "Son" John Mark* 325
- Examples of Saintly Love 325

ABBREVIATIONS

Common

cf – Latin "conferatur", compare, or see, or see also
ff – and following (pages or verses)
i.e. – Latin "id est", that is
e.g. – Latin "exempli gratia", for example

Books of the Bible

OLD TESTAMENT

Genesis	Gen	Esther	Est
Exodus	Exo	Job	Job
Leviticus	Lev	Psalms	Psa
Numbers	Num	Proverbs	Pro
Deuteronomy	Deut	Ecclesiastes	Ecc
Joshua	Josh	Song of Solomon	Song
Judges	Jdg	Isaiah	Isa
Ruth	Rth	Jeremiah	Jer
1 Samuel	1 Sam	Lamentations	Lam
2 Samuel	2 Sam	Ezekiel	Eze
1 Kings	1 Kgs	Daniel	Dan
2 Kings	2 Kgs	Hosea	Hos
1 Chronicles	1 Chr	Joel	Joel
2 Chronicles	2 Chr	Amos	Amos
Ezra	Ezr	Obadiah	Oba
Nehemiah	Neh	Jonah	Jonah

Micah	Mic	Haggai	Hag
Nahum	Nah	Zechariah	Zech
Habakkuk	Hab	Malachi	Mal
Zephaniah	Zeph		

New Testament

Matthew	Mt	Titus	Titus
Mark	Mk	Philemon	Phm
Luke	Lk	Hebrews	Heb
John	Jn	James	Jas
Acts	Acts	1 Peter	1 Pet
Romans	Rom	2 Peter	2 Pet
1 Corinthians	1 Cor	1 John	1 Jn
2 Corinthians	2 Cor	2 John	2 Jn
Galatians	Gal	3 John	3 Jn
Ephesians	Eph	Jude	Jud
Philippians	Phil	Revelation	Rev
Colossians	Col		
1 Thessalonians	1 Thess		
2 Thessalonians	2 Thess		
1 Timothy	1 Tim		
2 Timothy	2 Tim		

INTRODUCTION

In this you rejoice, though now for a little while, if necessary, you have been grieved by various trials, so that the tested genuineness of your faith—more precious than gold that perishes though it is tested by fire—may be found to result in praise and glory and honor at the revelation of Jesus Christ.

1 PETER 1:6-7

As Christians we are continually under attack; we face many trials that weigh us down because of our beliefs, which are founded in Jesus the Christ and his life. Jesus lived a perfect life but that does not mean he was immune to persecution, trials, and suffering; Jesus was tempted, beaten, betrayed and killed and yet still did not sin.

As believers we are the "elect exiles" who don't belong here. We await a new heaven and a new earth. Here, like our Lord, we will be rejected, suffering for our faith.

AUTHOR

Peter, one of Jesus' twelve disciples, wrote 1 Peter encouraging believers who were, and are, experiencing persecution (1:1). Peter's familiarity with the Old Testament and Jesus is evident in this book as he relates several teachings toward how believers should respond to persecution based on the life that Christ lived fulfilling the Old Testament.

Peter was once called Simon which means "one who hears." However, sometimes Simon seems to have had a difficult time listening on occasion. Jesus gave Simon his new name, Peter, which means "rock." Peter was the originally "Rocky"!

RECIPIENTS

The letter is addressed to Christians scattered in "Pontus, Galatia, Cappadocia, Asia, and Bithynia" (1:1). These names all referred to Roman provinces in Asia Minor, north of the Taurus Mountains in modern-day Turkey. These territories had been impacted by Greco-Roman culture and had been under Roman control from the mid-first century B.C.

Dispersion and exile are key themes. Peter addresses his Christians recipients as "elect exiles" (1:1) which very much carries on the theme of exile to Babylon during the 70 years of captivity. He closes the letter by giving greetings from the Christians in a metaphorical Babylon, referencing Rome where Peter would later die by being crucified upside down. The message is that we are not at home here on earth. We are in exile. He says those Christians in Babylon are "chosen." So Peter begins and ends with the theme of election. We may be rejected by the world, but we are chosen and loved by God.

THE CONTEXT OF 1 PETER

It was the mid-60s A.D. A tyrant named Nero was on the throne. He was just three years old when his father died. It was little loss to the boy. for his father had been a killer, a bully, and a cheat. His mother took over the family trade and continued the boy's education. She murdered his stepfather with a dish of poisoned mushrooms. He was reared in squalor and proved a notable son to his parents. While still young, he committed his first murder, killing a teenage boy who stood in his way and watching him die with callous indifference. He married at fifteen but soon had his wife killed. He married again and slew his second wife too. In order to marry a third time, he murdered the husband of the woman he wanted. His mother annoyed him; so he arranged her murder, first by guile, but when that was unsuccessful, without pretense. He was an ugly man with a bull neck, beetle brows, a flat nose, and a tough mouth. He had a pot belly, spindly legs, bad skin, and offensive odor. At the age of thirty-one he was sentenced to death by flogging. He fled to a dingy basement and, in the house of a slave, cut his own throat. He gave the infant church its first taste of things to come. He burned Rome to the ground in order to rebuild in his own name. They say he played the fiddle while Rome was burning, and he blamed it all on the Christians. He was the first of the persecuting Caesars of Rome.[1]

1 Peter was likely written prior to the persecutions by Nero, which began in A.D. 64, sometime between A.D. 61-64. Nero's persecutions are often associated with arenas in which Christians were thrown into battle against fierce animals. However, it is likely, Peter was not writing to address physical persecution taking place but verbal.

The epistle was probably written from Rome however uncertainty arises because the epistle states in 5:13 that it was written from Babylon but this was probably just a metaphorical reference for Rome.

SUMMARY

In the book of 1 Peter we find three main sections: salvation (1:3—2:10), submission (2:11—3:12) and suffering (3:13—5:11). Each of these sections were written to encourage believers to remain strong in the foundation that had been laid by Jesus through his disciple Peter. In the section about salvation Peter affirms that trials bring about renewal as they burn away our past way of living toward living holier lives in Christ. Chapters 2 and 3 begin to focus on our role in being submissive to the powers above us: roles between spouses, the government and God are explicitly mentioned in these passages. Finally, the book culminates in chapters 4 thru 5 about how to we should respond to suffering.

The book of 1 Peter emphasizes that suffering brings perseverance. It is by suffering that we are humbled and grow closer to the Lord. Christ allows suffering in our lives to mold us into the person he has created, conforming us to his image (Rom 8:29). As we go about life sometimes it can be discouraging, but it is important to recognize that the suffering we face develops perseverance in our lives and ultimately should sanctify us toward living holy lives.

Those who persevere in faith while suffering persecution should be full of hope. They will certainly enjoy end-time salvation, since they already enjoy God's saving promises through Christ's death and resurrection.

---

[1] John Phillips, *Exploring Revelation: An Expository Commentary*, The John Phillips Commentary Series (Kregel; WORDsearch Corp., 2009), Re 2:8–11.

1 | 1 PETER 1:1-2
ELECT EXILES

Peter, an apostle of Jesus Christ, to those who are elect exiles...
1 PETER 1:1A

Do you know what an exile is? It means you are not at home. You are "exiled" from your home. Some of us have been in very strange places, and we've felt out of place, like we didn't fit in. I remember moving from Chicago to Louisiana. In Louisiana, everybody talked funny. They said things like, "Y'all" and I'm "fixin'" to do something. The only thing I ever fixed was my bike, but in Louisiana, they're fixin' everything. In Louisiana, I learned how to eat red beans and rice and jambalaya. They were Cajuns there. It almost never snowed there. When they read the "Night before Christmas" Santa's sleigh had flying alligators instead of reindeer. I felt out of place.

Then later on, Jill and I moved to Spain. We felt out of place there too. We had to speak a language that made our head hurt and our tongues hurt. I remember going to the supermarket, and it seemed everyone went shopping at once. Everyone ran into everyone else. Every 30 seconds someone bumped my shoulder, and I would says in Spanish, *"Discúlpame,"* "Pardon me, sorry!" "Excuse me!" They just kept saying: *"Tranquilo"* which means *"Relax!"* I kept saying "Sorry!" and they finally said, "Why are you so polite?"

When I came back to Chicago, it was so funny. I went to the supermarket and was bumping into people, just getting the stuff I needed, not paying attention, like I was in Spain. They kept saying, "Excuse me! Pardon me." I was like: "Why are you so polite?"

There are sometimes when we feel out of place in on this earth, but for the Christian, Peter tells us that we are "out of place." We are foreigners and exiles on this earth.

> **1 Peter 1:1-2** | Peter, an apostle of Jesus Christ, to those who are elect exiles of the Dispersion in Pontus, Galatia, Cappadocia, Asia, and Bithynia, **2** according to the foreknowledge of God the Father, in the sanctification of the Spirit, for obedience to Jesus Christ and for sprinkling with his blood: May grace and peace be multiplied to you.

Peter says, we are "elect exiles." From God's perspective we are elect. We don't belong here on earth. We belong with him. From the world's perspective, we are exiles. We do not fit in here. We are "in the world, but not of the world" (Jn 17:16).

On the 19th of July, 64 A.D., Rome burned. It was a massive fire. Many historians believe Nero set the fire so that he could rebuild Rome in his name and receive more glory. He blamed the Christians as scapegoats, and we have those horrible stories of Nero putting Christians on poles and dousing them with oil, lighting them with fire as barbaric human lanterns, like the ones they had around the city of Rome. Unimaginable cruelty. Peter died in that persecution on October 13, 64 A.D. The result of this persecution is that as scattered as the people of God were when Peter wrote this letter, they became more scattered abroad upon this earth, like seeds for heaven.

This letter was likely written a year or so before 64 A.D., when Rome burned. The letter doesn't read like that kind of persecution is happening in the churches. It reads like it is on the horizon. Peter says, "Do not be surprised at the fiery trial when it comes upon you to test you, as though something strange were happening to you" (1 Pet 4:7). He must have been sensing something on the horizon. Peter seems to be writing from Rome since there is a reference to "Babylon" in chapter 5 which is codename (as in Revelation) for Rome. Peter wants to get something across to everyone in the church: we do not belong in this world. In a very real way, we are exiles.

IN RELATION TO THE WORLD, WE ARE EXILES (1:1)

1 Peter 1:1a | Peter, an apostle of Jesus Christ, to those who are elect exiles of the Dispersion.

Why does he use that nickname? It really brings us to the history of Israel. Twice in Israel's history the people of God were exiled.

Biblical History of Exile

Egypt – 400 years. You remember how the people of God were exiled in Egypt? They were slaves for 400 years until the Lord sent Moses to deliver them from bondage.

Babylon (and Persia) – 70 years. Then the people of God were taken away from their homes to Babylon for 70 years. Peter even refers to the nation they live in (Rome) as "Babylon" in chapter 5.

Your hometown – your lifetime. As a child of God, you are in exile on this earth. This world is not your home. I am not tied up in the idea that I need to go vacation in my exile. I have no desire to go to Florida or Arizona (for better weather or fun) when I get older. I don't think of life in those terms. I am in exile. I need to reach the people for Christ wherever God puts me.

Examples of Good Exiles

Daniel – Daniel is an excellent example of a good exile. There he was 70 years in Babylon. He didn't check out of the culture – instead he changed the culture. He pointed the King to the Lord and King Nebuchadnezzar was born again by God's grace. He was faithful during 70 years in exile in his earthly pilgrimage.

Joseph – Joseph is another excellent example of a good exile. He found himself in a prison, and by following the Lord, he was exalted to be prime minister of Egypt. He did not conform to this world but was transformed. He pointed the entire population to the Lord, and the Lord was with Joseph in Egypt that "land of the iron furnace" (Jer 11:4). As exiles in this world, hear the words of St. Paul: "Do not be conformed to this world, but be transformed by the renewal of your mind" (Rom 12:2).

Example of a Bad Exile

Demas – Paul says in 1 Timothy 4:10, "Demas has forsaken me, having loved this present world…" Demas, in love with the things of this world forsook Paul. He forsook the faith of Christ. Demas was an example of a bad exile. He didn't stay faithful to what he said was his home country of heaven. He showed himself to be first and foremost dedicated to seeking the things of this world. Demas was no exile at all, but made himself at home in his spiritual Egypt and Sodom.

What is an "Elect Exile"?

Peter says we are "elect exiles." A great synonym he gave us for what this means today would be something like "refugee millionaires." That's what he calls this church in the midst of this culture. You're like refugee millionaires. Here's what that means. You are at the same time the most despised and looked down upon in all of the world and yet the richest and most blessed in Jesus Christ of anybody on the face of the planet.

We are aliens. The language and values and customs and expectations of this world feel foreign to us. Something really radical has happened to us. Peter says in verse 3: God has caused us to be born again to a living hope—for another world, another, greater kind of existence. Paul put it this way: "You have died and your life is hid with Christ in God. When Christ who is our life appears, then you will appear with him in glory" (Col 3:3–4). Jesus said it this way – don't make it your main priority to get clothing and housing. You need to do that, but what should you do first? "Seek first the kingdom of God and his righteousness, and all these things shall be added unto you" (Mt 6:33).

Christians are out of place in this world. We don't fit. We are salt in a rotten world. We are light in a very dark world. We cause offence. We bear reproach for Christ's name. Jesus said Cursed are you when all men speak well of you. We are "pilgrims and foreigners in this earth"(1 Chron 29:15). We are citizens of heaven on this earth. We are not first citizens of this earth; we are citizens of heaven. This present evil world is not our home. We are pilgrims and strangers. We are rejected by this world. Jesus said, "if the world hated me, it will hate you also." Be instructed saint: you don't belong here. You don't fit in here. If you've been touched by God, you will never fit in here.

My brothers and sisters, the more you love and honor God, the more you expose the evil of those who do not. The more you expose the evil of those who dishonor God, the more they'll hate you. They'll hate you because of who you love, because of who you resemble. They hated Jesus and they'll hate those who are like Jesus.

The Place of Exile

1 Peter 1:1b | To those who are elect exiles of the Dispersion in Pontus, Galatia, Cappadocia, Asia, and Bithynia.

Peter is writing from Rome to those scattered throughout what is modern-day Turkey. He names states or provinces of Rome in today's Turkey. Peter is writing to the "elect exiles of the Dispersion in Pontus, Galatia, Cappadocia, Asia, and Bithynia" (1 Pet 1:1). So sad – today there are 52 million souls in Turkey, almost all without Christ. Turkey is about the size of Texas. This is like Peter saying, I'm writing to the elect exiles of Illinois, Indiana, Ohio, Pennsylvania, and New York. I'm writing to you Christians in the local churches scattered throughout the Roman empire.

Who are the Elect Exiles?

It's interesting that calls these Christians "exiles of the Dispersion." Right off the bat, we have to ask, what does Peter mean when he addresses the "exiles of the Dispersion"? They could be Jews exiled from Palestine or they could be Christians exiled from heaven.

The Jews Only?

Is Peter writing to Jews only in these Roman provinces? It could be. Peter is the apostle to the circumcision. Furthermore, in the Old Testament, this would have referred to the physical descendants of Abraham. They lived in the promised land, but because of their disobedience God sent them into captivity for 70 years, and they were scattered abroad. James uses this language opening his letter. "James, a servant of God and of the Lord Jesus Christ, to the twelve tribes in the Dispersion" (Jas 1:1). What a beautiful thing that God remembers his people who are no longer in their homeland.

More Likely, Christians of all Cultures

A more likely option is that this is more likely not referring to Jews away from Palestine, but indeed, Christians who are living away from heaven. Peter talks as if the Dispersed exiles include the Gentiles. Peter tells us a little later in 1 Peter 1:17, "conduct yourselves with fear throughout the time of your exile." They are no longer looking to go to Palestine, but to heaven. Or again in 1 Peter 2:11, "Beloved, I urge you as sojourners and exiles to abstain from the passions of the flesh, which wage war against your soul." This is the battle for sojourners from heaven, not just a geographic location on earth.

Outside 1 Peter we see the same idea. We are exiles from heaven. St. Paul says, "But our citizenship is in heaven, and from it we await a Savior, the Lord Jesus Christ" (Phil 3:20). The author of Hebrews connects Gentiles to God's people in the OT, saying "These all died in faith…having acknowledged that they were strangers and exiles on the earth" (Heb 11:13). Well, if we are exiles on earth, then what city are we seeking? Are we seeking Jerusalem on earth? No. "For here we have no lasting city, but we seek the city that is to come" (Heb 13:14).

The Jews of the Old Testament sought an earthly city. It was so tragic that the Jews were in the Dispersion, disconnected from their homeland in Jerusalem. Why? Because Jerusalem is where God's presence dwelled in the Old Testament. They wanted to get back to that place. But today we don't seek earthly Jerusalem. We seek the heavenly Jerusalem (*cf* Gal 4:25-26). Paul says the earthly Jerusalem in Israel is like Mount Sinai. It's got only laws and condemnation. But we seek the heavenly Jerusalem, which is free. We are seeking the city of God, not of man. Don't get me wrong, I would love to visit Jerusalem here on earth. But my eternal salvation is not there. My eternal salvation is in Christ and in heaven. That's where my inheritance is.

But in the New Testament times, in this age of grace, we no longer have to go to Jerusalem to partake in God's presence. Jesus has come. He is "Immanuel, God with us." God's presence in Jesus is with us! The Holy Spirit minister's God to us and in us. Peter says 2 Peter 1:4 that we have "become partakers of the divine nature." Peter views the Dispersion a little different than physical Israel. Peter views the church as Israel with the Gentiles grafted in who get to receive all the promises of Messiah. Christ is not only for Jews but for all the families of the earth! I'm included in that. So when Peter says we are "elect exiles of the Dispersion" he is talking to both Jews and Gentiles.

We are not in exile from Palestine brothers and sisters. Israel was the shadow promised land. It's like a black and white picture. The ultimate promised land is to dwell with God in a renewed heaven and earth. We are exiles from heaven. As Paul says in another place, "we are citizens of heaven."

IN RELATION TO GOD, WE ARE ELECT (1:1-2)

The Christian has been *chosen* by God – each person of the Trinity is involved in this work.

Chosen by God the Father

1 Peter 1:1-2a | Peter, an apostle of Jesus Christ, to those who are elect exiles ... according to the foreknowledge of God the Father.

We are elect exiles, chosen "according to the foreknowledge of God the Father" (1 Pet 1:2a). God the Father, who is every Christian's Father has taken the initiative to bring the Christian into his family. He did not merely '*know in advance*' the decision that they would make about him. Of course, he knew in advance, but it's deeper – he chose us according to His foreknowledge. The Scriptural idea is not mere intellectual knowledge but intimate knowledge. The word here means a vast and expansive and intimate knowledge of us – we could say God fore-*loved* us. He loved us from all eternity. Wow!

Before we jump to conclusions as to what this word means, let me help you understand the word "know." In many languages, there are two words fore and know. Greek has two primary words in the New Testament (*prognosis* and *oida*). Not many know Greek, so let me demonstrate in Spanish. You have *saber* and *conocer*. *Saber* means to know intellectually, to know ahead of time. *Conocer* means to know intimately. The Greek word here in 1 Peter 1:2 (πρόγνωσις *prognosis*) is to know intimately, not to know intellectually (*oida*) or merely ahead of time. God's love is much deeper than that. God knew you intimately. Of course, God knew you ahead of time, but this knowledge is an intimate knowledge, it goes beyond the English language concept of mere intellectual knowledge but is more like foreloving us.

Look up "foreknowledge" in a Bible Dictionary. I picked up Nelson's Bible Dictionary and here is the definition: "God's foreknowledge is much more than foresight. God does not know future events and human actions because he foresees them; he knows them because he wills them to happen. Thus, God's foreknowledge is an act of his will."[2] According to Warren Wiersbe, former Pastor of Moody Church, foreknowledge is not merely knowing something ahead of time.

---

[2] Youngblood, R. F., Bruce, F. F., Harrison, R. K., & Thomas Nelson Publishers. *Nelson's New Illustrated Bible Dictionary*. "Foreknowledge."

Foreknowledge does not suggest that God merely knew ahead of time that we would believe, and therefore He chose us. This would raise the question, "Who or what made us decide for Christ?" and would take our salvation completely out of God's hands. In the Bible, to foreknow means 'to set one's love on a person or persons in a personal way."[3]

Foreknowledge conveys the idea that God 'chose in advance to set his love personally upon each and every individual Christian.' Now when did our election take place? It took place in the secret counsel halls of eternity before we knew anything about it. A corresponding passage in Ephesians 1:4 says, "even as he chose us in him before the foundation of the world." Romans 9:11 says God chose Jacob and rejected Esau before they were "born and had done nothing either good or bad—in order that God's purpose of election might" stand. God has chosen us – elected us. Before you were born, before your father or mother, before the creation of the universe, God chose you. We were all equally deserving hell. He knew that we were part of the sinful world: "all have sinned and fall short of the glory of God" (Rom 3:23).

When I was younger, I moved from Chicago to Louisiana. I was the strange city boy! I can remember a game of stick ball on the playground, and I was the last one picked. I wasn't really that good. In the same way in life, I'm not good. I'm a sinner. If God looked at what was in me to choose me, he'd never pick me. He'd never pick anyone of us. Listen God doesn't choose us because of anything in us. It is because of his goodness and glory he chooses us.

The point of the doctrine of election is not theological debate. That never helped anyone to grow and change in Christ. The point of election is wonder and awe and worship. God loved be even when I was "dead in trespasses and sins," when I was a rebel "Christ died for me." God's choice is clearly the reason any of us can come to him.

I love him, because he first loved me. —*1 John 4:19*

Jesus said, "You did not choose me, but I chose you" —*John 15:16*

I chose him because he first chose me and not the other way around.

---

[3] Warren Wiersbe, *Bible Exposition Commentary*. Austell, GA: Victor Books, 1989), 1 Pet 1:2.

> But to all who did receive him, who believed in his name, he gave the right to become children of God, who were born, not of blood [*human birth*] nor of the will of the flesh [*human passion*] nor of the will of man [*human planning*], but of God. —John 1:12-13

You might say, "Well, God's not fair." And I'm glad God is not fair. If God was fair we would all be tormented forever in the lake of fire. Without the love of God electing us, we would all perish. Spurgeon said:

> On the outside of the gates of heaven it reads, "Whosoever will may come." And on the inside as you enter through it reads: "Elect from the foundation of the world."

God is sovereign, and man is responsible. It is true: "God is not willing that any should perish." He "takes no pleasure in the death of the wicked." God loves you. He set his affection on you before you were ever conceived. You were in the heart and the mind of God before he laid the foundations of this earth. Now that doesn't do away with human responsibility. Yet God chose us and that's why we came. You say, "Well, I don't understand that." Well, good, that's two of us. God's is sovereign and man is responsible.

Sanctified by the Spirit

1 Peter 1:2b | in the sanctification of the Spirit

The Father's choice was worked out in history by the activity of God the Holy Spirit who works to sanctify each believer. To be "sanctified" means to be "set apart" for God's purposes. It includes calling, conversion, cleansing and consecration. Sanctification is the Spirit's work to accomplish a full salvation, and it encompasses our entire life.

Before you were saved, from your mother's womb, you have been called by the Spirit. The Spirit uses your conscience and the Word of God and prayer to convict you of sin, righteousness, and judgment. And you say, "I'm really changing now." But you never do. You're not saved yet, but you are being called.

The Spirit not only calls, he converts your heart. There is a difference between calling and conversion. People say, "I prayed this prayer and now I'm saved." That's not how it works. You may be emotional and convicted of sin, and the Spirit is calling you. But many people after praying or going to church, it doesn't stick. That's because you have been called, but not converted. Conversion is described in Ezekiel

36:25-27 where God takes out the heart of stone and puts in a tender heart of flesh – he says, verse 27, "I will put my Spirit within you, and cause you to walk in my statutes and be careful to obey my judgments." In conversion, the Spirit gives the baby Christian the power to obey! Unless you have a heart to obey, you have no evidence that the Spirit has converted you.

> And by this we know that we have come to know him, if we keep his commandments. [4] Whoever says "I know him" but does not keep his commandments is a liar, and the truth is not in him, [5] but whoever keeps his word, in him truly the love of God is perfected. By this we may know that we are in him: [6] whoever says he abides in him ought to walk in the same way in which he walked. —*1 John 2:3-6*

How do we know we've come to know Christ? The Spirit puts a heart of obedience in us. Our obedience could never in a million years save anyone. But it is the evidence that we have a new heart and the transforming Spirit of God in us.

The Spirit is given to us to make us like Christ. Now this is very practical for you mothers. Listen to this. You are longing for your children to change. You are preparing them for high school and perhaps college. But nothing meaningful can happen to them until they are converted. You are trying to help them behave well, and that's good. But behaving well is not what gets them ready for eternity. Your children need Christ. Introduce them to the Holy Spirit. You say how do I do that? Show them how impossible life is without his life-giving power.

You are a refugee on earth – a spiritual exile from heaven. You belong somewhere, and God is moving you (by the Spirit of God) toward where you belong: You are a citizen of heaven living on earth. The Spirit of God is getting you ready to live with God. Heaven will one day come to earth and sanctify the whole earth. Sin and sickness will be banished. But until then, this world is not home.

This is not your home, so don't act like it's your home. You are an exile. You don't belong here. You don't fit in. So don't act like this is your permanent residence. "This world is not my home, I'm just a passin' through."

The work of sanctification means that the Spirit works supernaturally in you through the word and prayer and preaching or proclamation of the Gospel, and he "sets you apart" for God. When you hear this word "sanctification" I want you to think "miracle." This is something you can't do. This is a miracle gift from God. Mere human effort is not going to get you growing and changing. "Not by might, nor by power, but by my Spirit, says the Lord of hosts" (Zech 4:6).

This is a message for mothers for their children. You need the Spirit of God to do the work of crushing and transforming your heart and your children's hearts. Bible knowledge and church attendance are good and absolutely necessary. With great seriousness, I recommend them. But you need more than knowledge and commitment to see conversion and transformation. We need a miracle from God.

Think of a great poet. He has a pencil. That's good. He needs that to write. But the pencil will not be any good without the hand and inspiration of the poet. So it is that Bible knowledge and church attendance are necessary, they are nothing without the power of the Holy Spirit. We need the Spirit of Christ working deeply in us as moms and dads. "All is vain unless the Spirit of the Holy One comes down..."

Purchased for obedience by the Son

1 Peter 1:2c | for obedience to Jesus Christ and for sprinkling with his blood:

> I have given them your word, and the world has hated them because they are not of the world, just as I am not of the world. [15] I do not ask that you take them out of the world, but that you keep them from the evil one. [16] They are not of the world, just as I am not of the world. [17] Sanctify them in the truth; your word is truth.
> —John 17:14-17

You are not of this world. Christ has sent you into the world for you to live an obedient, sanctified life in spiritual response to the word of God. Why are we called to obedience "sprinkling with Christ's blood..."? Blood has to do with ownership and covenant. Three times in the Old Testament we see the sprinkling of blood. All have to do with ownership.

Sprinkling of Blood at Sinai Covenant

Let me explain. In the Old Testament in Exodus 24:3-8, Moses sprinkled blood on God's people, ratifying the covenant at Sinai. This nation accepted the terms of the covenant and became God's people at Sinai. So Moses took blood from the sacrifice of lambs and mixed it with water, and put it into containers, basins – and he splashed the blood on the people. They agreed to the covenant. They consecrated themselves to God that day. And as a sign and seal of the covenant, they were sprinkled or splashed with blood.

God's Part of the Covenant. This sprinkling pointed to God's ownership of them now. He brought them out of exile. His part of the covenant is that he would be God to them. He would comfort them and lead them and care for them and protect them.

God would be their God and Israel would be his people. Today, we are God's people, walking worthy of the blood that was shed for us on the cross. Peter says in 1:18-19, You were purchased "not with perishable things such as silver or gold, 19 but with the precious blood of Christ, like that of a lamb without blemish or spot."

The blood of bulls and lambs were a picture of the price God would be willing to pay to purchase his people. It is the purchase of us by the blood of Jesus that makes our obedience the proof that we are sealed by the Spirit and worthy of the blood of Christ.

> As obedient children, do not be conformed to the passions of your former ignorance, 15 but as he who called you is holy, you also be holy in all your conduct, 16 since it is written, "You shall be holy, for I am holy."
> —1 Peter 1:14-16

Sprinkling of Blood for a Leper

The second manner we see sprinkling of blood in the Old Testament was for a leper. When a person would have leprosy in the Old Testament, he would be facing a horrible death. He would have to live outside the camp. If they came into contact with anyone within 100 feet they would have to cry out, "Unclean, unclean" (Lev 13:45).

But there were times when God would work a miracle. And the cleansing of a leper is analogous to salvation, and a leper would be supernaturally, miraculously cleansed by the mercy of God. And then he would have to go show himself or healed by the mercy of God. And then he would have to go show himself to the priest for cleansing. And what the priest would take two live birds, and he would take a vessel, and put running water in that vessel. And he would take one bird and kill it and the blood would be mingled with the water in that vessel. Then he would take that other bird that had been captured and put him in that vessel and just put the water and the blood all over him and take him out and release him. And he'd fly away singing, "There's Power in the Blood." And so that leper, like the bird, would go free!

Sprinkling of Blood for the service of Priests

And the third place you would have the sprinkling of blood would be for the consecration of the priest in Exodus 29. He would be owned by God for God's service. They would offer a sacrifice and take the blood of the lamb and put it on his hands (his thumb) and on his feet (his toe) and poor oil on his head. That's what we are! We are kings and priests in the kingdom. We are a royal priesthood. We've been consecrated for service and obedience. We want to be faithful in our calling as priests to proclaim the word of pardon through the blood of our Lamb of God, Jesus Christ!

Being a Christian means you long for holiness. You long to live in such a way that is separate from this world.

> Do not love the world or the things in the world. If anyone loves the world, the love of the Father is not in him. [16] For all that is in the world—the desires of the flesh and the desires of the eyes and pride of life—is not from the Father but is from the world. [17] And the world is passing away along with its desires, but whoever does the will of God abides forever. —*1 John 2:15-17*

In other words, as A.W. Tozer said, you cannot come to Christ without accepting him fully as Savior and as Lord. You cannot divide his offices. If Christ is not your Lord and Master, then he is not your Savior. "By this we know that we have come to know him…" John says in 1 John 2:3, "if we keep his commandments." Child of God, are you walking worthy of the blood of Christ? Is your walk an evidence that a miracle has taken place in your heart by the Spirit of God? In the new covenant, we have the power to obey. We have the Spirit of God moving and working in us that obedience. We "work out our salvation in fear and trembling…" knowing "it is God who works to will and to do" of "His good pleasure" in and through us (Phil 2:10-11).

We are elected by the Father, sanctified by the Spirit, and purchased by the blood of the Son. And it is because we belong to Him that we will also experience a permanent 'exile' in this life. It is because Christ dwells within us, that the world hates us. This is a type of exile for us. We can never be completely home on this earth.

DESPITE OUR EXILE, CHRISTIANS ARE BLESSED (1:2D)

1 Peter 1:2d | May grace and peace be multiplied to you.

The apostle wished for his audience God's grace and its resultant peace (Rom 5:1) in maximum allotment or quantity. He wished for them all the best that God can offer believers, and that it would repeatedly increase to their advantage.[4]

Here is Peter's cosmic multiplication formula. I was never that great at complex math, but I sure do need this kind of multiplication in my life. Grace and peace superabound to us! Aren't you grateful for the resurrection of Christ that makes this possible for us? Grace is God giving us what we do not deserve. However great your sin is, God's grace is infinitely greater! Peace harkens back to the Old Testament word "shalom" – it doesn't just mean an absence of war. It means total well-being. God's grace and peace are upon you dear ones. They are multiplied to you! That's the kind of math program I want to be a part of!

Don't allow the tyranny and turmoil of living in "Babylon" get you down. Your blessing is not based on your circumstances: where you live, who's in charge in the government, or how much money you have in the bank. It's based on God's kindness to give you a full measure of gracious power and his heart calming peace and full reconciliation to the triune God. This is the Hebrew concept of shalom: complete wholeness and well-being.

Conclusion

As the world grows darker and darker, we must keep our focus on our heavenly home. We are in exile on this earth. We've been born again. I don't belong here. I'm a refugee millionaire. I look poor on this earth, but I have the riches of Christ!

---

[4] John F. MacArthur Jr., *1 Peter*, MacArthur New Testament Commentary (Chicago: Moody Publishers, 2004), 25.

2 | 1 PETER 1:3-5

BORN AGAIN

Blessed be the God and Father of our Lord Jesus Christ! According to his great mercy, he has caused us to be born again to a living hope through the resurrection of Jesus Christ from the dead.

1 PETER 1:3

When I was a child, my parents were constantly telling me, "Matt, slow down." "Matt, calm down." "Matt, stop shouting, I'm right here." They gave me a neat new title: they said I was a "hyperactive child." They gave me pills to try to make me calm, but it took away my personality, so they soon ceased that and just accepted me as I am! I had a personality that was filled with life and energy, but spiritually I was dead. The Bible says that we are "dead in our trespasses and sins" and we need God to wake us up. That's what we are talking about today: spiritual awakening. Have you been born again?

Once we are born again, the change is so radical that Peter tells us that we fell like "elect exiles." As far as this earth goes, we don't fit in. We are citizens of heaven. We are elect, but we are exiles. 1 Peter 1:1 "¹ Peter, an apostle of Jesus Christ, To those who are elect exiles of the Dispersion in Pontus, Galatia, Cappadocia, Asia, and Bithynia...

Ephesus is here. In fact, all of the seven churches are here – as well Colossae, Antioch, Iconium, Derbe, Phrygia, and Troas. This is the area where the most growth of the church was. Peter writes to them at Rome is burning. Nero blames the Christians. What if you were there? What would characterize your life? Worry? Anxiety? Bitterness. Peter points the believers to doxology because of the new birth.

THE SOURCE OF THE NEW BIRTH (1:3A)

> **1 Peter 1:3** | Blessed be the God and Father of our Lord Jesus Christ! According to his great mercy, he has caused us to be born again to a living hope through the resurrection of Jesus Christ from the dead.

Praise ought to characterize your life. Why? Because though we have so many trials and tribulation on this earth, we have all that we need. We have God as our Father and the Spirit as our Comforter and Jesus as our King. Peter writes to the "elect exiles" and says, "You are blessed!" Don't look to your circumstances but look beyond them to the God and Father who has caused you to be born again!

Doxology and praise are the products of this great life change that God has given. We have been born again into Christ, our living hope. We have a living hope named Jesus! Aren't you glad that because of the resurrection, as bad as things might be, this is not our final home? We have a living hope in Jesus Christ being raised from the dead! We have hope! He said, "I am he that lives, and was dead; and behold, I am alive for evermore, Amen, and have the keys of hell and of death" (Rev 1:18). There is hope in your trials. There is hope for your sins! Jesus is alive!! Let us "bless the Lord at all times" (Psa 34:1). Jesus has revealed the Father to us. The demons don't get redemption. But we fallen, weak humans do! We have so much to bless God for.

The Blessing of God the Father

Whenever the New Testament calls God Father, it primarily denotes that he is the Father of the Lord Jesus Christ.[5] There is only one true and living God. Allah is no god. Allah is a demon, pagan God of hatred and war. Allah of Islam in no way resembles the God of the Bible. There is only one true and living God who is exclusively revealed by Jesus Christ. As Christians we say: "Blessed be the God and Father of our Lord Jesus Christ!" There is no other way to heaven. Jesus is the

---

[5] MacArthur, *1 Peter*, 30–31.

"way, the truth, and the life" and no one comes to the Father, the one true and living God, but through the exclusive say of Jesus, so says Jesus in John 14:6. Jesus is the express image of the invisible God. He exegetes and reveals exactly who the Father is (*cf* Jn 1:18). We could not know him in a personal way without Jesus Christ.

Blessing Despite Suffering

There is deep blessing amidst deep suffering. All Christians are living a strange double life: Peter addresses his audience as 'foreigners', not because they have emigrated to where they now live but because they now have a dual citizenship. They are, simultaneously, inhabitants of this or that actual country or district (Pontus, Galatia, or wherever), and citizens of God's new world which, as he will shortly say, is waiting to be unveiled.[6] We are "chosen" or "elect" foreigners. Our home is in heaven. "But our citizenship is in heaven, and from it we await a Savior, the Lord Jesus Christ…" (Phil 3:20). Because of the transforming power of Christ's resurrection, we are no longer the same. Because of the resurrection, no matter what you are going through, you have hope! You have a living hope!

THE MOTIVE OF THE NEW BIRTH (1:3B)

If we look back, we have to bless God for his mercy in causing us to be born again "according to his mercy."

> **1 Peter 1:3b** | Blessed be the God and Father of our Lord Jesus Christ! According to his great mercy.

We are born anew is *by his great mercy*. The whole point of mercy is God had to have pity on us to save us. God got no help from us! God "caused us to be born again."

Metaphors of God's Mercy

In order to understand that we cannot decide when a person is saved, let us be reminded of some of the metaphors of regeneration in the Bible. In these metaphors God is the active mover and miracle worker. These metaphors draw attention to the glory of God's grace to powerless sinners who cannot help themselves.

---

[6] Wright, *James, Peter, John and Judah*, 49-50.

Resurrection: In the new life raised from the dead (Eph 2:1-6; Eze 37, i.e. "dry bones"), God brings the dead sinner to life.

Birth: In the new birth (Jn 3:3; 1 Pet 1:23) God makes a new person by conceiving faith in the sinner by the word of God.

Creation: In the new creation (2 Cor 4:6; 5:17), God speaks and creates something out of nothing.

Metamorphosis: In the conversion of heart (Eze 36:26-27; Deut 30:6) God transforms the heart of stone into a tender heart of flesh.

A Growing Harvest: In the miraculous increase of the harvest (1 Cor 3:6) Paul and Apollos plant and water, but it is God who gives the increase.

Back to Peter, it was according to his mercy he caused us to be born again. In all of these examples, including new birth, man is passive. God is active. I cannot raise myself from the dead. I cannot give birth to myself. I cannot create myself. I cannot give the increase of harvest. The new birth is passive. We weren't seeking God. God wasn't lost. We were lost, and God was seeking us!

One of the most profound illustrations of this is the story of Cedric and Nicole. I'll never forget sitting at their kitchen table on October 31, 2011. We had been studying through Ephesians for several weeks, and we got to that place in Ephesians 2, where it says we were "dead in our trespasses and sins" – and then it says, "But God who is rich in mercy raised us up with Christ..." I'll never forget, Cedric interrupted and said, "Pastor, I got to pray!" Nicole at that time being a proper Italian Catholic, said, "Cedric, don't interrupt the priest!" I told her – the Spirit is giving birth to Cedric. He is going to be a new creation. Cedric prayed with such an intensity and fervency, and he was swept into the glorious kingdom of God by faith in Jesus. And then Nicole followed right after. And you've seen the entirely new disposition.

The Recipients of God's Mercy

Regeneration is God imparting to us a new nature to spiritually dead sinners. As Ezekiel says (Eze chs 36-37), it's God giving us a new heart. It's God taking the dry, dead bones, and raising us up and causing us to live. It's God quickening us with life. Ephesians 2:1 says that we by nature were "children of wrath." But now we have a new nature. We have a new heart and a renewed mind. Ephesians 2:10 says we were "created in Christ Jesus" with a new nature that loves God and obeys him. Let me illustrate this with several Scripture passages.

In mercy, God sends his Spirit to transform our hearts. Jesus says in John 3:3, "unless one is born again he cannot see the kingdom of God." The one entering the kingdom must experience an absolute miracle. He goes on in verse 6, "That which is born of the flesh is flesh, and that which is born of the Spirit is spirit." So if you are born of the flesh, that is physically, that's all you are. Fallen flesh like that doesn't inherit the kingdom of God. You need a miracle. You need the Spirit to make you alive and birth you spiritually. Jesus goes on to say in John 3:7-8, "Do not marvel that I said to you, 'You must be born again.' 8 The wind blows where it wishes, and you hear its sound, but you do not know where it comes from or where it goes. So it is with everyone who is born of the Spirit." Being born of the Spirit happens not by human design, which is very predictable, but it happens like the wind, which is surprising and unpredictable. When someone is born again, you are like, "Whoa! How did that happen! It's a miracle!"

John tells us how the new birth is not of man, but of God. "But to all who did receive him, who believed in his name, he gave the right to become children of God, 13 who were born, not of blood nor of the will of the flesh nor of the will of man, but of God" (Jn 1:12-13). All who believe are born of God. They are born "not of blood" – they didn't get the new birth through natural descent. They were born, "not of the will of the flesh" – they didn't get the new birth through personal choice or human decision. Neither were they born "of the will of man" – they didn't get the new birth through, or more literally, the will of a husband. Your mom and dad cannot just decide for you to be born again. Instead, you are "born of God." You are born by the miracle mercy of God.

John tells us in 1 John 5:1, "Everyone who believes that Jesus is the Christ has been born of God, and everyone who loves the Father loves whoever has been born of him." We need to define the belief John speaks of. It means to trust. It doesn't mean merely intellectual understanding, but intentional dependence. So the one who has been "born of God" – here is the sign: Faith. Belief. Trust. Trust in what? In Jesus as Christ. Christ means "Anointed One." Anointed for what? To be King. So one of the signs that a person is born of God is faith. Ephesians 2:8 says faith is "a gift from God." And 1 John 5:1 says that the sign for one being born of God is that they trust Jesus as their King.

The Message of God's Mercy

What does God use to cause us to be born again? The word of God. "You have been born again, not of perishable seed but of imperishable, through the living and abiding word of God" (1 Pet 1:23). God uses his word to bring people to faith. It's specifically the "good news" that Jesus substituted himself for us that saves us.

> For the word of God is living and active, sharper than any two-edged sword, piercing to the division of soul and of spirit, of joints and of marrow, and discerning the thoughts and intentions of the heart.
> —*Hebrews 4:12*

> Of his own will he brought us forth by the word of truth, that we should be a kind of firstfruits of his creatures. —*James 1:18, KJV*

James is referring to the new creation. We are the first things created for the new earth. We don't belong here.

The Blessing of God's Mercy

The believers Peter is writing to are suffering, yet he says, "Bless God! The God who changed your life should be praised and adored and worshipped! "Blessed be… God!!!" Praise Him! No matter what you are going through, bless Him for your transformed life.

Peter encourages his readers to praise God, a helpful remedy for hearts weighed down with discouragement because of suffering. He then lists the reason for praise: *By his great mercy we have been born anew*. The word for 'born again (*anagennaō*) has a more active sense than our translation (ESV) indicates, for the root word (*gennaō*) often refers to a father's role in the birth of a child. In blessing God, Peter thinks first of the new spiritual life that God has given to his people. Let's bless Him for it![7]

One of the best things you can do is get your eyes off yourself. That's what resurrection power is all about. It's about helping those who are hurting around you. No matter how much you are hurting, you have the promise that your pain will end. God will wipe away all tears.

Many don't have that hope of the resurrection. I want to fervently urge you to share your faith. Share what God has done for you! Bless the one who has given you Jesus, who is our Living Hope!

---

[7] Wayne Grudem, *1 Peter: An Introduction And Commentary*, Vol. 17 (Downers Grove, IL: InterVarsity Press., 1988), 59–60.

THE REWARD OF THE NEW BIRTH (1:4)

The reward that we are called to in the new birth is God himself.

1 Peter 1:4 | Born again... to an inheritance that is imperishable, undefiled, and unfading, kept in heaven for you.

God Himself is Our Inheritance

What is this inheritance? Our inheritance is not merely the streets of gold, the crowns of glory, or the celestial cities. Oh yes, we get all that. But that is like the wrapping on the candy bar. Our inheritance is God. It is communion with Him forever and ever. We are heirs of God and joint heirs with Christ. What did Christ have before the worlds were created? He had the Father. The Father and the Son and the Spirit is our inheritance. Remember what God told Abraham? Genesis 15:1, "The word of the LORD came unto Abram in a vision, saying, Fear not, Abram: I am your shield, and your exceeding great reward." What is our reward in paradise, in heaven? We get God!

Or course we get a future share in the kingdom! The New Testament regularly uses 'inheritance' (*klēronomia*) to refer not only to an earthly inheritance but also to a believer's 'share' in the heavenly kingdom, his or her future heavenly reward.[8] When we think about our inheritance, we ought not look forward to merely the streets of gold and the celestial city. Those things are like wrapping for a candy bar. You don't eat the wrapping. You aren't satisfied by the wrapping. the gold and the jewels and the city are just wrapping. What is our inheritance? Remember God's promise to Israel in Exodus 6:7, "I will take you to be my people, and I will be your God." God in the Abrahamic covenant says in Genesis 17:7, "And I will establish my covenant between me and you and your offspring after you throughout their generations for an everlasting covenant, to be God to you and to your offspring after you."

Revelation 21:1-7 echoes the cry of God through all of Scripture. The living God is our inheritance. All the crowns and gold and cities are just wrapping.

> Then I saw a new heaven and a new earth, for the first heaven and the first earth had passed away, and the sea was no more. ² And I saw the holy city, new Jerusalem, coming down out of heaven from God, prepared as a bride adorned for her husband. ³ And I heard a loud voice

---

[8] Ibid., 61.

from the throne saying, "Behold, the dwelling place of God is with man. He will dwell with them, and they will be his people, and God himself will be with them as their God. ⁴ He will wipe away every tear from their eyes, and death shall be no more, neither shall there be mourning, nor crying, nor pain anymore, for the former things have passed away." ⁵ And he who was seated on the throne said, "Behold, I am making all things new." Also he said, "Write this down, for these words are trustworthy and true." ⁶ And he said to me, "It is done! I am the Alpha and the Omega, the beginning and the end. To the thirsty I will give from the spring of the water of life without payment. ⁷ The one who conquers will have this heritage, and I will be his God and he will be my son. —*Revelation 21:1-7*

God the Father is my inheritance.

The Holy Spirit is Our Inheritance

He's given me a down payment of my inheritance. Look over at Ephesians 1:13-14, "In him [Jesus] you also, when you heard the word of truth, the gospel of your salvation, and believed in him [Jesus], were sealed with the promised Holy Spirit, ¹⁴ who is the guarantee [down payment, earnest money] of our inheritance until we acquire possession of it, to the praise of his glory."

The New Creation is Our Inheritance

God has, through the resurrection, inaugurated a whole new world. At the moment it is being kept safe, out of sight, behind the thin invisible curtain which separates our world (earth) from God's world (heaven). But one day the curtain will be drawn back; and then the 'incorruptible inheritance', at present being kept safe in heaven, will be merged with our earthly reality, transforming it and soaking it through with God's presence, love and mercy (verse 4). And if that new world is kept safe for us, Peter assures us that we are being kept safe for it.[9]

An Imperishable Inheritance

1 Peter 1:4a | He has caused us to be born again ... to an inheritance that is imperishable.

Our stake in the future kingdom is not subject to decay. It is unable to be worn out with the passage of time. The New Testament uses this word only of eternal heavenly realities, such as God himself (Rom 1:23;

---

[9] Wright, *James, Peter, John and Judah*, 50-51

1 Tim 1:17), God's word (1 Pet 1:23), and our resurrection bodies (1 Cor 15:52; *cf* 1 Cor 9:25; 1 Pet 3:4).

All earthly possessions will ultimately decay and be destroyed (Lk 12:33; Rom 1:23; 2 Cor 4:16; Col 2:22; 1 Pet 1:18), for the creation now is in 'bondage to decay' (Rom 8:21).[10]

An Undefiled Inheritance

1 Peter 1:4 | He has caused us to be born again ... to an inheritance that is... undefiled.

Peter invites contemplation of a heavenly inheritance unpolluted by even our own sin and containing nothing unworthy of God's full approval.[11] Our place in God's kingdom is secured by Christ alone! It is undefiled because it is secured by Christ's unfailing and perfect righteousness. Because you are robed in His righteousness, you are completely worthy in Christ of that undefiled inheritance! You are unpolluted in Christ!

An Unfading Inheritance

1 Peter 1:4 | He has caused us to be born again ... to an inheritance that is ... unfading, kept in heaven for you,

Peter next describes our inheritance as "unfading"—that which is not subject to fading or decay. Unlike earthly wealth (Jas 1:11), it will never wither, grow dim, or lose its beauty or glory (*cf* 1 Pet 5:4).[12]

Not being as young as I used to be, I am learning that the human body fades. Presently mine is falling more quickly than I would like into a state of decay. Gravity is taking over. My skin is no longer taut. The inevitable descent toward the earth from which it came is noticeably underway. In contrast, the inheritance toward which Christians are said to be moving is said to be "unfading." It will never be subject to decay. What good news! When our own bodies, long since expired, are reunited with Christ on that final day, we will be made incorruptible

---

[10] Grudem, *1 Peter*, 62.
[11] Ibid.
[12] David R. Helm, *1 & 2 Peter and Jude: Sharing Christ's Sufferings* (Wheaton, IL: Crossway Books, 2008), 34-35.

forevermore, restored, new, complete. This is the inheritance that awaits all who are in Christ.[13]

The form of the verb 'kept' (perfect passive participle) indicates a completed past activity (by God) with results that are still continuing in the present: God himself has 'stored up' or 'reserved' this inheritance in heaven for believers and it continues to be there, 'still reserved' for them. [14]

Christians possess some of the benefits of salvation in this life, but the great fullness of redemption is yet to come. God has promised unfathomable glories in the eternal perfection of heaven that will one day be the conscious experience of every believer.[15]

THE RECEIVING OF THE NEW BIRTH (1:5)

> **1 Peter 1:5** | He has caused us to be born again ... **⁵** who by God's power are being guarded through faith for a salvation ready to be revealed in the last time.

It is God's power that gives us salvation, but it is through faith that we appropriate that salvation. It is true that being born again is a miracle of grace. We didn't come up with it, and so we do not keep it for ourselves. We access that salvation (our union with the triune God) through faith, both to be saved and to continue being sanctified. God guides us and keeps those who are born again. This is God's work. Jesus is risen from the dead, and it makes all the difference.

Guarded by Faith

Guarded (*phroureō*) means 'kept safe, carefully watched', and is frequently used in military contexts. The word can mean both 'kept from escaping' and 'protected from attack', and perhaps both kinds of guarding are intended here: God is preserving believers from escaping out of his kingdom, and he is protecting them from external attacks.[16]

Ephesians 2:1-3 says we used to be enslaved to self, Satan, and the world. Now we are safe from those old enemies, even our own fleshly, sinful nature. No one is able to pluck us out of the Father's hand! Even our own selves! Jude 1:24-25, says it so well, "Now to him who is able to

---

[13] Grudem, *1 Peter*, 62.
[14] Ibid.
[15] MacArthur, *1 Peter*, 38.
[16] Grudem, *1 Peter*, 63.

keep [guard or imprison] you from stumbling and to present you blameless before the presence of his glory with great joy, 25 to the only God, our Savior, through Jesus Christ our Lord, be glory, majesty, dominion, and authority, before all time and now and forever. Amen." You are imprisoned by the power of God from falling away!

Empowered by Faith

I love how Peter says we are "guarded through faith" in verse 5. The present participle, which Peter uses, gives the sense 'you are continually being guarded'. He stresses that this is *by God's power*. Wayne Grudem says of this verse: "God's power in fact energizes and continually sustains individual, personal faith."[17] This mystery is expressed in Philippians 2:12-13, "work out your own salvation with fear and trembling, 13 for it is God who works in you, both to will and to work for his good pleasure." We might call this "grace empowered faith."

It is God's power that is illumining our minds and strengthening our faith. We love him because he first loved us. We came to him because he drew us to himself by his Spirit. We are kept by the power of God, which is a fountain for our faith. We might say we are kept by the grace, or power of God. In other words, it is the grace that empowers and enlightens our faith to understand who God is. It is God graciously revealing himself to us that empowers our faith.

Conclusion

Philippians 1:6 says, "He who began a good work in you will complete it." The word of God implanted the Spirit and a new nature in you! God is not done. I remember we wanted to plant grass in our yard in Spain. We hauled out the rocks, put down dirt, and planted grass seed. We watered it. Katie was about six years old and Krissy was four. They came out of the house and were so excited. They asked, "Why isn't the grass growing?" It is. Over time the evidences will come forth, and the seed will have a miracle of life. That's what it is to be born again. God's giving the increase!

---

[17] Ibid.

3 | 1 PETER 1:6-9
GLORIOUS SUFFERING

> *In this you rejoice, though now for a little while, if necessary, you have been grieved by various trials, so that the tested genuineness of your faith—more precious than gold that perishes though it is tested by fire—may be found to result in praise and glory and honor at the revelation of Jesus Christ.*
>
> 1 PETER 1:6-7

Someone once asked the great Renaissance sculptor Michelangelo what he saw when he approached a huge block of marble. Michelangelo stood back and looked at that big square block of white marble, rubbed his chin thoughtfully, and replied, "I see a beautiful form trapped inside and it is my responsibility to take my mallet and chisel and chip away until the figure is set free." I love that illustration because you can relate to it. God is forming "Christ in you, the hope of glory" (Col 1:27). The Spirit is forming Christ in us. Our Heavenly Father is a little like a sculptor. He wants to form his Son in us. He uses affliction like a hammer and trouble just like a chisel, and he chips and cuts away at us through trials to reveal Jesus' image in you. God chooses as his model his Son. Romans 8:29 says: We born again believers are all "predestined to be conformed to the likeness of his Son."

I have lot of hard marble in my life that needs to be chipped away before Christ can be seen in me. We all have that marble. That hammer hurts, doesn't it? Those trials, that chisel bites! After time, the rough form begins to take shape. What does this sculpture look like? God uses suffering to purge sin out of your life and strengthen your commitment to him, and force us to depend on his grace.

God uses affliction to put your focus on the sufficient grace of Jesus, to transform your character to be like Jesus, and also to build compassion towards others who are hurting. That hammer and chisel makes you dig deep in God's word to find comfort. The pain of God's hammer increases your faith and strengthens your character. And oh brothers and sisters, that is a beautiful image. That's Christ in you! Peter tells us we can rejoice in the midst of suffering.

> **1 Peter 1:6-9** | In this you rejoice, though now for a little while, if necessary, you have been grieved by various trials, **7** so that the tested genuineness of your faith—more precious than gold that perishes though it is tested by fire—may be found to result in praise and glory and honor at the revelation of Jesus Christ. **8** Though you have not seen him, you love him. Though you do not now see him, you believe in him and rejoice with joy that is inexpressible and filled with glory, **9** obtaining the outcome of your faith, the salvation of your souls.

Trials come in various ways. Personality conflicts in marriage. Loss of income. Loss of health. Retirement. The expectations and disappointments of people. People who once confessed Christ are going to fall away back into the world. This is happening at all times. Demas was with Paul as a close companion in ministry but ended up forsaking the faith because he was "in love with this present evil world." So sad. Expect trials and testings.

THE PROMISE IN OUR SUFFERING (1:6)

> **1 Peter 1:6** | In this you rejoice, though now for a little while, if necessary, you have been grieved by various trial.

The promise of God in our suffering is that he is in control, and that is why we can rejoice.

The Delight of God's Promise

1 Peter 1:6a | In this you rejoice.

Rejoice in trials? Huh? What are we rejoicing in? In God's plan that he just explained in 1 Peter 1:1-5. It's through those difficulties and problems of life that God fulfills his plan. It's God's ultimate plan to make us like Christ that we can rejoice in. God's plan is to save you and make you like Christ. You were dead in sin, but he caused you to be born again. It was a plan that he put into play in eternity past. You are chosen. We can't trust our own understanding of things. We need to insist on trusting God's good plan for us, which includes all the tragedies and triumphs (*cf* Pro 3:5-6).

The Design of God's Promise

We rejoice in the promise laid out in verses 1 through 5. We are foreknown and eternally loved by God the Father, sanctified by the Holy Spirit, and washed in the blood of Christ. Because of that we are blessed to an inheritance that will never fade because it is God himself.

David said of God in Psalm 23, "He leads me beside quiet waters. ... he guides me in the paths of righteousness for his name's sake" (Psa 23: 2-3). And though we go through the valley of the shadow of death, God is "right there with us." He's got a plan. He's in control. When God took his people into captivity in Babylon, he said in Jeremiah 29:11, "For I know the plans I have for you," declares the Lord, "plans to prosper you and not harm you, plans to give you hope and a future." Ultimately God's plan is to conform us to the image of Jesus Christ (Rom 8:28-30).

The Dependence on God's Promise

1 Peter 1:6 | In this you rejoice, though now for a little while, if necessary, you have been grieved by various trials.

We depend on God through all the suffering, rejoicing in him, and in his plan to do us good in the midst of all the suffering. Peter is giving us the foundation underneath all our trials, so that we don't fall apart, but we instead rejoice, since "for a little while" we are going to be "grieved by various trials." The idea is continual here. You have been and are being "grieved by various trials" (1:6). It's like 2 Corinthians 6:10, "as sorrowful, yet always rejoicing." How is this paradox possible?

How can I rejoice even though I am filled with grief and sorrow? Your child has chosen the wrong path, yet you are rejoicing in Christ. You have suffered betrayal, yet you are rejoicing in Christ. Your job isn't what you thought it would be yet you are rejoicing. You have failed at times as a parent or as a spouse, yet you are rejoicing in Christ. Why? Because day by day, you are looking to God's power and ability to fulfill his good purpose through the mess on this earth.

Aren't you glad trials are only for "a little while"? That is another way of saying, "during the course of your short life." It's just a "little while" before Jesus returns. He's coming soon saints. Don't be discouraged, but be encouraged!

THE PURPOSE OF GOD'S SUFFERING (1:7)

To Be the Prototype of Christ

What's the point? Where are we going with all the suffering? Can't we bypass the pain part? No. The pain and suffering and trials occur "so that" our faith might grow and mature through testing. Pain leads us to a greater conformity to Jesus Christ.

> **1 Peter 1:7** | So that the tested genuineness of your faith—more precious than gold that perishes though it is tested by fire—may be found to result in praise and glory and honor at the revelation of Jesus Christ.

God is refining your faith to be truly genuine. And this refined and tested faith of yours is "more precious than gold that perishes though it is tested by fire." That is, the more you refine gold through fire, the more precious it is. The more costly and valuable and rich it is.

If we have the right expectations of the Christian life, we are better equipped to persevere in it. We are going to suffer in this life until Christ comes again. Suffering for Christ is temporary, but it will not let up in this life. Suffering is not a mistake, or even an expression of our Father's displeasure. It is for your growth in faith. Your friendship with God is to deepen and mature.

Of course, there are some wrong views of suffering. We might think, suffering comes only when I've been bad. God is punishing me. No! That's not correct thinking. There is no condemnation (Rom 8:1). All suffering in the Christian life is based on God's love. Your suffering is never punitive. Christ was given the full retribution for your sin. Your suffering is formational. God is using your suffering to help you grow.

Think about the little boy who saw a butterfly struggling to emerge from its cocoon. It was straining with all it's might to get out, so the little boy thinking that he would help, took a knife, and slit the cocoon. But to his dismay, he found the butterfly came out with small and shriveled wings, and unable to fly. That's what happens when we try to cut our time in the cocoon short. We have this fat body that cannot fly.

We need to let the cocoon of trials get all the ugly sinful habits out of us. God uses that cocoon to squeeze those sinful habits out so that when we emerge with wings, we can fly!

To Bring Praise to Christ at His Coming

> **1 Peter 1:7** | So that the tested genuineness of your faith...may be found to result in praise and glory and honor at the revelation of Jesus Christ.

The trials and testings of this earth are only temporary. This sin-cursed earth is not our final destination. Jesus is coming again to make heaven and earth as one, where God dwells here again with man, as he did with Adam and Eve in the garden of Eden.

Until that time, our suffering brings a refined genuineness to our faith, so that when Jesus returns, he will get all the praise and glory and honor. Jesus is coming again! When he comes again, Jesus will turn to us and say something amazing.

> Well done, good and faithful slave. You were faithful with a few things, I will put you in charge of many things; enter into the joy of your master. —*Matthew 25:21, NASB*

Good? Faithful? I can say that none of us has been perfect, but in Christ, he will have done a work in us that will have made each of us good and faithful. Christ will be praised, and we will be commended. Truly behind anything good and faithful will be the work of the Holy Spirit and the purchase of my soul by Jesus' blood. All praise and honor go to him, even when we are rewarded and commended. We must all confess that from beginning to end, salvation is all of grace (Eph 2:8-10). We are merely his workmanship, his masterpiece. He does the work, he gets the praise, and we get eternal salvation.

I am looking forward to that day when we see Jesus returns again in power and glory. It could be at any moment. All our tears will be wiped away. The power and penalty for sin will be defeated. The very presence of sin will be removed. There will be no more temptation, no desire for sin whatsoever. There won't even be the possibility for sin when Jesus returns. There will be a new heaven and a new earth, and heaven and earth will be one. Even so, Lord Jesus, come soon!

The trials in life grow us so that at the coming of Jesus, our lives bear proof that he is our Savior, our Redeemer, and our God. Trials prove that God is doing a good work in you. Philippians 1:6, "I am sure of this, that he who began a good work in you will bring it to completion at the day of Jesus Christ."

THE PARADOX IN OUR SUFFERING (1:8-9)

The paradox is that the more we suffer, the more we know Christ. Trials are the crucible that strengthen our relationship with Christ. He's got an overall plan for our suffering that is breathtaking. Look at what Peter says about the outcome of faith in suffering.

> **1 Peter 1:8-9** | Though you have not seen him, you love him. Though you do not now see him, you believe in him and rejoice with joy that is inexpressible and filled with glory, **9** obtaining the outcome of your faith, the salvation of your souls.

This is a paradox. You would think we would be growing farther and farther away from Christ because of pain, sorrow, and suffering. But instead, we are sharing in Christ's suffering. "But rejoice insofar as you share Christ's sufferings, that you may also rejoice and be glad when his glory is revealed" (1 Pet 4:13). We get closer and closer to Christ even as we suffer. Here are a few truths we can depend on during suffering.

We cannot see Christ, but we love him.

It surely would be amazing to have Christ in bodily form with us during suffering.

> **1 Peter 1:8a** | Though you have not seen him, you love him.

Here and now, though we do not see him, we love him. And though we do not see him, we experience him in other ways. We see his providential guidance in our lives (Eph 2:10, 1:11; *cf* Pro 3:5-6; Psa 37:23-

25). We see his constant answers to prayer (Jn 15:7). We see his transformation of our character (Rom 8:29). We can't see him with our eyes, but we see him in our lives, and it makes us love him more and more.

It seems trials should blind us to Christ, but it makes us instead draw nearer to him. In the world, suffering makes people bitter. But for the Christian focused on Christ, it makes us love him more. How? Because it is during suffering that we draw so much nearer to Christ. Our pride is such that if trials did not come, we would hardly walk with him. We see him most manifestly during our suffering, because it is during suffering that we are humbled. Since "God resists the proud

We cannot see Christ, but we joyfully trust him.

We cannot experience Christ with our eyes, but we are experiencing Christ, nonetheless.

> **1 Peter 1:8b** | Though you do not now see him, you believe in him and rejoice with joy that is inexpressible and filled with glory.

The idea here is that in trials, we suffer with Christ, and we have a joy that is not from this world. It is joy that is "inexpressible and glorified joy." Joy inexpressible comes when you believe that he loves you. You have not seen him, but you love him. You are already obtaining the outcome of your faith – that relationship with him – the salvation of your soul!

We cannot see Christ, but he's still working on us.

> **1 Peter 1:9** | You believe in him and rejoice... [9] obtaining the outcome of your faith, the salvation of your souls.

Daily, we believe and rejoice in him, and daily, we are obtaining the final product of Christ's work: our salvation, which is conformity to Christ. When we think of salvation, we often think of it in the past tense, merely a forensic or judicial way. We are no longer condemned. We are justified. Amen! But our salvation is not merely a past tense legal transaction, but that legal transaction results in a present tense transformation. We are adopted into God's family, and we draw close to Christ. Trials are the crucible that strengthen our relationship with Christ. In trials, our soul is being transformed by our relationship with Jesus. He draws us closer and closer. In our pain, there is peace and blessing. This is a paradox. You would think we would be growing farther and farther away from Christ because of pain, sorrow, and suffering. Instead, we rejoice, because he is still working on us.

There is an eschatological attitude about suffering for the Christian. We are looking to the final victory, not focused on merely on our pain. We are not to be overcome by any trial, but awaiting that moment that Jesus pierces the clouds and brings the "outcome of our faith, the salvation of our souls."

Conclusion

So many times, God has used trials for me, personally. He knows what he is doing. We have physical ailments. I was born premature. I had open heart surgery as a young boy. I've had so many eye problems. I was diagnosed with ADHD as a child. My parents divorced when I was a young. My mom died when I was only fifteen. But the truth is all these things have made me more like Christ. These trials are difficult, like a chisel hitting us! But God uses every tiny detail for the advancement of his kingdom and to conform my soul to Christ's image.

One day, God's work will be finished. One day Christ will come again and take his bride away. One day the church is going to forever put off the garments of sin. We will meet Christ in the air. We will put off suffering and difficulties and trials. We will put off our sinful flesh. One day, we will come with Christ from "heaven... prepared as a bride adorned for her husband" (Rev 21:2). There will be no spot or wrinkle or any such thing! And we will all be changed into his glorious holy image! O come quickly Lord Jesus! Come and glorify your saints. Be exalted O Christ among us. Though we cannot now see you, when you will come, we will see you face to face!

4 | 1 PETER 1:10-21

BE HOLY

As obedient children, do not be conformed to the passions of your former ignorance, but as he who called you is holy, you also be holy in all your conduct, since it is written, "You shall be holy, for I am holy."

1 PETER 1:14-16

The theme of this passage and of the whole Bible is holiness. The angels in Isaiah 6 cry out "holy, holy, holy." But what is holiness, really? In one word it describes that our God is set apart and unique. It is his "God-ness." No one compares to him. "There is none holy like the Lord" (1 Sam 2:2). As David says in Psalm 40:5, "Lord my God, no one can compare with you." Can you witness with me that *"No one compares to my Jesus"*?

Holiness speaks of God being set apart from his creation. And yet, God calls us from the beginning to "be holy," he says for "I the Lord am holy." We need to know what that means. We are not naturally like God. We are fallen. We are sinful. God calls us to reflect him. We are his image bearers. We are to reflect the moral attributes of God. We cannot reflect his infinite attributes. That's what separates him from us. He is eternal, immutable, and infinite in his knowledge, power, and presence. But what God does call us to imitate and reflect is his morality. God is love. God is light (morally perfect). God is gracious and merciful, abounding in his relentless love. Oh, the ocean of God's love and kindness. We are not naturally like that until we meet God. God must reveal himself to sinful creatures. He is able to transform us by his love.

Holiness Encountered

We see various examples of how holiness is displayed in the Old Testament. Consider Moses. When Moses encounters God's presence in the Old Testament, he is told to take off his sandals, and is also told not to come any closer. Moses covers his face in fear. Consider the temple. In the same way, the temple was the main place where God's holy presence was. God's name is so holy, that when you come to him, you must be pure. God's holiness is deadly – a lamb or a goat must be slain vicariously for the worshipper. Sacrifices shout: without holiness you will die.

On the other hand, God's name is not treated with holy reverence. His name is tramped through the dirt of this world. God's name functions as a curse word, a platform for the obscene. That the world has little respect for God is clearly seen by the way the world regards his name. No honor. No reverence. No awe before him.[18]

If anyone would ask, what is the top priority of our church? Some would say, "Evangelism. The preaching of the word. Spiritual nurture." But I believe that the top priority is to be conformed to God's image. In other words, to be holy. This is what ought to fill our prayer lives. What is the first petition of the Lord's Prayer? Jesus said, "When you pray, pray like this: 'Our Father, which art in heaven....'" The first line of the prayer is not a petition. It is a form of personal address. The prayer continues: "Hallowed be thy name. Thy kingdom come."[19]

Peter tells us in 1 Peter – we are elect exiles. We have been chosen. We have an inheritance guarded for us in heaven. Our faith that will bring us to heaven is being guarded. Trials will come to grow you and train you. Why? Because you are to be holy. This is the theme of the Bible. A holy God chooses an unholy and wicked people and makes them holy.

---

[18] Sproul, *The Holiness of God*, 18–19.
[19] Ibid.

God is calling us into his holiness! We are called to live a separate, holy life from this world. God keeps you believing. He's in you preserving you from this sinful world. Peter wants us to be holy, first by seeing our great privilege. We were sinners, but now we are saints.

THE PRIVILEGE OF HOLINESS (1:10-12)

Oh, what privilege we have in Christ. We have a greater privilege than the Old Testament prophets and even greater than God's holy angels. God has brought us to a great salvation that the prophets longed to inquire into.

The spiritual blessings now experience are greater than anything that was envisioned by Old Testament prophets or even by angels.[20] No matter what you are going through, are you thankful for the supreme privilege of holiness? I know life hurts. I know you are going through many trials. But look at the awesome privilege that God has included you in his plan of redemption. Gratitude should motivate us to be like our holy God.

A Privilege Greater than the Prophets

Peter says, as New Testament saints, you are more privileged than the Old Testament prophets.

> **1 Peter 1:10-12a** | Concerning this salvation, the prophets who prophesied about the grace that was to be yours searched and inquired carefully, **11** inquiring what person or time the Spirit of Christ in them was indicating when he predicted the sufferings of Christ and the subsequent glories. **12** It was revealed to them that they were serving not themselves but you.

The Old Testament prophets experienced much, but they wrote of things which fascinated them. They revelations of the coming Christ were better than what they experienced. Abraham heard the voice of God. Jacob wrestled with God. Moses had the burning bush and saw the glory cloud by day and night. Elijah rode in a chariot of God's glorious presence. Isaiah saw the Lord in all his glory and majesty. But we who live after the resurrection of Jesus have it better than them. They longed to know the details of Christ's suffering on the cross and his resurrection. They looked "searched and inquired carefully."

---

[20] Grudem, *1 Peter*, 72.

From Moses to Malachi, all of the Old Testament prophets were fascinated by the promises of salvation. However, they did not merely *wish* to receive that salvation; they *actually* obtained it. But they received the gift of God's salvation without seeing its full accomplishment (*cf* Heb 11:39–40), without seeing Jesus Christ. Though the prophets wrote of Messiah, they never fully comprehended all that was involved in Christ's life, death, and resurrection.[21] They wrote in detail about Christ's life, death and resurrection, not for themselves, but for you! "It was revealed to them that they were serving not themselves but you" (1 Pet 1:12a).

God invites you to partake in this fuller new covenant revelation of himself. The Old Testament prophets had the privilege of knowing him, but you partake in a much deeper, richer way than they ever could. They looked forward to the coming of Christ. For you these glories are not predictions – they are realities! We as New Testament saints are more privileged than the Old Testament prophets.

A Privilege Greater than the Angels

Peter says in verse 12, the glorious events of Christ's work of redemption that the prophets wrote about are now revealed and announced.

> **1 Peter 1:12** | It was revealed to them that they were serving not themselves but you, in the things that have now been announced to you through those who preached the good news to you by the Holy Spirit sent from heaven, things into which angels long to look.

The angels hear about this redemption that has been announced to you, and they peer over the rail of heaven with curiosity. They long to look into this redemption and understand it. We see the angels cry day and night, "Holy, holy, holy, the whole earth is filled with his glory" (Isa 6:3). How could a holy God redeem sinful man? Fallen angels don't get redeemed. Why fallen man?

This grace of holiness that we have is something the angels long to look into. If you think about it, none of the fallen angels will ever be redeemed, but God has chosen to redeem mankind. Oh how grateful

---

[21] MacArthur, *1 Peter*, 51–52.

we are to have the privilege of holiness, a privilege greater than all the Old Testament prophets and even the angels themselves.

A Privilege to Thank God for

How about you, are you seeking God's holiness by being grateful, or are you focused on the negatives in your life? Whatever you are going through is not worthy to be compared with the glorious privileges you have in Christ. It's so sad to hear Christians who love to complain about just about everything. They complain about their marriage. They complain about their job or their health. Brothers and sisters, we have nothing to complain about. Our suffering is only temporary. We've been delivered by Christ. For eternity we will live in all the perfections of God. Our short, difficult life is like a vapor that appears and then vanishes (Jas 4:14). Our glorious eternity with Christ will be forever. We are more privileged than the prophets and angels, and we have nothing to complain about. Your suffering will last a little while on this earth and then will be removed at the revelation of Christ at his second coming.

THE PRACTICE OF HOLINESS (1:13-16)

How are we to be holy? Remember, holiness is God's "God-ness." It is his infinite and moral attributes. We can't put God's omnipotence or his omniscience, but we can put on his purity, love, goodness, kindness, and faithfulness. That's holiness. It's being conformed to God's likeness. When God says, "Be holy for I am holy," he is calling for the image of God in us that was corrupted to be restored by our relationship with Christ. The first thing Peter says is to prepare for battle. The Christian life is a fight. We are to fight with five attitudes: preparation, sobriety, expectancy, humility, what I will call "identity".

Fight with Preparation

1 Peter 1:13a | Therefore, preparing your minds for action.

Peter is literally saying, "*roll up the robe of your mind.*" In ancient times in Israel, soldiers wore a long tunic that flowed down to the ground. The tunic was an outer garment that served as his primary clothing. Ordinarily it flowed down to the ground. But when it came time to fight, the soldier would pick up his tunic and tuck it into his belt for mobility in battle. The battle that every Christian has is in the mind. In many ways, this belt of truth affects the eyes since the truth crystalizes our worldview, how we see the world. How can you fight in a robe? You have to roll it up and tuck it into your belt. Prepare yourself for a fight because you are living in a wicked world. Be ready to fight for holiness by rolling up the robe of your mind into the belt of God's word. We have to be committed to walk by faith in the word of God and not be deceived or discouraged by our own thoughts (Pro 3:5-6).

What is your mind consumed with? Are you focused on your rights and your comforts and your security? That's mental focus will make any Christian miserable. We are not made for this world. Let us focus on "things above." Listen to Paul in Colossians 3.

> Set your minds on things that are above, not on things that are on earth. ³ For you have died, and your life is hidden with Christ in God. ⁴ When Christ who is your life appears, then you also will appear with him in glory. —*Colossians 3:2-4*

We have to be intentional with the attitudes and emotions of our inner being. So many are hardened by a low-level anger and pride, and remain ignorant of Satan's plans to use that pride to harass them with anger, anxiety and despair. Be prepared for action by constantly fighting with the sword of God's word (Mt 4:4; Heb 4:12). We are often lazy with our minds and wonder why Satan harasses us so much! I've heard Christians tell me that the only time they read God's word is on Sunday morning during church. Imagine if that was the only time we got a meal for the week. We would be emaciated.

If we are to truly live out a life of holiness, we must be in God's word "day and night" (Psa 1:1-3). God's word must be the "light unto our feet and a light unto our path" (Psa 119:105).

Fight with Sobriety

> **1 Peter 1:13b** | Therefore, preparing your minds for action, and being sober-minded.

He says first to be "sober-minded." Be on guard. You are always under attack. We are to take the battle seriously every day. The Christian life is not a vacation. That's why the prosperity gospel is a lie from hell. Our rest comes later. Right now we are at war. You have a bunch of Christians who are telling God's people to take a vacation in a war zone. That's reckless. You have to take this battle seriously. How do you do that? By putting God first above everything in your life where He belongs.

Holiness means we follow our King no matter where He leads us. Being a Christian is a change of citizenship, a change of governments, a change of allegiance. Holiness means that we let Christ rule in our lives and transform us and train us to be like Him, good, loving, faithful, kind, just, and filled with self-control.

This world is a fight. It's a battle. Your unsaved friends and family are going to be pulling you and tempting you constantly to come back to the world. You must gird up the robe of your mind and focus your heart on Jesus. Are you sober-minded? When people meet you do they see above all that Jesus Christ is at the control center of your life? Are you taking this war against your soul seriously? It takes sobriety. "being sober-minded, set your hope fully on the grace that will be brought to you at the revelation of Jesus Christ" (1 Pet 1:13b).

Fight with Expectancy

Peter is telling us how to fight the battle. It takes hope. Jesus Christ is coming at any moment, and you should be ready and filled with joy considering Christ's coming.

> **1 Peter 1:13c** | Therefore, preparing your minds for action... set your hope fully on the grace that will be brought to you at the revelation of Jesus Christ.

As you hope in Christ and look for his coming, you will have a transformed life. Jesus is coming again! He may come today! When he comes the battle will be over.

> We know that when he appears we shall be like him, because we shall see him as he is. —*1 John 3:2*

The hope that we have is a certain and unshakable expectation. It's not wishful thinking, but certainty. This brings overwhelming confidence. Like someone who's already seen the end of a movie, we are not torn apart by the plot twists of life.

Until Jesus returns, we are in a battle, and you can't do this alone. You can't do it in your own power. You need God's power. Grace is not just God's unmerited favor, but it is his transforming power. In order to live a life of holiness, separate from this world, you must focus your mind fully on the transforming grace of Jesus at his second coming. You have this grace right now.

This hope of Christ's coming creates a great deal of effort. Paul says in 1 Corinthians 15:10, "But by the grace of God I am what I am, and his grace toward me was not in vain. On the contrary, I worked harder than any of them, though it was not I, but the grace of God that is with me." Grace is not merely unmerited favor but transforming power. God's grace leads not only to our forgiveness, but our empowerment to live holy lives as we await the second coming of Jesus.

Where is your hope? – Is it in the grace you have in Christ? Or is it in something else? Is it in a job promotion? Don't get bogged down with the exhaustion of your work and employment. Do your best. But your ultimate hope is not in an earthly paycheck. It's not in a bigger house. Soon Christ will redeem the planet and cleanse it from the filth of sin. Is your hope in worldly entertainment? Is that where you go when you are hurting? Be filled with the hope of Christ. Don't settle for worldly substitutes. Don't get caught up in this world's entertainment. Learn what you can in this information age, but don't be info junkies. Instead, be addicted to worship. Be addicted to grace! Or when you hurt are you a shopper? There's not enough stuff at Stuff-mart to fill the emptiness in your soul. Don't set your hope in the obtaining of this world's goods. When Jesus' glory is revealed, your stuff will be worthless. Don't lay up junk on this earth. Sell your junk and invest the proceeds in missions. What are you doing with your money? Is your money going toward holy purposes? If you hope in earthly relationships, you will be cruelly disappointed. Christ alone is our hope. His grace is sufficient!

Fight with Humility

> **1 Peter 1:14** | As obedient children, do not be conformed to the passions of your former ignorance.

I love how Peter says the final way to fight with grace is to be helpless as a child. Rest in God as an obedient child. Don't be conformed to your "former ignorance" but instead be like an obedient child, humbly resting in the command of the Father.

In Matthew 18:3, Jesus called a little child to sit on his lap and proclaimed, "Truly, I say to you, unless you turn and become like children, you will never enter the kingdom of heaven."

Do you have the attitude of an obedient humble child? So often we act as if we know so much, but without humility we confuse holiness with self-righteousness and spiritual pride. Without humility, we are also prone to "be conformed to the passions of your former ignorance" (vs. 14). Without humility, you are going to fall into your former lifestyle.

Listen you can't do it alone. You need the Lord and you need the saints. Don't be too proud to ask for help. Have the attitude of an obedient and humble child if you want to be holy.

How many times do we know exactly what is in the Bible, but we make excuses? We are a proud person, not an obedient child. We have a temptation to question the all-wise God. His way is perfect!

Fight with Identity

1 Peter 1:15-16 | But as he who called you is holy, you also be holy in all your conduct, **16** since it is written, "You shall be holy, for I am holy."

When Peter tells of our call to be holy, he is referring to our identity. God has called us to "be" something. We are to "be holy". To be holy means "to be set apart" for something special. We get that. God did that for Israel and set them apart from all the other nations.

The command, it is written, "You shall be holy, for I am holy" is from Leviticus 11:45, "I am the Lord who brought you up out of the land of Egypt to be your God. You shall therefore be holy, for I am holy." God goes into the land of Egypt with a glory cloud and appoints Moses to lead the children of Israel out of Egypt. God took a sinful people out of the world to reflect his holiness.

God's ultimate call for holiness comes through Christ. All the ceremonies and sacrifices of the Old Testament were insufficient. God's ultimate plan for holiness comes through Christ's righteousness. The Spirit of God who is holy calls us to be holy and creates in us a new heart for holiness. We have the power now because of Christ to "be holy" in all our "conduct."

We as Christians are chosen as a remnant out of this world to be holy. Jesus said it in other ways on the Sermon on the Mount. "You are the light of the world" – you are to be holy by shining in a dark and sinful world. He also said, "You are the salt of the earth" – you are to be holy by preserving a rotten world.

Our holiness is something God has accomplished ultimately through Jesus Christ. God calls us to himself by his Spirit. He grants us faith and repentance. He separates us from all the peoples of the world. And he takes ownership of the believer's heart by his Holy Spirit (Eph 1:13-14; *cf* Eze 36:25-27). In Christ we are who God says we are. In Christ, we are called and made holy. This is our identity. We belong to him. We are adopted into his family. Our holiness is not generated by white knuckling it through fleshly human self-will. Our holiness is possible by the power of the Spirit within us. The Spirit's power is accessible through faith, understanding our identity is in Christ, and not of our own making.

THE PRICE OF HOLINESS (1:17-21)

Finally, we consider the price for holiness. God wants you to be holy, and you as a sinner are to die to your old life and be holy. But it comes at a price. You were ransomed by the blood of Christ.

Conduct Yourselves with Fear

Peter begins with a sober outlook for the Christian life. Since Christ has paid such an infinitely high price, Peter says "fear" should be the overarching attitude of our lives. We should live and conduct our lives with reverence and sobriety.

Fear the Lord as Father

1 Peter 1:17 | And if you call on him as Father who judges impartially according to each one's deeds, conduct yourselves with fear throughout the time of your exile.

We should fear the Lord because he is our Father. As our good Father in heaven, to whom we cry out "Abba" or "da da", like a little child, he loves us and will not allow us as his children to live carelessly. Indeed, he judges his children in several ways that are for our good and his glory. His judgment is certainly not condemnation, for there is no condemnation in Christ (Rom 8:1).

His judgment is first an *examination* (1 Cor. 3:10–15) at the end of our lives. All our deeds will be examined at the judgment seat of Christ, whether they are good or worthless. Some will be like gold and silver and precious stones. Others will be worthless and burn like wood, hay, and stubble.

His judgment is manifested presently in our lives through his loving *discipline* (Heb 12:5–11). God will not allow his children to stray, but "lead them in paths of righteousness for his name's sake" (Psa 23:3). Indeed, all believers are "predestined to be conformed to the image of his Son" (Rom 8:29). We are his "masterpiece," created unto good works which God foreordained that we should walk in them (Eph 2:10). In other words, God will do whatever it takes to make his children holy in this present life. Sometimes God's discipline of his children even includes death if they are unwilling to submit to him (1 Cor 11:30-32). Some of God's discipline is carried out by his church (Mt 18:15–20).

Fear the Lord as Foreigners

1 Peter 1:17b | Conduct yourselves with fear throughout the time of your exile.

Peter reminds us we are in exile. This world of sin and rebellion is not our ultimate home. God is our Father, and we long to be with him. Jesus is coming soon to institute righteousness on the earth. This world is quite uncomfortable for the believer. The world laughs at sin, but the believer soberly grieves, for soon the Judge of all the earth will arrive and hold court. We are not at home here but gather at local churches which are outposts of the New Jerusalem, where we gather encouragement from other sober-minded citizens of heaven.

Fear the Lord as Forgiver

1 Peter 1:18-19 | Conduct yourselves with fear... **18** knowing that you were ransomed from the futile ways inherited from your forefathers, not with perishable things such as silver or gold, **19** but with the precious blood of Christ, like that of a lamb without blemish or spot.

Another thing that ought to bring a deep reverence to our hearts as followers of Christ is the price Christ paid on the cross. God sent his Son for us. He gave the blood of the Son for you. God will judge each person based on how we have appropriated the sacrifice of Christ.

We are redeemed from *wrath*. Peter says, "Conduct yourselves with fear... knowing that you were ransomed" (1:18a). Scripture makes clear the truth that all believers were once in bondage to sin and wrath, and that only Christ's redemption broke that bondage (Rom 6:6, 17–18).

We are also redeemed from *futile religion*. Peter says we are "ransomed from the futile ways inherited from your forefathers" (1:18b). So many religious people will meet Christ on judgment day and be shocked when he says: "I never knew you; depart from me, you workers of lawlessness" (Mt 7:23). They had known religious traditions, and even the word of God, perhaps, but they did not know the God of the word. The religious and non-religious are both under God's wrath and need redemption. All works done outside of the Spirit of God are merely dead works, done for self, and are under the condemnation of God. Futile religion is deceptive because it has "the appearance of godliness, but denying its power" (2 Tim 3:5). True religion is always done from the heart for the glory of God and the good of humanity (Jas 1:27).

We are redeemed by *the blood of Christ*. Peter says we know that we "were ransomed... not with perishable things such as silver or gold, but with the precious blood of Christ, like that of a lamb without blemish or spot" (1:18c-19). We count the blood of Jesus as precious. When we speak of the blood, we are talking about the substitutionary atonement of Christ. It is the blood that gives you a righteous standing before God for all eternity.

> He made him who knew no sin to be sin on our behalf, so that we might become the righteousness of God in him. —*2 Corinthians 5:21*

The price Christ paid is not like gold or silver. No amount of earthly treasure could ever take away our sins. No amount of money could deliver us from hell. But Christ willingly gave his life to satisfy God's just wrath against our sins. Christ fulfills the Levitical sacrificial system where a lamb had to be spotless and without blemish.

What is our response to this awful price Christ paid for our sins? Fear God my brothers and sisters. Consider the Almighty God in the person of Christ hanging there on the cross of Golgotha. Never be flippant about that. We are forever changed once we've seen such an awful price. Fear God as you consider the awful price that was paid for your soul. Don't trample underfoot the blood of Christ. Don't play around with grace. The author of Hebrews says in Hebrews 10:29, "How much worse punishment, do you think, will be deserved by the one who has trampled underfoot the Son of God, and has profaned the blood of the covenant by which he was sanctified, and has outraged the Spirit of grace?"

Conduct Yourselves with Faith

On the one hand there is fear when it comes to the blood of Christ. We don't want to trample Christ's blood underfoot. Yet there is also deep comfort as we entrust ourselves to the one who loved us and gave his Son for us.

Faith in God's Plan

1 Peter 1:20 | He was foreknown before the foundation of the world but was made manifest in the last times for the sake of you.

Christ's sacrifice was planned from the foundation of the world but has been revealed in these last days for you! God loves you. He has planned for your redemption before the world was formed. In other words, Christ's sacrifice was never "Plan B." God knew the universe would fall into the chaos of sin when he created it. In his sovereignty he allowed us to choose, even though we would choose wrongly. When Peter says God foreknew his Son Jesus before the world was formed, it does not mean that God merely "knew ahead of time" that Christ would be the sacrifice for the world, but that God foreordained it in his eternal decree. This plan of redemption that the prophets of the Old Testament spoke about had always been the plan in the counsels of the divine Trinity in eternity past. The Father planned it, the Son would pay for it, and the Spirit would be the agent to transform those who would by faith enjoy redemption. How amazing it is that "in these last times" and for our sake, God has revealed his Son to believers. By "last times" Peter means the final epoch of human history. This is the time period between the cross of Christ and the consummation at the second coming.

Faith is God's Gift

1 Peter 1:21 | Who through him are believers in God, who raised him from the dead and gave him glory, so that your faith and hope are in God.

It is Christ who has given you faith to believe. God the Father raised Christ from the dead so that that you could have the gift of faith and hope! To put it more simply: You are to hold on to God, but more importantly, God is holding on to you. He's got you. He'll never let you go.

He'll never leave you and never forsake you. Oh, saint, be holy for your Lord is holy. Don't be conformed to the world but be transformed by the renewing of your mind.

Conclusion

Dear saints, we are called to holiness. This is your purpose and destiny. No child of God can live comfortably in sin for any length of time. The Christian life reminds me of the sweet and unique ermine, or the northern weasel. He's like an albino squirrel. "In the forests of northern Europe and Asia lives little animal called the ermine, known for his snow-white fur in winter. He instinctively protects his white coat against anything that would soil it. Fur hunters take advantage of this unusual trait of the ermine. They don't set a snare to catch him, but instead they find his home, which is usually a cleft in a rock or a hollow in an old tree. They smear the entrance and interior with grime. Then the hunters set their dogs loose to find and chase the ermine. The frightened animal flees toward home but doesn't enter because of the filth. Rather than soil his white coat, he is trapped by the dogs and captured while preserving his purity. For the ermine, purity is more precious than life."[22]

God has called us to holiness and provided the way. Let us be like that ermine who would rather die than soil ourselves with this world. Let us live holy and separate lives from this depraved planet.

---

[22] Henry G. Bosch. "Holy Blue" (Grand Rapids, MI: Our Daily Bread, April 21, 1997), https://odb.org/US/1997/04/21/holy-blue.

5 | 1 PETER 1:22-25
THE LIVING WORD

The grass withers, and the flower falls, but the word of the Lord remains forever." And this word is the good news that was preached to you.

1 PETER 1:24-25

Jill and I are approaching 25 years of marriage. At our 10-year anniversary I decided to make her a custom anniversary ring. I had no money, so I gathered all the gold around the house. I also had one diamond. A friend of mine, my friend, Miles Crouse gave me two diamonds that his wife had. I gave all that to the jeweler and he melted it down and made a beautiful custom anniversary ring for Jill. That jeweler did an amazing job. I gave him a bunch of random pieces and he turned it into a beautiful ring through the furnace. He melted it down and transformed it.

That's how God's word is. God melts our hearts through his word and transforms us! How can God's word do this? How come it can transform us so effectively? Peter gives us the answer in 1 Peter 1:22-25. God's word is powerful, alive, and lasting, and it brings lasting change to the life of every believer.

1 Peter 1:22-25 | Having purified your souls by your obedience to the truth for a sincere brotherly love, love one another earnestly from a pure heart, ²³ since you have been born again, not of perishable seed but of imperishable, through the living and abiding word of God; ²⁴ for "All flesh is like grass and all its glory like the flower of grass. The grass withers, and the flower falls, ²⁵ but the word of the Lord remains forever." And this word is the good news that was preached to you.

The flag that we have "nailed to the mast" of our churches is the uncontested authority and sufficiency of the word of God for faith and practice-for living it out in obedience to our Lord. The 16th Century Reformers called this doctrine "Sola Scriptura" or "Scripture Alone." Scripture alone is our sole and final authority for faith and practice. The Bible alone is God's revelation of himself and tells us how to be saved and in right relationship with him. There is no possible way to know the God who created us apart from his self-revelation in the 66 books of our Bible. God's word is powerful to enlighten our hearts and bring us to salvation in Jesus Christ.

GOD'S WORD IS POWERFUL (1:22-23)

1 Peter 1:22-23 | Having purified your souls by your obedience to the truth for a sincere brotherly love, love one another earnestly from a pure heart, ²³ since you have been born again, not of perishable seed but of imperishable, through the living and abiding word of God.

The whole premise of verse 23 is that you have been born again. There is power in the word of God! Peter presents three evidences of the power of the new birth: power for purity, power to obey, and power to love. The word of God is powerful, so says the author of Hebrews.

> For the word of God is living and active, sharper than any two-edged sword, piercing to the division of soul and of spirit, of joints and of marrow, and discerning the thoughts and intentions of the heart.
> —*Hebrews 4:12*

Power for Purity

1 Peter 1:22a-23b | Having purified your souls... through the living and abiding word of God.

God's living word, the Bible, is powerful to cleanse our souls. So much of what is wrong with society comes from the toxic consequences of sin. People are heavy with guilt. Their hearts are filled with anxiety, anger, and despair. They are trying to turn this off through worldliness, lust, and addictions. But only God's word can cleanse us from our sin and guilt. Jesus said, "Sanctify them through your truth: your word is truth" (Jn 17:17). Paul says we are "washed by the water of the word" (Eph 5:26). David says, "as far as the east is from the west, so far does he remove our transgressions from us" (Psalm 103:12). It is the word of God that Peter says purifies our souls! When you are born again, your soul is purified. You believe the word that Jesus gave to his disciples before he went to the cross. You are cleansed by his word. Let that word of cleansing wash over you.

> Already you are clean because of the word that I have spoken to you.
> —John 17:3

A person can't work their way to that kind of soul cleansing. You don't work your way into God's favor.

> For by grace you have been saved through faith. And this is not your own doing; it is the gift of God, [9] not a result of works, so that no one may boast. —Ephesians 2:8-9

Only in Christ can we be fully cleansed and accepted. Only God is pure. What John said is true: "God is light, and in him is no darkness at all" (Jn 1:5). That's true. So we think, I must not be accepted, because I am so unholy. I've believed, but I've backslidden. God's word to you is this: It is finished. Christ's righteousness is upon you. Repent of your selfish living and turn back to God. There is no period of penance. Yes, you must repent. You must see your sin as God sees it. You must hate your sin and your old life as God hates it. But then you are immediately restored. Your soul is cleansed by the blood of Jesus. It is finished. Believe it! We are cleansed through Christ alone.

We need to have a daily bath in God's word, or we will slowly fade away from fellowship with the Lord. Sometimes we are too weak or dry to help ourselves. This is why fellowship is so important. We need to have rich encouragement and accountability through the saints who are filled with God's word and can help cleanse us by reminding us of God's word. Worshipping with God's people every Lord's day is also vital for the cleansing of God's word.

Power for Obedience

1 Peter 1:22b | Having purified your souls by your obedience to the truth...

Someone said wisely, "Either this book will keep you from sin, or sin will keep you from this book." We are called, through our soul's purification to obey the truth of Jesus' death and resurrection. I love how he doesn't say "faith" or "belief in the truth." That's maybe what we might say. But Peter emphasizes obedience because it is the outcome or fruit of true faith. The Bible defines mature faith as "faith accompanied by action," not just the verbal expression of one's belief (Jas 2:14-26). Here, action means obedience to God's word. Faith can be measured through obedience. Obedience is the visible expression of invisible faith. As we assimilate God's word to our heart to love God and his way, it will manifest in our lives through obedience. In other words, we are not merely receptacles for biblical information, but we are those who are called to walk in the word, not just hearing, but taking action (Jas 1:22-25).

Immersion in God's word will keep us from sin. David said, "Your word have I hid in my heart, that I might now sin against you" (Psa 119:11). Put the word in your heart through true surrender and faith, and power to obey will take root in your heart. If you lack power, then search your heart for sin. The first word in the gospel is *repent*.

If you come by faith, the word gives you power to obey. You believe Christ, and his word to you is get up and walk. His word to you is "Lazarus, come forth." Don't stay in that grave a moment longer. You are alive! The word of God is living and active. Rise up and walk! Stretch forth that dead hand because it can now function. God's word give you a heart to obey. Ezekiel says that God takes out your old, dead heart of stone. He puts in a tender living heart of flesh. He gives you his Spirit and he causes you "to walk in his statutes and to keep his judgments" (Eze 36:25-27). In other words, you now as a Christian have the power and the impulse to obey. When you are in the flesh, you are weak and unable to obey God. If you feel that way right now, believe and receive his word. Obey saint of God. The Spirit in you will do the work. Surrender to the Spirit and he will make you his instrument.

Power for Love

1 Peter 1:22c | Having purified your souls...for a sincere brotherly love, love one another earnestly from a pure heart.

Peter says another effect of the word of God is you love the brothers. Verse 22 says you've obeyed the truth of God's word that it is finished and Christ has paid it all, and then we see the result: love. Your faith works itself out "for a sincere brotherly love, love one another earnestly from a pure heart."

This is the command: "love one another." How? Sincerely. Don't put on an act. Love one another. Let me make a couple of distinctions. This is Agape love. It's not the love of feeling that is constantly in flux. It is not the love of passion or romance that can change from day to day. This is the constant love of choice. It is a God kind of love. It is the love of sacrifice and choice, not based on whether the person is loveable, but because they are in Christ.

Love needs to be sincere – you can't fake it until you make it. In beanbag toss, you might be a total newbie. I'm scared to play beginners. They always win. They fake it. They just aim, and somehow that beanbag goes into the hole. You can fake it in cornhole, but you cannot fake it in the Christian life.

The word "earnestly" or fervently (*ektenōs*) is a physiological term meaning to stretch to the furthest limit of a muscle's capacity.[23] It's a supernatural love that goes beyond human capacity. People are so messed up. I'm messed up. How can we love purely when there's so many warts? The love of Christ flows from broken people. He didn't say, "Come, you who have your life together." He called the weary and those burdened with sin (Mt 11:18-30).

The apostle John tells us plainly how brotherly love is an evidence of the new birth. "Everyone who loves the Father loves whoever has been born of him" (1 Jn 5:1b). This isn't humanly manufactured but divine. Human love is always mixed with selfish motives. But divine love is pure and unconditional. This is the blazing center of our evangelism. John 13:35 says, "By this shall all people know you are my disciples, that you love one another." This is the evangelism tool that Jesus

---

[23] MacArthur, *1 Peter*, 90.

says is authentic. The greatest key to evangelism is a healthy local church—a forever family that love one another.

The world will know that God has sent Jesus by our love for one another. What does that mean? Do you know someone in the Body of Christ who is hurting? Are they sick? Are they lonely? Minister to them! Do you know a brother or a sister in need? Provide for them! Is there a believer who has gone astray? Go after them and don't judge them. Show them the unconditional love of Calvary. Are you slipping in your love for the brothers? Get back into the word of God. It will empower you to love.

Our forever family in Christ is the physical manifestation of Christ in the earth. Remember when Saul of Tarsus was persecuting the church? Jesus said, "Saul, Saul, why do you persecute me?" Jesus says in Matthew 25:40, "Truly, I say to you, as much as you did it to one of the least of these my brothers, you did it to me." Just as Jesus walked in this world and blessed people, so you are now the body of Christ in this world. As he loved, so you should love.

GOD'S WORD IS ALIVE (1:23)

> **1 Peter 1:23-25** | Since you have been born again, not of perishable seed but of imperishable, through the living and abiding word of God; **24** for "All flesh is like grass and all its glory like the flower of grass. The grass withers, and the flower falls, **25** but the word of the Lord remains forever." And this word is the good news that was preached to you.

Martin Luther said, "The Bible is alive, it speaks to me. It has feet, it runs after me. It has hands, it lays hold of me." God's Word is alive in three ways: like a birth, a seed, and a roommate.

God's Word is Alive like a Birth

> **1 Peter 1:23a** | You have been born again... through the living and abiding word of God.

The new birth is monergistic; it is a work solely of the Holy Spirit. Sinners do not cooperate in their spiritual births *(cf* Eph 2:1–10) any more than infants cooperate in their natural births. Jesus told Nicodemus, "The wind blows where it wishes and you hear the sound of it, but do not know where it comes from and where it is going; so is everyone who is born of the Spirit" (Jn 3:8; *cf* Jn 1:12–13; Eph 2:4–5; Phil 2:13).[24]

God's word has caused you to be born again. What does that mean? Essentially, it is a nature change. You used to never have power to obey God. You used to be not only powerless to obey, but powerless to get clean. But something new happened to you. You were born again by believing and trusting the word of God.

The Bible says, "Abraham believed God, and it was counted to him for righteousness" (Gen 15:6; *cf* Rom 4:3). The word of God came to him, and he trusted God. Now it was an infantile trust. Jesus said, "if you have the faith of a mustard seed, you can move a mountain" (Mt 17:20). We don't have fully developed faith immediately, just the faith of a mustard seed. But it's so powerful it can move mountains. The greatest mountain is your old nature that is dead in trespasses and sins. You can't love God because you love sin so much. God comes in through the word of God and kills your old self. You are crucified with Christ.

God's Word is Alive like a Seed

> **Peter 1:23b** | Since you have been born again, not of perishable seed but of imperishable...

God's word is like seed that gives imperishable fruit. There are many things we plant, and they go bad. We have a grape vine by our home. Concord grapes. I love them when I remember to pick them. Jill's made this amazing concord grape juice. It's that purple grape juice, so sweet! Sometimes I get busy and forget to pick the grapes when they are ripe and they perish. They're no good. They have a shelf life. They have a limited life. God's word is not that way. It's like a seed that gives imperishable fruit. Imagine the perfect apple tree. You plant it and every apple is perfect, and it's good after it's been on the vine ten years or a hundred years. Can you imagine? That's how God's word is. God's word is alive! It never goes bad!

These verses remind me of one of Ezekiel's prophesies in the valley of dry bones. The prophet was told to preach over a cemetery of dead soldiers in Israel. He preached, and as the word of God went forth, the dry bones came alive and were clothed with flesh, and they lived (Eze 37). What a picture of the new covenant when the spiritually dead are

---

[24] MacArthur, *1 Peter*, 92.

brought to life! Ezekiel tells us how exactly people are brought to life as well. The stubborn and hard heart of stone is taken away, and a new living heart is replaced by the power of the Spirit through the word of God. God then causes the fruit of faith and obedience, causing us to "walk in his statutes and keep his judgments" (Eze 36:26).

God's Word is Alive like a Roommate

> **Peter 1:23b** | ... through the living and abiding word of God.

I love the language Peter uses. He says it's a living word that "abides" or literally "moves in." God promises to "never leave... or forsake you." He says, "no one can pluck you out of my hand." He's moving in. When you were born again, God moved in to constantly remind you of his word.

Have you ever had a roommate? When I got married a roommate-socks on the floor. She doesn't really nag me – she is gentle. She doesn't say "Matt you left your socks on the floor." But she does encourage me when I do not leave my socks on the floor. You see God's word is not just pages in a book or words on a page. When God's word enters your heart, it is like God moving in (*cf* Jn 15:1-7). That's why it's the living and abiding word. It's God moving into your heart and revealing himself to you.

I love Psalm 119:105, "Your word is a lamp to my feet and a light to my path." The Lord who dwells in you uses the word to light the pathway of your life. Without the word, you are lost in a forest without a light. You cannot see the right trail!

GOD'S WORD IS LASTING (1:24-25)

Here Peter contrasts our weak flesh with the powerful word of God. What the flesh can accomplish is temporary. What the word accomplishes is lasting. But unlike the living word, all flesh withers away.

What Doesn't Last

> **1 Peter 1:24** | For "All flesh is like grass and all its glory like the flower of grass. The grass withers, and the flower falls."

"All flesh" refers to all humans and animals, and "grass" refers to the wild grass of the typical Middle Eastern countryside. The phrase "glory like the flower of grass" denotes the beauty of that scenery in which colorful flowers (*cf* Mt 6:28–29) occasionally rise above the grass. So Peter noted that whether something is as common as grass or as uniquely lovely as a flower, it eventually withers or falls off—it dies. Human life is brief in this world. Ten out of ten people die. It's the ultimate statistic.

People pass away like dry grass under a withering east wind. In their graves, the poor and illiterate of no influence are equal to the wealthy and highly educated of great influence (*cf* Job 3:17–19). In Christ, however, whether people are common or uncommon, they will never deteriorate or die spiritually. Instead, they are like the word of the Lord which endures forever.[25]

What we can do in our flesh will never last! We can't change people. We can't even change ourselves. If you want lasting change you need the word. This contrast is made throughout the word of God. Jesus says in John 6:63, "It is the Spirit who gives life; the flesh profits nothing. The words that I have spoken to you are spirit and life." Paul says the same thing. He contrasts the flesh and the spirit. Let's look at two places.

> 2 Corinthians 4:16, "Though our outer self is wasting away, our inner self is being renewed day by day."

> Romans 8:6-8, "For to set the mind on the flesh is death, but to set the mind on the Spirit is life and peace. ⁷ For the mind that is set on the flesh is hostile to God, for it does not submit to God's law; indeed, it cannot. ⁸ Those who are in the flesh cannot please God."

What are you investing in? Here we see the two sides of the human being. The outer man is like the flower of the field, which is mortal and will pass away, whereas the inner man lives forever by the power of the living God.[26]

What Lasts

1 Peter 1:25a | "But the word of the Lord remains forever."

It is true that "the word of the Lord remains forever" (1:25). Peter begins by quoting Isaiah 40:6-8 which tells us all flesh (all living things) are powerless to save themselves from death. God's word is eternal, but

---

[25] MacArthur, *1 Peter*, 93.
[26] Hilary of Arles in Gerald Bray, *James, 1-2 Peter, 1-3 John, Jude* (Downers Grove, IL: InterVarsity Press, 2000), 81.

our flesh is not. We are temporal. We are here today and gone tomorrow.[27] Don't try to accomplish anything with a fleshly mindset in your own human power. That mindset is like the grass or like flowers. It's not going to last. Only God's word can bring about lasting change. How? It begins with the gift of faith. "Faith comes from hearing, and hearing through the word of Christ" (Rom 10:17; *cf* Jas 1:18).

The word of God creates faith in fallen sinners. It is this faith that connects us to the work of Christ, which atones for our sins. It is this faith that the Spirit of God honors and regenerates our heart. The word of God transforms us so that we are not only saved, that is justified, but we are being saved, that is sanctified.

What Love!

1 Peter 1:25b | And this word is the good news that was preached to you.

Someone loved you and cared enough to give you the good news about Jesus, and you believe and trusted your life to him, and now you are eternally saved. The work that the word does in you will bring fruit that lasts forever (Phil 1:6). Indeed, you are God's masterpiece, and he will never stop working on you (Eph 2:10). You are forever born again into God's family. Your sins are forever forgiven. You will be forever conformed to Jesus. You are forever adopted into God's family. You are forever an heir of God and a joint heir with Christ. The grass and flowers of this life fade. You get various things in life – a home, a family, children perhaps. A career. Many things can be enjoyed in this life. But they are all going to fade away like grass in a drought or a flower on a hot day. Everything in this life is fading. But what God does in your heart by the word – conforming you into the image of Christ – that lasts forever!

Conclusion

The word of God is alive! God lives inside you! He will never leave you or forsake you. His Spirit who resides in you made you alive by the word of God. That enlivening or as the old word is, quickening, is sometimes referred to as conversion.

---

[27] Helm, *1 & 2 Peter and Jude*, 68.

In our local church, before people become members, we have them give the story of their conversion. Many people are awakened from time to time and drawn to God, but for every true believer, they go beyond the mere calling, and they are converted by the word of God. There is a radical change that takes place. That change is forever. It's lasting. It's a metamorphosis performed by the word of God.

Do you have a testimony of conversion? Are you able to articulate how God moved into your heart by the Holy Spirit because of the death and resurrection of Jesus? When were you made alive by the Spirit through the word?

6 | 1 PETER 2:1-3
DESIRING GOD

Like newborn infants, long for the pure spiritual milk, that by it you may grow up into salvation— if indeed you have tasted that the Lord is good.
1 PETER 2:2-3

Don't get disconnected. The other day my phone is about out of battery. So I'm in the car and I plug it in, but I don't realize the cable is not connected to the charger (It's in my glove box so I couldn't see it. How terrible it is when you think you have a fully charged phone, and then you pick it up and it's almost dead. That's how we get sometimes in our Christian life. There are blind spots that make us think we are farther along in our Christian life than we are.

We've got to be desiring God, being connected to him if we are going to grow into the image of Jesus.

1 Peter 2:1-3 | So put away all malice and all deceit and hypocrisy and envy and all slander. ² Like newborn infants, long for the pure spiritual milk, that by it you may grow up into salvation— ³ if indeed you have tasted that the Lord is good.

I want us all to be plugged in to our Lord. I want us to be at full power. I want us as Peter says to be craving the spiritual milk of the Word. Perhaps you've lost your desire and you want to get it back.

WHAT HINDERS OUR APPETITE FOR GOD? (2:1)

1 Peter 2:1 | So put away all malice and all deceit and hypocrisy and envy and all slander.

Peter describes the self-life that hinders our relationship with God (*cf* Gal 5:19-24). The whole idea of Peter's message is that we are born again. He's going to tell us we are living stones in God's temple. We are a body. Therefore, rid yourselves of all malice and all deceit, hypocrisy, envy, and slander of every kind. What do all these bad vices have in common? They involve relationships, how we treat others.

When carnal fighting or sin of any kind is present, it will hurt your love for others and hinder our desire for God. We are to crave God's spiritual food with the tenacity of a hungry infant. If you want to know what will kill your spiritual walk with God, it's the self-life. Selfishness is demonstrated here five ways but could be demonstrated in five thousand ways. Paul says put away selfishness. Take it off like a dirty garment.

Residing with undetected sin will destroy your appetite.

1 Peter 2:1 | So put away all malice and all deceit and hypocrisy and envy and all slander.

The one thing that all these things Peter listed have in common is that they are activities of the heart that we cannot see with our physical eyes. They are easily hidden. Peter says to "put away" these sinful attitudes of the heart. Stop living with respectable sin. Take it off like a filthy garment. Put these things away.

"Put Away" Illustrated

In ancient Christian baptism ceremonies, those being baptized customarily took off and discarded the clothes they wore to the ceremony. Following their baptisms, they put on new robes they received from the church. Exchanging clothes symbolized the salvation reality of laying aside the old life and taking up the new (Rom 6:3–7; 2 Cor 5:17; Eph 4:24).[28] Those who would wear the white robe of regeneration must lay aside the filthy garments (Zech 3:3) of the old carnal life. So St. Paul bids us put off the old man and put on the new (Eph 4:22, 24; Col. 3:8,

---

[28] MacArthur, *1 Peter*, 97.

10). So as Romans 13:14 says most simply: "Put on the Lord Jesus Christ."[29] The things we are to "put away" have one thing in common. They all undo the bonds we have with people. They destroy relationships. In contrast love builds others up; love strengthens relationships.[30] You cannot put on the love of Christ and wear selfishness at the same time. Get the stinking, filthy garments of the self-life off you, and put on the sweet-smelling garment of Christ.

"Put Away" Practiced

The idea of "put away" is a continual action. Some translations say, "having put away" to bring this to light. A true believer cannot life with the selfish life as a practice. No true believer can continue in ongoing habits of unrighteousness. You will never be what you once were. We should never treat each other as if we were lost. You are not rebels. You are saints. You should characterize each other as saints. You are the chosen of God. You were bought with a price.

Paul says, you may struggle with these five sins (and many more) but they do not characterize you. They cannot characterize you. You have the Spirit of God dwelling in you. He's your roommate. He's your comforter and the One who brings conviction. Take off these five forms of selfishness and lay them aside like a dirty garment. They'll destroy your desire for God's word. You won't want to walk with God if these things are in your life. The first is malice or ill-will toward others. Sin destroys our appetite for spiritual food. You've heard the saying, "This book will keep you from sin, or sin will keep you from this book." That's what Peter is saying. You need to properly apply the word to your life.

This book will keep you from sin, but if you neglect the book and don't act upon it, then that sin will rob you of your appetite for the word of God. There are many sins that will quench and stifle our appetite for God's word. Peter names five here.

"Put Away" Personalized

We often think the problem is in someone else. It's my work. It's my spouse. It's a church member. Peter says, no! Begin with yourself. Almost always it's me! Not my brother or sister, but it's me O Lord. It's

---

[29] H. D. M. Spence-Jones, (ed.) *1 Peter* (London; New York: Funk & Wagnalls Company, 1909), 68.
[30] Helm, *1 & 2 Peter and Jude*, 69.

almost always sin that has entered into our life. Sin that is justified, sin that is minimized, sin that is overlooked, sin that is ignored will take away our desire for God and his word. Put away anything in your life that is contrary to the revealed word of God. Sin is sin, whether we recognize it or not. Sin is crossing the line of the boundary of God's will, and it effects our relationship with God. We need to breathe a prayer to the Spirit that he would reveal sin in my life.

"Put Away" Commanded

1 Peter 2:1a | So put away...

1 Peter 1:22 told us to "love one another earnestly from a pure heart." We are to love each other deeply. Therefore, we have to put off these relationship killers. They are a cancer to the body of Christ, and they stifle our devotion and craving for God.

To "put away" something requires purposeful action. "Rid yourselves" "Cast aside" "Strip off your garment." Lay aside like a garment. Strip off your clothes like those who would strip off a jacket that was filled with maggots. We hear this command constantly echoed throughout Scripture.

> Put off your old self, which belongs to your former manner of life and is corrupt through deceitful desires, [23] and to be renewed in the spirit of your minds, [24] and to put on the new self, created after the likeness of God in true righteousness and holiness. —*Ephesians 4:22*

> Do not lie to one another, seeing that you have put off the old self with its practices [10] and have put on the new self, which is being renewed in knowledge after the image of its creator. —*Colossians 3:9-10*

> Let us also lay aside every weight, and sin which clings so closely, and let us run with endurance the race that is set before us, [2] looking to Jesus, the founder and perfecter of our faith. —*Hebrews 12:1-2*

What is in your life that is not pleasing to the Lord? Lay it aside like a filthy, stinking garment. Put it away.

Rationalizing respectable sin will destroy your appetite.

Notice Peter uses the word "all" here. We cannot rationalize away any little bit of sin. It all has to go. The only way to do that is to expose it. Let's look at these areas of sin in depth.

1 Peter 2:1 | So put away all malice and all deceit and hypocrisy and envy and all slander.

These are all sins that destroy relationships within the family of God. Peter's not dealing with the big sins, we can see those. In most places Christians put those big sins, drunkenness, fornication, etc. off first. But these so called "respectable sins" are the sins that destroy relationships in the Body of Christ. These are five areas that you say at first you don't have a problem. That is because we are blinded in our flash by spiritual pride and self-righteousness. Peter names the scariest because they are common to man. These are relationship killers in the body of Christ. It's not just these five sins, but any sin that keeps us from desiring God. "If I regard iniquity in my heart, the Lord will not hear me" (Psa 66:18). That means if I sin, my covenant with God is still intact, but my relationship with him is hindered. We ought to pray with David.

> Search me, O God, and know my heart! Try me and know my thoughts! [24] And see if there be any grievous way in me, and lead me in the way everlasting! —*Psalm 139:23-24*

When I was a teenager, we would walk around the mall sometimes and smell the aroma of popcorn. Oh, when you are hungry have you ever smelled that aroma? It may be you are in your neighborhood, and you don't know what to make for dinner, and you smell the delightful aroma of grilled steak. There are certain things that whet the appetite. There are other things that destroy our appetite. For me if you talk about something gross at the dinner table, my family and close friends will tell you, I lose my appetite. If you were eating rice, and all the sudden you saw a maggot moving, you'd lose your appetite. So today we are going to talk about what make us lose or gain our spiritual appetite.

Hurting Others (Malice)

1 Peter 2:1a | So put away all malice.

All malice has got to go. Malice is hatefulness or ill-will. It's a desire to inflict pain on others. It's the exact opposite of Jesus. Jesus laid down his life for us. He knew the worst about us and did the best for us. Jesus has good will toward all people. Malice is a response, that when I am hurt, I am prone to hurt others. You know the old saying, "Hurting people hurt people." That's not the attitude of a Christian. When someone hurts us, we want to hurt them. That's not the way a true Christian acts. If someone hurts you, that does not give you the right to hurt them back.

> Cleanse out the old leaven that you may be a new lump [of dough], as you really are unleavened. For Christ, our Passover lamb, has been sacrificed. ⁸ Let us therefore celebrate the festival, not with the old leaven, the leaven of malice and evil, but with the unleavened bread of sincerity and truth. —*1 Corinthians 5:7-8*

How do we put off malice? Jesus and the apostles talk a lot about how we should deal with relationships. Remember our culture as Christians is not first and foremost as Americans. We are first and foremost citizens of heaven! So our culture is from the Bible. And the culture of Christ is one of love and sacrifice – compassion and empathy. We are to lay down our lives, not win the argument. How do we put off malice? Here are some ideas.

1. Don't try to avenge yourself. Overcome evil with good. "Bless those who persecute you; bless and do not curse them" (Rom 12:14). "Repay no one evil for evil, but give thought to do what is honorable in the sight of all. ¹⁸ If possible, so far as it depends on you, live peaceably with all. ¹⁹ Beloved, never avenge yourselves, but leave it to the wrath of God, for it is written, "Vengeance is mine, I will repay, says the Lord" (Rom 12:17-19). "Do not be overcome by evil, but overcome evil with good" (Rom 12:21).

2. Love those who wrong you. Practice non-resistance. "You have heard that it was said, 'An eye for an eye and a tooth for a tooth.' ³⁹ But I say to you, Do not resist the one who is evil. But if anyone slaps you on the right cheek, turn to him the other also" (Mt 5:38-39). As a believer in Christ, you are to be non-resistant. Obviously, this does not include such things as domestic abuse where the person should call for the law to deal with person. But this is talking about those personal wrongs that hit us the wrong way. We are to turn the other cheek. "Love your enemies and pray for those who persecute you, ⁴⁵ so that you may be sons of your Father who is in heaven. For he makes his sun rise on the evil and on the good, and sends rain on the just and on the unjust. ⁴⁶ For if you love those who love you, what reward do you have? Do not even the tax collectors do the same? ⁴⁷ And if you greet only your brothers, what more are you doing than others? Do not even the Gentiles do the same?" (Mt 5:44-47). Lost people can love their family and friends

when they are nice to them. But God calls us to love our enemies. Love those who do wrong to us.

3. Trust God. You've got to leave your hurt to God. God will repay. Most of the nitpicky stuff we deal with we need to trust God. We must never be malicious or vengeful. We must wait for the glorious day of Christ when "he will judge the living and the dead" (2 Tim 4:1). "Beloved, never avenge yourselves, but leave it to the wrath of God, for it is written, 'Vengeance is mine, I will repay, says the Lord'" (Rom 12:19).

4. Remember who you are. Malice is not like Jesus. The mindset of malice is always thinking good of myself and evil of others and to act on it. To meet out evil toward others. To be malicious is to do something on purpose for another person's harm.[31] It means to have "ill will." The word *malice* signifies ill will that originates in our sinful nature.[32] Malice is not at all who we are in Christ. In Christ we love those around us, especially our forever family in Christ. "Whoever says he is in the light and hates his brother is still in darkness" (1 Jn 2:9). "But whoever hates his brother is in the darkness and walks in the darkness, and does not know where he is going, because the darkness has blinded his eyes" (1 Jn 2:11). "Everyone who hates his brother is a murderer, and you know that no murderer has eternal life abiding in him" (1 Jn 3:15).

You can't fight the brothers and sister in your family or at church and think you are a mature Christian. You can't fight with your spouse continually and think you are growing and changing. Take off ill-will and put on good will. Love hopes the best. Love does not "rejoice in iniquity" in ill-will but rejoices in the truth.

Hiding Your Sin (Deceit)

1 Peter 2:1b | So put away ... all deceit.

Are you blameless? Is there deception in your life? Maybe self-deception. Don't be playing games at church. This isn't real to you. Are you blameless?

The word "deceit" means to "bait" people with "a fishhook." Are you fooling people? Are you fooling yourself? Do you have clean hands and a pure heart? If not, repent. Fake your spiritual life if you want to

---

[31] Grudem, *1 Peter*, 99.
[32] Simon J. Kistemaker, & William Hendriksen, *Exposition of the Epistles of Peter and the Epistle of Jude*, Vol. 16 (Grand Rapids: Baker Book House, 1953-2001), 78-79.

dry up your cravings for God. If all your worship at church is nothing but "fish bate" then you are going to dry up.

Be who you are. Be vulnerable. Come clean. Don't hide your sins. Often when people get right with God the sewer comes out! Tons of sins are confessed, and you come clean. Stop trying to hide your sins and come clean! Often someone will confront you with a pattern of sin, and you become defensive and crafty, dancing around the reality of your sin. Come clean! Admit your sin. Put off deceiving yourself and deceiving others. Come clean about your sin. How can you come clean? Talk to a spiritually strong person today. Be vulnerable about any area of your heart that is hardened. Don't wait. Do it now.

Impressing Others (Hypocrisy)

1 Peter 2:1c | So put away all ... hypocrisy.

Hypocrisy is the masking of inward evil by an outward show of righteousness.[33] It means living a double life.[34] Hypocrisy often acts out by not focusing on our sins and repentance, but instead, trying to impress others. In not admitting our sins, we try to be people pleasers and live a double life of impressing others. Instead of transparency we "wear a mask" or "cover up our faults" or "pretend to be what we are not."[35] We all have this tendency to impress others, and we need to get rid of it if you are going to grow. The hypocritical person pretends to be what he is not; he is a person with a double heart and a lying tongue.[36] Jesus said, "You hypocrites! Isaiah was right when he prophesied about you: 'These people honor me with their lips, but their hearts are far from me'" (Mt. 15:7–8; *cf* Isa 29:13).

Don't act like everything is ok with God when your heart is far from him! This will kill your spiritual life. We should be humble and childlike. A child is often innocent and honest. They have a need – they don't try to impress. I can have important people in my kitchen, and I hear my little child shouting from the bathroom, "Mommy, daddy come wipe me!" We ought to be humble, sincere, and authentic and not hypocritical. Instead of hypocrisy, be open.

---

[33] Grudem, *1 Peter*, 99.
[34] MacArthur, *1 Peter*, 98.
[35] D.C. Arichea & E.A. Nida, *A Handbook On The First Letter From Peter* (New York: United Bible Societies, 2004), 50.
[36] Kistemaker, *1 Peter*, 80.

High Mindedness (Envy)

1 Peter 2:1d | So put away all ... envy.

Envy is a form of high-mindedness and superiority. It will kill your growth and your craving for God and his word. When we think of envy, we think jealousy, but this word is a bit more personal. Envy in this verse is a resentful discontent.[37] Envy is "the feeling of displeasure produced by the advantage of others."[38] Envy is the toxic emotion of always wanting to be on top. Envy[39] can come out in a number of ways, often in spiritual pride and self-righteousness. Thinking we are far more knowledgeable than we are – thinking we are more spiritual and more mature than we really are. This kind of pride creates a superiority that always puts one on top. There is always a "resentful discontent" and jealousy that "no one understands me."

Do you always think you are right? In a disagreement, are you always trying to win instead of compassionately listening to the other person? If you are good at cutting people off when they talk, you are more acquainted with envy than you think.

John MacArthur says this word envy "is the spirit of superiority and resentment and defensiveness and often leads to grudges, bitterness, hatred, and conflict (*cf* 1 Cor 3:3; 1 Tim 6:4; Jas 3:16).[40] This is the kind of defensiveness that puts others down while holding any sin against them. One great test of envy is how well you listen. Are you able to listen to someone who is hurt without judging them? When you are filled with envy, you don't want to listen. You merely want the advantage for yourself in an argument. You don't want to listen; you just want to win. Envy has the idea of judging others harshly while holding yourself to an easy standard.

Instead of nursing on the sincere milk of the word, you may be nursing a wound. You think you are the important one, and you should be treated a certain way. Give your wounds to Jesus. Let him heal you.

---

[37] David Walls and Max Anders, *I & II Peter, I, II & III John, Jude*, vol. 11, Holman New Testament Commentary (Nashville, TN: Broadman & Holman Publishers, 1999), 29.

[38] Hiebert, *1 Peter*, 111.

[39] In Greek, this word is actually the name of a Greek god (*Phthonus*) who had a great many wives but killed each one eventually, on suspicions of adultery. He was suspicious that they were not completely devoted to him.

[40] MacArthur, *1 Peter*, 98.

Don't let your wounds keep you from compassion towards others. There is unforgiveness and envy in your heart.

Hurtful Speech (Slander)

1 Peter 2:1e | So put away .... all slander.

Slander refers essentially to defamation of character (*cf* 2:12; 3:16; Jas 4:11).[41] The idea here is insulting language. This includes any disparaging remark or gossip. It referred essentially to defamation of character behind a person's back.[42] Literally the word means "evil speech." It is especially prevalent when a rumor is passed around. This disparaging gossip destroys our confidence in an individual and can weaken that person's reputation.[43]

This is the opposite of love. Love thinks the best and hopes the best. You should always talk about people as if they are right there in the room with you. Instead of badmouthing, gossiping (through a prayer request) or casting aspersion, we need to follow Matthew 18 and speak to the person directly. Don't talk to your family member, your friend, or even your pastor. Go directly to the person.

Matthew 18 is violated so often, and it is a shame, because if we followed it there would be no slander and gossip, and there would be a greater level of peace in the body. It's every member's responsibility to live out Matthew 18.

> If your brother sins against you, go and tell him his fault, between you and him alone. If he listens to you, you have gained your brother. [16] But if he does not listen, take one or two others along with you, that every charge may be established by the evidence of two or three witnesses. [17] If he refuses to listen to them, tell it to the church. And if he refuses to listen even to the church, let him be to you as a Gentile and a tax collector. —*Matthew 18:15-17*

Most people skip the first two steps. They go straight to an elder or pastor. Take time to go to the person you are offended with and get things right. Otherwise, you'll end up bad mouthing and slandering a brother for whom Christ died! Don't do it. Get things right privately. If

---

[41] Ibid.
[42] Ibid.
[43] Charles R. Swindoll, *Insights on James and 1 & 2 Peter* (Grand Rapids, MI: Zondervan, 2010), 165.

you can't settle it, bring an impartial witness. If you still can't settle it, bring it to an elder or pastor. Be diligent about this. Put off slander. Do whatever it takes to keep the peace in the body. If you are lazy in this, it will stunt your growth. There is nothing harder than loving confrontation and conflict resolution. If you are badmouthing other Christians, you are going to kill your appetite for God's word.

WHAT HELPS OUR APPETITE FOR GOD? (2:2-3)

1 Peter 2:2-3 | Like newborn infants, long for the pure spiritual milk, that by it you may grow up into salvation— ³ if indeed you have tasted that the Lord is good.

Peter uses the illustration of a baby to demonstrate the normal appetite of a truly born again Christian. Peter speaks of an infant that has just emerged from its mother's womb and is crying for milk from her breast.[44]

A New Heart

1 Peter 2:2a | Like newborn infants...

True believers can no longer live in the filthy of the old self life. They have a new heart and can no longer live comfortably in sin. Instead of living the self-life – take that filthy garment off. Why? Since, "indeed you have tasted that the Lord is good" (2:3). Psalm 34:8 is quoted here because the craving is the evidence that one has *tasted that the Lord is good*. [45] In order to put off sin, you must first be a new creation. You must have a new heart and a new spirit. You cannot "put away" sin in your life if it's not already forever defeated by Jesus on his cross.

New Desires

1 Peter 2:2 | Like newborn infants, long for the pure spiritual milk, that by it you may grow up into salvation.

---

[44] Ibid.
[45] David H. Wheaton, "1 Peter," in *New Bible Commentary: 21st Century Edition*, ed. D. A. Carson et al., 4th ed. (Leicester, England; Downers Grove, IL: InterVarsity Press, 1994), 1376.

In speaking of milk, he's not talking about immaturity but instead intensity. He's talking about the spiritual craving a true believer has for the word of God. It's like a newborn baby desires his mother's milk. True believers crave milk that is *Logicon*, or milk that is spiritual or "of the word." Milk that is of the *logos* or of the word. It's something we cannot live without. Jesus affirmed this when he told Satan in the wilderness, "It is written, 'Man shall not live on bread alone, but on every word that proceeds out of the mouth of God' " (Mt 4:4; *cf* Deut 8:3; Lk 4:4).

We need *logos* milk! Is that what you drink? It is notable what Peter did not command. He did not charge believers to read the Word, study the word, meditate on the word, teach the Word, preach the word, search the word, or memorize the word. All of those things come from desiring to be fed (cf Psa 1:1-3).

In view of postmodern culture's relentless output of informational junk food through radio, television, films, the Internet, computer games, books, periodicals, and even so-called Christian pulpits—all of which causes spiritual malnourishment and dulls appetites for genuine spiritual food—believers must commit to regular nourishment from God's word.[46]

New Experience

1 Peter 2:3 | If indeed you have tasted that the Lord is good.

The language alludes to Psalm 34:8. The psalmist exhorts others to "taste and see that the Lord is good." Peter assumes these Christians have already tasted that goodness.[47] Peter's point is that Christian maturity is impossible without a vital relationship with the Lord (*cf* Jn 15:1-7). No one can grow apart from daily experiencing (taste, sight) the Lord.

A New Family

1 Peter 2:4-5 | As you come to him, a living stone rejected by men but in the sight of God chosen and precious, **5** you yourselves like living stones are being built up as a spiritual house, to be a holy

---

[46] Ibid.
[47] A. Black, *1 & 2 Peter*, 1 Pe 2:3.

priesthood, to offer spiritual sacrifices acceptable to God through Jesus Christ.

No Christian can grow in isolation. You are to be with the Living Stone, Jesus Christ. You are to be built up into him as a living temple. "Rather, speaking the truth in love, we are to grow up in every way into him who is the head, into Christ, 16 from whom the whole body, joined and held together by every joint with which it is equipped, when each part is working properly, makes the body grow so that it builds itself up in love" (Eph 4:15-16). Are you having regular, weekly, serious conversations not only with your family but with the saints of God?

True believers make progress in their lives by receiving and obeying the word of God. You need knowledge and grace (power from God) to grow., "But grow in the grace and knowledge of our Lord and Savior Jesus Christ" (2 Pet 3:18). You have a new nature, but you need to grow in the use of it. The Bible becomes your culture, and you grow in it. You become conformed more and more to Christ.

Applications

Are you in the word? Here are several ways you can get in the word. How do we grow? First and foremost, you need to know Christ – you cannot grow if you are not yet born again. Assuming the new birth, the following are helpful guides to grow in the word.

1. Meditate and fellowship in the word. You can do this by nourishment and Christian fellowship. "Let the word of Christ dwell in you richly, teaching and admonishing one another in all wisdom, singing psalms and hymns and spiritual songs, with thankfulness in your hearts to God" (Col 3:16). Are you on a reading plan? Are you sharing the treasures you are learning with others? Be proactive. If you don't have a reading plan, you can get the YOUversion Bible App on your smart phone and it has simple Bible reading plans based on subject or if you just want to read the Bible in a year.

2. Be faithful to the church services. Be there whenever the word is opened. "Seek first the kingdom of God and all these things shall be added unto you" (Mt 6:33).

3. Be accountable to a more mature person in the congregation. Discipleship means you are working through areas of growth in your life with a more mature Christian that can pray for you and counsel you

in your areas of struggle. This is also vital for married couples. You cannot grow solo. Satan will isolate you and discourage you.

Conclusion

Every Christian must be vitally connected to the word of God, drinking it's nourishment like a newborn infant.

Don't get disconnected. The other day flooding came through our neighborhoods in Elgin. Some of our houses were flooded. When I was coming home that day, there were trees down that disconnected the electricity in the storm. Some of you are spiritually like those who are temporarily without electricity. You need to ask him to restore power to your life and heart.

7 | 1 PETER 2:4
JESUS OUR CORNERSTONE

Behold, I am laying in Zion a stone, a cornerstone chosen and precious, and whoever believes in him will not be put to shame.
1 PETER 2:6

Jesus is our cornerstone. He places us where he wants us. Peter has told us in 2:1-3, that we are to grow individually, but being nourished by Jesus through the spiritual milk of the word. Now he tells us we need to grow corporately as a living temple. In order to become a "living stone" you first have to see Jesus as a "living stone." This is peculiar. Peter is talking about an organic temple – a living, breathing abode for God. Have you given your life to Christ? That's where we go from being dead to alive.

Are you making sure there are no cracks in the foundation? The house where one family in our congregation lived once had a bad foundation. They had to lift up the house and pour a new foundation. I'm not in the construction industry, but I know I need Jesus as my foundation. Jesus is my cornerstone! Consider Jesus' construction advice in Matthew 7. He's not talking about physical, but spiritual construction.

> Everyone then who hears these words of mine and does them will be like a wise man who built his house on the rock. ²⁵ And the rain fell, and the floods came, and the winds blew and beat on that house, but

it did not fall, because it had been founded on the rock. ²⁶ And everyone who hears these words of mine and does not do them will be like a foolish man who built his house on the sand. ²⁷ And the rain fell, and the floods came, and the winds blew and beat against that house, and it fell, and great was the fall of it. —*Matthew 7:24-27*

I want to build my life on Jesus my cornerstone! That's what Peter says. Peter says whoever builds their life on the living Cornerstone will not be disappointed (or "put to shame," 2:8, ESV). Some of you have been very disappointed after you purchased a house. Can I tell you if you've been placed into the spiritual house of Jesus, you'll never be disappointed with the Architect! Consider God's construction plan for your life in 1 Peter 2.

> **1 Peter 2:4-10** | As you come to him, a living stone rejected by men but in the sight of God chosen and precious, ⁵ you yourselves like living stones are being built up as a spiritual house, to be a holy priesthood, to offer spiritual sacrifices acceptable to God through Jesus Christ. ⁶ For it stands in Scripture: "Behold, I am laying in Zion a stone, a cornerstone chosen and precious, and whoever believes in him will not be put to shame." ⁷ So the honor is for you who believe, but for those who do not believe, "The stone that the builders rejected has become the cornerstone," ⁸ and "A stone of stumbling, and a rock of offense." They stumble because they disobey the word, as they were destined to do. ⁹ But you are a chosen race, a royal priesthood, a holy nation, a people for his own possession, that you may proclaim the excellencies of him who called you out of darkness into his marvelous light. ¹⁰ Once you were not a people, but now you are God's people; once you had not received mercy, but now you have received mercy.

So how do we build our lives on Christ our cornerstone? First we have to "come to him" as Peter says in verse 4. He must be the stone that makes us alive. Have you given your life to Christ? In order to become a "living stone" you first have to see Jesus as a "living stone." This is peculiar. Peter is talking about an organic temple – a living, breathing abode for God. Jesus gave the grand invitation.

> Come to me, all who labor and are heavy laden, and I will give you rest. ²⁹ Take my yoke upon you, and learn from me, for I am gentle and lowly in heart, and you will find rest for your souls. ³⁰ For my yoke is easy, and my burden is light. —*Matthew 11:28-30*

If you have tasted the Lord is good, that he's merciful, kind, generous, loving then come, and keep coming to your living stone. Remember when your sins were forgiven. Keep coming to him. Keep touching him and be rid of your deadness. How do I do that? Four ways: recognize Jesus as the living stone, the rejected stone, the chosen stone, and the precious stone.

JESUS IS THE LIVING STONE (2:4A)

1 Peter 2:4-5 | As you come to him, a living stone rejected by men but in the sight of God chosen and precious, **5** you yourselves like living stones are being built up as a spiritual house, to be a holy priesthood, to offer spiritual sacrifices acceptable to God through Jesus Christ.

These are stunning words and elevating beyond measure. In one sentence Peter grasps the entire wealth of Israel's identity and applies it not to Jesus alone, but to any man, woman, or child who comes to faith in Christ! When we come to Jesus—not the city of Jerusalem—we come to the "living stone." When we come to Jesus—not to Judaism—we come into God's kingdom. When we come to Jesus—not the ornate temple—we become God's "spiritual house" and "holy priesthood."[48]

Peter builds 2:4–10 around stone and building imagery. Jesus began the use of this metaphor by his appropriation of Psalm 118:22 ("The stone the builders rejected has become the capstone"—cited by Jesus in Matthew 21:42 and parallels).[49]

Jesus is the cornerstone, but Peter adds that he is a living cornerstone. He's alive in the Spirit, without sin from birth. He's conquered death through his resurrection. He is the Prince of Life who has destroyed sin, death, hell, and the devil. Historically, there were more than 500 eyewitnesses that testified Christ was raised from the dead (1 Cor 15:5), but Peter is referring to something more than this in calling Jesus the living stone.

---

[48] Helm, *1 & 2 Peter and Jude*, 74–75.
[49] A. Black, *1 & 2 Peter*, 1 Pe 2:4.

Humanity, Dead Stones

We are all brought into this world as dead stones. The stone is relating to the nature of our humanity. Normally stones are dead, unless you are watching a children's film with talking rocks. In reality, stones are dead. All humanity, like stones were dead until Jesus came. Jesus was born as the first "living stone." As you pursue the living stone, you will live. We are made alive at our regeneration. But we experience that life by the work of the Spirit.

Jesus, the Living Stone

Why is Jesus called a "living stone"? The implication is that all human beings are born as "dead stones" and Peter is pointing to Jesus as the one man who was born with a nature unstained by sin. The Old Testament designates God as the only rock (Deut 32:3–4, 31), the foundation and strength of His people. In the New Testament, Jesus Christ is the rock (2:8; 1 Cor 10:4) and the stone on which the church rests.[50] He is the one and only living stone. Anyone who "comes to him" in repentant faith will be transformed from a dead stone to a living stone. By nature and by choice we are in rebellion against God. We are depraved coming out of the womb. This is why people are born proud and self-centered. They have hardened their hearts to God. This is our nature. This is why Paul says "no one is good... no one seeks after God" (Rom 3:11-12). We're all dead stones. Coming to know Christ, our deadness as a stone is turned to life. Jesus came into this world and put on the nature of what looked like a dead stone, yet he wasn't a dead stone. He was "made in the likeness of men..." "...yet without sin" (*cf* Phil 2:4-11). Hallelujah. He didn't come as a dead stone. He came as the living stone.

Jesus is the only one to be born a living stone. His father wasn't Joseph – that was his stepfather. Jesus' father was God, conceived by the Holy Spirit in the womb of the virgin Mary. It was no ordinary birth; it was a miracle birth. "He came unto his own and his own received him not" (Jn 1:11, KJV). His birth was unique – he wasn't a dead stone, but a living stone.

---

[50] MacArthur, *1 Peter*, 104–105.

The Church, a Living Temple

Peter cements his thought in an architectural metaphor. Notice: he is moving beyond the idea of the church being God's family (1:1–2:2). Further, he will leave to the Apostle Paul the metaphor of the church as Christ's "body." What he takes for himself, though, is the architectural metaphor of the church as God's building.[51]

When sinners come in faith to Christ, the "living stone," they too become living stones; when someone believes in Christ he shares his life (*cf* Jn 17:21, 23; 2 Cor 3:18; Eph 4:15–16; 1 Jn 3:2). To be living stones means that believers have the eternal life of Christ. They are united with him, which is their first spiritual privilege. They do not just worship him, obey him, and pray to him; they are united with him as stones in a spiritual building of which he is the cornerstone.[52]

"As you come to him" refers not to our initial conversion, but to our drawing nearer to God through our spiritual growth in fellowship with God and others. The Greek verb "coming" is a present participle connected to the main verb of the sentence in verse 5—"you ... are being built up." So, Peter declares that by drawing nearer to Christ, we get built up.[53] If you have come to Christ and been made alive by touching the living stone, then keep coming. He came to give you "life, and life more abundantly" (Jn 10:10). Where are you seeking life right now? The world cannot satisfy the deep need of your heart. The deep need of your cavernous heart is fellowship with God. Nothing in this world can satisfy that. Walk with the living stone. Brothers and sisters, come to him, pursue him. Make the pursuit of Jesus the blazing center of your life. Put away all lesser things. Let those lesser things become dull and faded and embrace the joy of Jesus be an outflow of your adoration and worship of him! Let Jesus be the living stone who as you are connected to him, he constantly breathes life into you.

Let me get personal now. I want to address some things that concern me about this generation. This generation takes the congregation of believers so casually. We don't mind if we are late to church or miss this service or that service. Listen you are a living stone connected to the living cornerstone. Be where his people are. Who put you in the

---

[51] Helm, *1 & 2 Peter and Jude*, 75.
[52] MacArthur, *1 Peter*, 106.
[53] Charles R. Swindoll, *Insights on James and 1 & 2 Peter*, Swindoll's New Testament Commentary (Grand Rapids, MI: Zondervan, 2010), 169.

temple of God, in the Body of Christ? Who placed you there? Jesus did. Be in the place Jesus wants you to be. He wants you to be with the saints every Sunday morning. Every time the church meets you should be there. Why aren't you here for prayer meeting? Some of you used to come. You used to love the prayer meeting of Christ's little flock. Some of you aren't in a small group. You need to be a living stone! You need to be active! Some of you are undercover Christians! You don't invite the brothers to your home. You need to do that. Be built up into Christ the cornerstone.

JESUS IS THE REJECTED STONE (2:4B)

1 Peter 2:4 | As you come to him, a living stone rejected by men but in the sight of God chosen and precious.

Jesus "came unto his own, and his own did not receive him" (Jn 1:11). Jesus came into the world to "save his people from their sin" (Mt 1:21), but instead he was "rejected" and "despised" (Isa 53:3). In spite of the fact that Jesus is precious to God and to his church, he's not precious to all people. Indeed, he is rejected. He was rejected by Israel, and unless the Holy Spirit draw a person, they will not come to the Father (Jn 6:44-45). That means not everybody is going to love the Lord Jesus Christ. Jesus himself said that not everyone would believe on him. He said, "The gate is narrow and the way is hard that leads to life, and those who find it are few" (Mt 7:14). The Bible here plainly and clearly prophesies that there are some who are going to reject the cornerstone. There are some who are going to refuse Jesus as the foundation of their life.

Some people say, "Pastor Matt, what about a person, a man, a woman, a boy or girl who dies without ever hearing of Jesus Christ? What happens to them? Can they go to heaven without Christ?" That's a big question. And there's a Bible answer to it in Romans 1. But let me tell you something that's even a greater question than that: What is God going to do with people who sit in an air-conditioned, upholstered church, and hear a pastor tear his heart out and preach Jesus Christ, and they examine Christ and say, "I don't want him"? What's going to happen to those people? I want to tell you that the hottest part of hell is reserved for those who, having examined God's precious cornerstone, reject it; those who, having seen God's precious Son, slight Him and reject the Lord Jesus Christ. Listen to Christ's warning to people who would reject him in the bright sunlight of truth.

> That servant that knew not his master's will and did things worthy of stripes shall be beaten with few stripes. But he who knew his master's will, and then did things worthy of stripes, shall be beaten with many stripes. For unto whomsoever much is given, of the same shall much be required. —Luke 12:47–48, KJV

And Jesus Christ said in Matthew 11 to the city where he did his most wonderful works.

> And you, Capernaum, will you be exalted to heaven? You will be brought down to Hades. For if the mighty works done in you had been done in Sodom, it would have remained until this day. [24] But I tell you that it will be more tolerable on the day of judgment for the land of Sodom than for you. —Matthew 11:23–24

A good way to know if you are a living stone connected to Christ as part of his living house, his spiritual temple, is if the world rejects you like it rejected Christ. "Yea, and all that will live godly in Christ Jesus shall suffer persecution" (2 Tim 3:12). Dead stones don't like living stones. Every true Christian should expect that his new pattern of life will be rejected in some way by the world. The apostle John says we should not be surprised. "Do not be surprised, brothers, that the world hates you" (1 Jn 3:13). Jesus said, "If the world hates you, know that it has hated me before it hated you" (Jn 15:18). The world hates Christians. They might talk nicely to your face, but they are no longer comfortable around you if God dwells in you. They don't like you because they don't like your divine roommate, the Holy Spirit. They are comfortable in their sin, and the Spirit of righteousness in you is like an alarm clock awakening them out of their sinful slumber.

Your friends and family don't like the "new you" if they are enslaved to this world. They want the "old you" back. They want the person back that wasn't so different from them. They liked the dark you, but now your light is making them uncomfortable. You used to carouse and curse, and you used to make them feel pretty good about themselves. Now that you protest against the world, you make them uncomfortable. You have the Spirit living in you, and you reject the world, so the world rejects you.

> If the world hates you, know that it has hated me before it hated you. [19] If you were of the world, the world would love you as its own; but because you are not of the world, but I chose you out of the world, therefore the world hates you. [20] Remember the word that I said to

you: 'A servant is not greater than his master.' If they persecuted me, they will also persecute you. If they kept my word, they will also keep yours. —*John 15:18-20*

Your worldly friends don't like you because they don't like Jesus. They like being their own master, but you are surrendered to a New Master, and they don't like that. They don't want Jesus Christ to be Lord.

JESUS IS THE CHOSEN STONE (2:4C)

1 Peter 2:4 | As you come to him, a living stone rejected by men but in the sight of God chosen and precious.

What does it mean that in the sight of God Jesus is the stone that was "chosen" and precious? This goes back to Jesus' baptism when the Father speaks from heaven and says that he "delights" in his Son, and that everyone needs to listen to Jesus. Christ is the chosen Messiah.

What was Jesus chosen for? To be our Messiah, Savior and Redeemer. Job said, "For I know that my Redeemer lives, and at the last he will stand upon the earth" (Job 19:25). Jesus was chosen to be the Savior of the world. "We love him because he first loved us" (1 Jn 4:19, KJV). Jesus Christ in eternity past covenanted with his Father to redeem humanity. Paul says, "This is a faithful saying, and worthy of all acceptance, that Christ Jesus came into the world to save sinners; of whom I am chief" (1 Tim 1:15). He came into the world to redeem us. "Even as the Son of man came not to be ministered unto, but to minister, and to give his life a ransom for many" (Mt 20:28). Jesus was chosen and elected to be "the Lamb slain from the foundation of the world" (Rev 13:8).

Jesus is the chosen stone. What does that mean for you and me? It means we are called to recognize Jesus as our chosen Savior. Where do you go when you are hurting? Where do you go when you are betrayed? Where do you go when you have indignation in your heart and maybe it's legitimate? Do you try to save yourself through escapism, anger, or self-righteousness? None of it works. Nothing can fill that cavernous heart of yours but the love of Jesus. Your spouse isn't your savior. Your kids or job or church, etc., isn't your savior. Jesus is "the way, the truth and the life." He's the exclusive way to the Father's salvation (Jn 14:6). "And there is salvation in no one else, for there is no other name under heaven given among men by which we must be saved" (Acts 4:12). Choose him. Put away all your idols. Our hearts are an idol making factory (Calvin). Let Jesus be the

JESUS IS THE PRECIOUS STONE (2:4D)

1 Peter 2:4 | As you come to him, a living stone rejected by men but in the sight of God chosen and precious.

Unto you who have found him to be precious. Oh, how precious Jesus is. How blessed is his communion! How blessed it is to be "filled with all the fullness of God," filled with "joy unspeakable and full of glory;" to have the "peace that passes understanding;" and to "know the love of Christ." How wide, how deep, how long, how high is the love of Christ! Oh he is precious! As we continue our study, we will see many things that Jesus is and why he is precious to us. He brings us into union with himself. He gains us access to God, his Father. He makes us priests who offer spiritual sacrifices. He gives us a position and security that will not disappoint us! He gives us a place of honor with him as God's children. He grants us a place as a chosen race.

Some of you know the story of my friend Dr. Ahmed Joktan, a medical doctor who grew up in Mecca, Saudi Arabia as an angry young man filled with hatred. Now he is the most loving, gentle, patient, and humble man I know because his life touched the living stone, and now Jesus is the cornerstone of Dr. A's life. I once asked him, "Dr. A, how do you adjust to western culture having such an extreme upbringing?" His answer was profound and simple: "Brother Matt, the Bible is my culture." Wow. How true. Let's crave the living word that comes from the livingstone. Let your life intersect with his. Let him be your foundation stone who gives you life. Be built up and grow in these ways – conform your mind to think of life in these ways. Let the "Bible be your culture." Live in the reality of these truths.

Conclusion

When I came to know Christ, I gave all to Christ. I was like a dead stone taken from the trash heap. But God made me a living stone. I had one goal: know Christ. I wanted to be radical, and I was willing to lose all for Christ. Listen don't hang on to dead stones or crumpled buildings in this world. Be founded on Christ. He is the cornerstone! Be founded on Christ, our cornerstone!

8 | 1 PETER 2:5-9
GOD'S SPIRITUAL TEMPLE

You yourselves like living stones are being built up as a spiritual house, to be a holy priesthood, to offer spiritual sacrifices acceptable to God through Jesus Christ.
1 PETER 2:5

My four-year-old daughter Ava and I love to play games. Her favorite is called, "you are what I say you are." You can imagine that's most children's favorite. She says, "You're a cow." I say, "Mooooooo!"

"You're a duck!"

"Quack. Quack," but I love to throw her off.

She says: "You're a sheep!"

"Ok, "Cock-a-doodle-doo!"

"No Daddy, you're a sheep," she insists.

"Ok, baaaaaa!"

That's a sweet and childlike way of illustrating a more majestic and powerful reality. We are whatever God says we are. And here in 1 Peter 2 he says we are his house, Jesus is our cornerstone, and he is the architect of his church.

> **1 Peter 2:5-10** | You yourselves like living stones are being built up as a spiritual house, to be a holy priesthood, to offer spiritual sacrifices acceptable to God through Jesus Christ. **⁶**For it stands in

Scripture: "Behold, I am laying in Zion a stone, a cornerstone chosen and precious, and whoever believes in him will not be put to shame." ⁷ So the honor is for you who believe, but for those who do not believe, "The stone that the builders rejected has become the cornerstone," ⁸ and "A stone of stumbling, and a rock of offense." They stumble because they disobey the word, as they were destined to do. ⁹ But you are a chosen race, a royal priesthood, a holy nation, a people for his own possession, that you may proclaim the excellencies of him who called you out of darkness into his marvelous light. ¹⁰ Once you were not a people, but now you are God's people; once you had not received mercy, but now you have received mercy.

So how do we build our lives on Christ our cornerstone? Christians must grow together not just as individuals, but as living stones, which, when joined together with others, become integral parts in God's building of a spiritual house.[54]

WE ARE GOD'S HOUSE (1:5)

1 Peter 2:5 | You yourselves like living stones are being built up as a spiritual house, to be a holy priesthood, to offer spiritual sacrifices acceptable to God through Jesus Christ.

A House of Living Stones

Be built up in your union with Christ as "living stones." What are we housing? We are housing God's presence, the Holy Spirit. We have an obligation to manifest him with our lives. We are not just any house – we are God's house. Paul asked, "Do you not know that your body is a temple of the Holy Spirit within you, whom you have from God? You are not your own" (1 Cor 6:19). As those who house God's Spirit, God has made us "living stones." We are alive in Christ, founded on Christ our cornerstone.

A House that is Growing

1 Peter 2:5a | You yourselves like living stones are being built up as a spiritual house.

---

[54] Walls, *I & II Peter, I, II & III John, Jude*, 29.

We've never seen an organic temple, but that's what God says we are. That means unlike every other building, we are a building that is growing and being built up. You are not a finished temple. You are growing in holiness and love and faith. The more you grow, the more you are unified – the more you have one heart and one mind. Speaking of a body, Paul says something similar in Ephesians 4:15-16, "we are to grow up in every way into him who is the head, into Christ, 16 from whom the whole body, joined and held together by every joint with which it is equipped, when each part is working properly, makes the body grow so that it builds itself up in love."

We are coming to Christ, the living stone. Christ is the living, resurrected, and life-giving God. Each person accepts or rejects this "living stone." When anyone comes to Christ, as the living stone, a new stone is added to God's spiritual building—Christ's church. As a spiritual building, the church is to be influenced or dominated by the Holy Spirit in a local assembly.

A child does not reach their full-grown height overnight. Neither does a child of God achieve spiritual maturity overnight. Sanctification is a process. Yet there is marked progress, measured and steady. Indeed, Jesus said, "I will build my church and the gates of hell shall not prevail against it" (Mt 16:18). Jesus is not only the architect of the church, but because we are stones that are alive, he is like a gardener cultivating us. He is watering us with the word and pruning us by the Spirit's conviction.

Because of our union with Christ, believers have spiritual resources to meet their every need. That is why Paul could pray on behalf of the Ephesians, "Now to him who is able to do far more abundantly beyond all that we ask or think, according to the power that works within us" (Eph 3:20). You lack nothing because of your union with Christ! You are "citizens of heaven" (Phil 3:20), "heirs of God and joint-heirs with Jesus Christ" (Rom 8:17). You are blessed with "every spiritual blessing in heavenly places in Christ Jesus" (Eph 1:3). Jesus said, "I came to give you life and life more abundantly" (Jn 10:10). God has plans for us! "For I know the plans I have for you, declares the LORD, plans for welfare and not for disaster, to give you a future and a hope" (Jer 29:11).

A House with Priests

1 Peter 2:5 | You yourselves like living stones are being built up as a spiritual house, to be a holy priesthood, to offer spiritual sacrifices acceptable to God through Jesus Christ.

Now Peter shifts the metaphor and says we are not only God's temple, but we work in God's temple as priests offering sacrifices. As God's priests, what are we doing? We are to be helping others in evangelism and edification. That's the job of priests – to bring people to a meaningful relationship with God.

As Priests, We Have Access

The whole imagery of the temple is access to God. As New Testament believers, we have unlimited and unfettered access to God as priests – we "are being built up as a spiritual house, to be a holy priesthood" (1 Pet 2:5b). We used to be his enemies, but now we are his priests. What does it mean to be a priest? As priests, we have access to the Holy of Holies… In the Old Testament only the high priest could actually go into the holy of holies once a year (Lev 16:2, 29–34; Heb 9:1–10, 25). Anyone who presumptuously crossed over into the priestly function without fully meeting the requirements and qualifications of the priesthood suffered severe judgment. The high priest once a year would have to go into the holy of holies with bells and a rope. If he did anything improperly the Lord could kill him. We don't have to approach God with bells and a rope. "Let us therefore come boldly to the throne of grace, that we may obtain mercy and find grace to help in time of need" (Heb 4:16).

As Priests, We Offer Sacrifices

1 Peter 2:5c | … a holy priesthood, to offer spiritual sacrifices acceptable to God through Jesus Christ.

Christ being our cornerstone means we do what pleases the Father. We are the manifestation of God on earth. We have a calling as living stones to offer up spiritual sacrifices to the Lord. The primary function of the Old Testament priests, as they ministered in the tabernacle and then the temple, was to offer animal sacrifices to God (Exo 29:10–19; 2 Chron 35:11). But when Christ inaugurated the new covenant, animal sacrifices were no longer necessary (Heb. 8:13; 9:11–15; 10:1–18). Now the only sacrifices remaining for the priesthood of believers to offer up, according to Peter, are spiritual sacrifices.[55]

There were at least five common offerings in the Levitical system as seen in the illustration below.

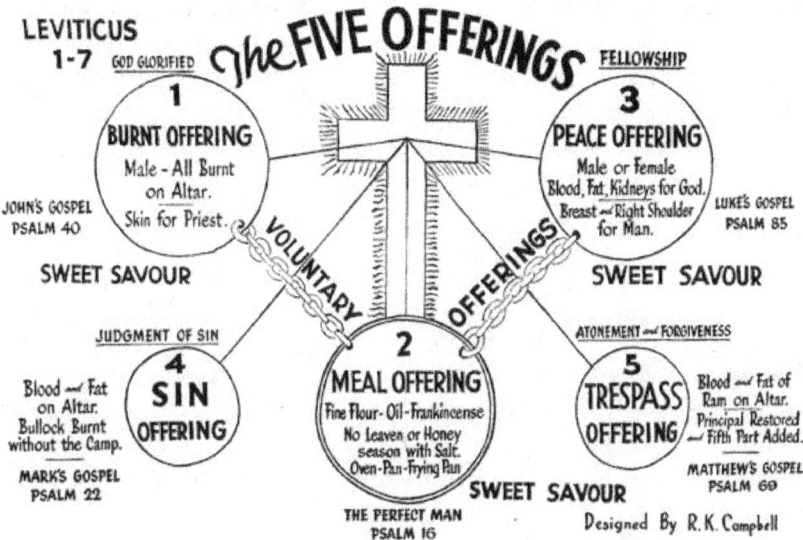

First, you had the *whole burnt offering,* an offering of lambs or goats (Lev 1). This points to the fact of *justification* by grace through faith in Christ alone. We read in Leviticus 1:9, "the priest shall burn all of it on the altar, as a burnt offering, a food offering with a pleasing aroma to the Lord." If you were poor, you could bring turtledoves or pigeons.

Second, there was the *bread offering* (Lev 2). The grain or bread they offered points to *sanctification* through feeding on Christ's word and communing with him as the "bread of life." We see this in Leviticus 2:13, "You shall season all your grain offerings with salt. You shall not let the salt of the covenant with your God be missing from your grain offering; with all your offerings you shall offer salt."

---

[55] MacArthur, *1 Peter*, 113-114.

Third, you had the *peace offering* of oxen or cattle (Lev 3,7). This sacrifice pointed to *fellowship with other believers*. This was a community offering that pointed to the fellowship we have as a congregation. We show ourselves to be God's forever family as we feast with the people of God. In this offering, the breast of the animal was waved in the form of a cross. This is recorded in Leviticus 7:15-16, "And the flesh of the sacrifice of his peace offerings for thanksgiving shall be eaten on the day of his offering. He shall not leave any of it until the morning. **16** But if the sacrifice of his offering is a vow offering or a freewill offering, it shall be eaten on the day that he offers his sacrifice, and on the next day what remains of it shall be eaten." It is as the author of Hebrews says.

> Through him then, let us continually offer up a sacrifice of praise to God, that is, the fruit of lips that give thanks to his name.
> —Hebrews 13:15

Fourth there was the *sin offering* (Lev 4) where a young bull or a goat was sacrificed (pigeons if you were poor). This was done outside camp. This sacrifice pointed to *restoration of fellowship with God*. This reminds us that our relationship with God is hindered by a guilty conscience and can be restored. John tells us that though sin no longer condemns us to hell, it does affect our relationship with God, and it needs to be confessed and forsaken.

> If we confess our sins, he is faithful and just to forgive us our sins and to cleanse us from all unrighteousness. —1 John 1:9

Finally, we see the *guilt or trespass offering* (Lev 6) where a ram plus 20% was offered to make restitution. This sacrifice pointed to *restoration of fellowship with fellow believers*. Here sin is looked at as a trespass against the government of God which affects the fellowship of the congregation. Amends had to be made for the wrong done and the fifth part added to it. Atonement was made by the blood of the offering, and the trespasser was forgiven. This offering presents Christ who died for our sins and trespasses on the cross restoring that which he took not away (Psa 69:4). He has not only answered to God for our sins and paid our debt by his shed blood, but has added the fifth part, as it were, bringing more glory to God and more blessings to man than were had before sin was committed. We see this in Leviticus 6:6-7, "And he shall bring to the priest as his compensation to the Lord a ram without blemish out of the flock, or its equivalent, for a guilt offering. 7 And the priest shall make atonement for him before the Lord, and he shall be forgiven for any of the things that one may do and thereby become guilty."

As New Testament saints, be hold to the priesthood of all believers. J.V. Fesko describes this doctrine as follows.

> The doctrine of the priesthood of all believers states that all believers in Christ share in his priestly status; therefore, there is no special class of people who mediate the knowledge, presence, and forgiveness of Christ to the rest of believers, and all believers have the right and authority to read, interpret, and apply the teachings of Scripture. [56]

Another place our priesthood is mentioned is in the book of Revelation.

> And they sang a new song, saying, 'Worthy are you to take the scroll and to open its seals, for you were slain and by your blood you ransomed people for God from every tribe and language and people and nation. —*Revelation 5:9*

What is an implication of Christ's redemptive work? What is one of the things he accomplishes through his shed blood?

> You have made them a kingdom and priests to our God, and they shall rein on the earth. —*Revelation 5:10*

Believers united to Christ share in all that he is and does, and in this case, they share in his priestly office. Unlike the Old Testament priests, who offered sacrificial animals, New Testament believers rest in the finished work of Christ, the one true sacrifice. Now, as Peter writes, we proclaim the excellencies of the God who called us out of darkness into light and offer spiritual sacrifices to God through Christ, the sacrifices of our bodies as "living sacrifices" (Rom 12:1) and praise to God, that is, "The fruit of lips that acknowledge his name" (Heb 13:15). [57]

I once knew a man named Ed Fisher when I lived in the inner city of Philadelphia during my college years. Ed Fisher was a fisher of men!

---

[56] J.V. Fesko, "The Priesthood of All Believers", Concise Theology Series (Austin, TX: The Gospel Coalition, 2019). Retrieved September 10, 2021, from https://www.thegospelcoalition.org/essay/the-priesthood-of-all-believers/.

[57] Fesko, ibid.

What was his secret? Praise. He would say, "There are many gods. But there's no other name under heaven whereby we can be saved. Don't just preach God. Preach Jesus. Woe is unto me if I preach not the gospel." Brother Ed Fisher would get so excited when he would talk about Jesus! He would literally jump, "Preach Jesus! Praise Jesus!" We ought to be like Brother Ed, offering spiritual sacrifices of praise. Put on your praise saints! Be living stones! Live out the culture of Jesus in your lives.

JESUS IS THE CORNERSTONE (1:6)

Peter adds to the list of spiritual privileges by introducing Isaiah 28:16 with the phrase this is contained in Scripture, testifying to the inspiration and authority of the prophetic book.

> **1 Peter 2:6** | For it stands in Scripture: "Behold, I am laying in Zion a stone, a cornerstone chosen and precious, and whoever believes in him will not be put to shame."

Isaiah said that Jesus Christ would be the cornerstone of God's new spiritual house, which is made up of believers (Isa 28:16; *cf* Matt. 21:42; Acts 4:11; Eph. 2:19–22).[58] Everything God has promised is true. Who put you in the Temple of God, in the Body of Christ? Who placed you there? Jesus did. Be in the place Jesus wants you to be. Be built up into Christ our cornerstone!

In Christ we have many privileges. Jesus brings us into union with himself. He gains us access to God, his Father. He makes us priests who offer spiritual sacrifices. He gives us a position and security that will not disappoint us! He gives us a place of honor with him as God's children. He grants us a place as a chosen race. Have you founded your life upon him?

GOD IS THE ARCHITECT (1:7-9)

You don't do the building. You submit to the builder. God is the architect of this building. Whoever believes in Christ becomes a living stone! You become built up in Christ. What an honor to be displayed as God's Temple!

---

[58] MacArthur, *1 Peter.*, 120.

Honor the Architect

> **1 Peter 2:7** | So the honor is for you who believe, but for those who do not believe, "The stone that the builders rejected has become the cornerstone."

Peter quotes Psalm 118:22 and basically says, "Let's honor the architect of the church." It's such an honor to follow Christ, isn't it? We know who he is. The world doesn't recognize him, so they use his name as a curse word. But we know who he is. Jesus is the Messiah. He is our deliverer. He delivers from sin and death. He destroys the work of the devil. We understand the honor of being called a Christian. For the world he is a rejected stone, but for us, he is our cornerstone.

Fear the Architect

> **1 Peter 2:8** | And "A stone of stumbling, and a rock of offense." They stumble because they disobey the word, as they were destined to do.

A new quote is given by the apostle Peter. He quotes Isaiah 8:14, and he is essentially saying, fear the architect of the church. He calls people to salvation, but he also hardens people.

Destined to Stumble

He says there are some who "stumble because they disobey the word, as they were destined to do." Whoa. Wait. Destined to disobey? That's what Peter says. In other words, God doesn't open the eyes of all in the human race. When Isaiah said in Isaiah 6:8, "Here I am! Send me." God said that he was calling Isaiah to harden the hearts of some in Israel (Isa 6:9-10). What a shock.

> Go, and say to this people: "'Keep on hearing, but do not understand; keep on seeing, but do not perceive." [10] Make the heart of this people dull, and their ears heavy, and blind their eyes; lest they see with their eyes, and hear with their ears, and understand with their hearts, and turn and be healed. —*Isaiah 6:9-10*

Jesus said something similar in Matthew 11.

> At that time Jesus declared, "I thank you, Father, Lord of heaven and earth, that you have hidden these things from the wise and understanding and revealed them to little children; [26] yes, Father, for such was your gracious will. [27] All things have been handed over to me by

my Father, and no one knows the Son except the Father, and no one knows the Father except the Son and anyone to whom the Son chooses to reveal him. ²⁸ Come to me, all who labor and are heavy laden, and I will give you rest. ²⁹ Take my yoke upon you, and learn from me, for I am gentle and lowly in heart, and you will find rest for your souls. —*Matthew 11:25-29*

Destined to Salvation

We as believers are not destined to disobey the gospel. God has graciously opened our eyes and given us a new nature like little children. So Peter can say that we are not destined to stumble, but chosen for salvation.

> **1 Peter 2:9** | But you are a chosen race, a royal priesthood, a holy nation, a people for his own possession, that you may proclaim the excellencies of him who called you out of darkness into his marvelous light.

God passed over some in the human race. They disobeyed the word, and that's all any of us would ever do had not God made us living stones! Live in the reality of these privileges. You are living stones. The Bible is your culture. The Bible is the air you breathe and the life you live! We might say that we as God's people are predestined for praise to "proclaim the excellencies of him who called you out of darkness into his marvelous light." Amen and amen.

Conclusion

As a spiritual house, the command is to "be built up" into Christ. Have you ever had a leaky roof? With all the rain we have in springtime, we've found out where the leaks are in our foundation and our roofs. In the same way, when the wind and storms of trials come, they show where we are weak in our walk with the Lord. Walk close to Christ! Don't let the world leak into you. Found your life on Christ the cornerstone and be built up in him.

9 | 1 PETER 1:9-10
PRAISING OUR CORNERSTONE

But you are a chosen race, a royal priesthood, a holy nation, a people for his own possession, that you may proclaim the excellencies of him who called you out of darkness into his marvelous light.

1 PETER 1:9

One of the marks of a believer is a heart of praise. When our focus is not on Christ, we tend to be unhappy, and the "crabby-meter" gets to dangerously high levels if you know what I mean. "The heavens declare the glory of God and the skies display his handiwork" (Psa 19:1). If nature can praise God so should we. If we don't, then the "rocks will cry out" (Lk 19:40).

Jesus is worthy of all glory, honor, and praise. Listen if you don't praise him, it shows your focus if off. If you are a complainer or a crabby person, you need to readjust your vision to Jesus. That's what this message is all about – stop looking at all your problems. Anxiety never increased your stature by even an inch. You don't grow taller by worrying. But you will grow spiritually by praising Jesus. Praise him! He's worthy.

Let everything that has breath praise the LORD! Praise the LORD!
—*Psalm 150:6*

> Rejoice in the Lord always; again I will say, rejoice. —*Philippians 4:4*
>
> I will bless the Lord at all times: his praise shall continually be in my mouth. —*Psalm 34:1, KJV*

Theologian Wayne Grudem concurs.

> The answer to our search for ultimate meaning lies in declaring the excellencies of God, for he alone is worthy of glory. Salvation is ultimately not man-centered, but God-centered. To declare God's excellencies is to speak of all he is and has done ... This purpose is too often thwarted by our silence or pride, but even brief associations with a Christian whose speech fulfills this purpose invariably refreshes our spirits.[59]

From beginning to end, our salvation is all of grace, and therefore God deserves all the honor and glory.

> **1 Peter 2:9-10** | But you are a chosen race, a royal priesthood, a holy nation, a people for his own possession, that you may proclaim the excellencies of him who called you out of darkness into his marvelous light. **10** Once you were not a people, but now you are God's people; once you had not received mercy, but now you have received mercy.

We are called to praise God at all times. We often complain about so much. Some of us ought to have an honoring doctorate in murmuring because we complain so much. The Bible says we are to put off "murmuring and complaining" and to put on the praise of God. Church of Jesus, do you have your praise on? Here Peter begins by quoting Exodus 19:4-6 and says we are God's treasured possession. Why else wouldn't we praise him?

YOU ARE A CHOSEN RACE (1:9A)

> **1 Peter 2:9** | But you are a chosen race...

The people of Israel did not like life in the wilderness, and they complained and grumbled. They said in Numbers 14:2, "Would that we had died in the land of Egypt! Or would that we had died in this wilderness!" They complained and grumbled against the Lord and against Moses and Aaron. Peter is quoting Moses' words. The context is the

---

[59] Grudem, *1 Peter*, 112.

Exodus. He says in Exodus 19:4-6, "You yourselves have seen what I did to the Egyptians, and how I bore you on eagles' wings and brought you to myself." These people who were once abandoned in Egypt for 400 years are now adopted into God's family. Egypt was a dark place. It was a place where they no longer had freedom but were torn from their homes into slavery. They didn't have family life, only slave life. Remember when you were in a spiritual Egypt? Remember when you were spiritually orphaned? Remember when you were dead in your trespasses and sins? You were forgotten? You were alone. Remember when your heart was not yet transformed by the Spirit – it was still a stubborn heart of stone?

God tells Israel: "You were slaves in the Egyptians houses and I brought you into my home. You were not a people, but now you are a chosen race." In the same way, we know that God adopted us. We have a new name Jesus is our banner. Jesus is our identity. We no longer belong to Pharaoh. We now belong to the living God, the God of unrelenting love and abundant in mercy. We are now God's "chosen race." He could have passed over us, but he chose to love us. He could have justly forgotten us forever, but he chose to bear us up on eagles' wings. He brought us to himself.

> They who wait for the Lord shall renew their strength; they shall mount up with wings like eagles; they shall run and not be weary; they shall walk and not faint. —Isaiah 40:31

We are a chosen race precious family of God. Now we are to "proclaim the excellencies of him who called you out of darkness into his marvelous light." Are you a part of God's forever family? Praise him! Are you adopted with a new name and a new identity? Praise him! Hasn't he engravened your name on his hands? Praise him! You are a chosen race! Praise him! Display the light of Christ. Be the aroma of Christ!

We are a Chosen People

God identifies those who believe in Christ as chosen, just as God had chosen Israel to demonstrate his redemption (*cf* Isa 43:21). They didn't deserve it, and neither do you. It is crucial for you as a Christian to understand that your salvation is based not based on your good deeds. You'll never do enough to be worthy. You are not worthy. You'll never be worthy. God doesn't choose us based on a merit system. He chooses you based on his own sovereign, electing purposes according to his glorious grace. You are a race of people chosen by God. You are no longer "in Adam" but "in Christ." Your family, race, is Jesus. Know Jesus. Love him. Embrace him. Proclaim him. Exalt him! Now here is another reason praise him.

We are a Transformed People

We are a "chosen generation." The idea of the word "generation" is that they have been generated by their fathers. As believers, we have also been generated through the power of the Holy Spirit. You are a new and chosen generation. You were brought to life by the Holy Spirit. Theologians call this concept "regeneration" or the "new birth" (*cf* Jn 3). Think of Ezekiel 36 and 37. You have a new heart. The heart of stone has been taken out, and you've been given a new tender heart of flesh. Consider Ezekiel 37. You were nothing but dead bones in a valley of dry bones. You were "dead in your trespasses and sins" and Christ made you alive (Eph 2:1-4). You are a chosen generation, a new humanity (Eph 2:15). You are a new creation (2 Cor 5:17). You are not what you once were, and you will never be what you once were.

YOU ARE A ROYAL PRIESTHOOD (1:9B)

1 Peter 2:9 | But you are a chosen race, a royal priesthood...

We've gone from rejected to received. You were once dead in your sins. You were rejected. But now you are received. Before you had no access to God. Now you are a kingdom of priests!

We are in a war, and we are to minister Christ's grace through praise and intercession like the priests of old. As priests, we participate in the high priestly ministry of Christ.

As one who is born again, you don't need a special status as pastor or elder to have access to God. We all have access to God and we "come boldly to his throne of grace, and obtain mercy, and ask for grace and help in time of need" (Heb 4:16).

The Power of the Priesthood

You have the power of the priesthood. It is the power of grace. You have the power to point wanderers to Christ. Go after Christ's lost sheep. Bring them back into the fold.

The power of the priesthood is the power of prayer. You can ask whatever you want according to Christ's will and he will do it for you. "Ask, and it will be given to you; seek, and you will find; knock, and it will be opened to you" (Mt 7:7). Jesus "ever lives to make intercession for us" (Heb 7:25).

The power of the priesthood is the power of a new position. God said to Israel: "you shall be to me a kingdom of priests" (Exo 19:6). Now a priest has an exalted position in Christ. Remember when you were stuck, and the Lord "brought you up out of a horrible pit, out of the miry clay"? (Psa 40:2a). Remember you could say, "And set my feet upon a rock, and established my steps. 3 He has put a new song in my mouth— Praise to our God; Many will see it and fear, and will trust in the Lord" (Psa 40:2b-3). You were so low in your position. You were an enemy of God, separated from the Holy One. You were never allowed to enter. But our high priest went in before us! Jesus entered into the most holy place in heaven and having paid the full price as sacrifice and High Priest, he sat down at the right hand of God and granted all of us access to God our Father.

The power of the priesthood is the power of praise. The Father took off his judicial robe, and we were transformed from criminals to his dear children. Our Father in heaven opened his arms because Jesus gave us access as priests. Oh how he loves us. I don't understand it, but I don't need to go to a priest. I am a priest.

We don't have a priestly line of one certain family, like the family of Levi. No, we are an entire kingdom of priests. We are a priesthood of God's royal kingdom.

The Power of Praise

The power of the priesthood is the power of praise. I'm no longer abandoned! I'm an ambassador. The blood of Christ grants entrance to me, but also to all who believe. Proclaim the praises of Jesus everywhere you go. "Let everything that has breath praise the Lord! Praise the Lord!" (Psa 150:6). "Rejoice in the Lord always; again I will say, rejoice" (Phil 4;4). "I will bless the Lord at all times: his praise shall continually be in my mouth" (Psa 34:1, KJV).

Royal means we have authority in Jesus' name, we utilize the power of Jesus' kingdom. Priesthood means we stand in the place of Christ in this world, interceding and pointing people to God. This is an office of evangelism. You were called to praise the name of Jesus as a royal priesthood. Preach the gospel to every creature. Have you ever witnessed to someone? When is the last time you witnessed to someone?

Do you realize the power you have? You remember my friend from Saudi Arabia? Well, he called me and said the police were going crazy in his home country looking for him. He said, "please pray!" And we did. We gathered as deacons and elders that night, and we put on the ministry of the priesthood, and we prayed. We prayed that God would blind the eyes of his enemies. And my persecuted friend called me later and said the Lord had blinded the eyes of his persecutors. They said because of his telephone number and the fact that they were talking only in English, they are looking for an American. It's in all the news reports that an American is evangelizing in this persecuted country. God answered our prayers to blind the eyes of his enemies! What a privilege to have the power of the priesthood.

YOU ARE A HOLY NATION (1:9C)

1 Peter 2:9 | But you are a chosen race, a royal priesthood, a holy nation...

We go from idolatry to identity. God's people were a nation of slaves. Their names were forgotten. They were no longer a people group, but a group of tools for Egypt. This was a nation of idols. They built perhaps the pyramids, who knows. But they were enlisted as slaves they lost their identity for idolatry. They were used to build Temples and pyramids for the gods of Egypt.

This goes back to Moses and the burning bush. God's people were not a nation. They lost their identity. They were slaves. And all the sudden, God speaks to Moses from a burning bush. He says, "Take off your shoes, for you are standing on holy ground." "Now Moses, you go to Egypt, and you tell Pharaoh, Let my people go, so they may worship me." He says to Moses, "I don't want them building idol shrines in Egypt anymore. I want my people to be free to worship me." And God promises them in Exodus 19 – after they were delivered, didn't I tell you, "You shall be to me … a holy nation" (Exo 19:6)?

A New Nation

Now Peter in the New Testament designates the same title to believers are separated to Christ as a holy nation. The word nation translates *ethnos*, which means "people," as an ethnic group (Lk 7:5; 23:2;

Jn 11:48, 50–52; Acts 2:5; 10:22; Rev 5:9).[60] St. Paul says, "But our citizenship is in heaven, and from it we await a Savior, the Lord Jesus Christ" (Phil 3:20). God's nation is ethnically diverse. We are from "every nation, from all tribes and peoples and languages" (Rev 7:9).

Christians are out of place in this world. We don't fit. We are salt in a rotten world. We are light in a very dark world. We cause offence. We bear reproach for Christ's name. Jesus said Cursed are you when all men speak well of you. We are "pilgrims and foreigners in this earth." We are citizens of heaven on this earth.

A Holy Nation

You have gone from idolatry in this world to a new identity in Christ. In Christ, we are positionally perfect before a holy God. That makes Christians a holy nation before God because His own righteousness is imputed to them. And practically, they are progressing in holiness by the work of the Spirit (*cf* 2 Cor 3:18).[61]

> *No guilt in life, no fear in death*
> *This is the power of Christ in me*
> *From life's first cry to final breath*
> *Jesus commands my destiny*
> *No power of hell, no scheme of man*
> *Can ever pluck me from His hand*
> *Till He returns or calls me home*
> *Here in the power of Christ I'll stand*

What are ways we can praise God by being a holy nation? Meet together for fellowship and prayer. Never miss. When you are on vacation, find a body of believers and live in the truth that you are a holy nation. Praise the Lord with other Christians everywhere.

YOU ARE A TREASURED PEOPLE (1:9-10)

We now belong to God as his treasured people, a people of his own possession. That means he has ownership of us by the Holy Spirit.

A People Possessed by God

1 Peter 2:9d | A people for his own possession...

---

[60] MacArthur., *1 Peter*, 128-129.
[61] Ibid, 130.

Remember the people of God were worthless slaves in Egypt, but God bought them with a price. He says, "I brought you out of Egypt." How did he do it? Through the blood of the lamb. He said to put the blood on your doorposts and on the header, and "when I see the blood, I will pass over you" (Exo 12:13).

Remember the Lamb of God is now revealed. Jn 1:29, "John saw Jesus and exclaimed, 'Behold the Lamb of God who takes away the sin of the world!'" You may be complaining today and hurting and saying, "I feel worthless!" But you are not worthless. You have nothing to worry about. You were bought with a price! You are bought with the precious blood of Christ. You are now *worthy* child of God. "You are not your own, 20 for you were bought with a price. So glorify God in your body" (1 Cor 6:19-20).

At Sinai God promised the Israelites, "If you will indeed obey My voice and keep my covenant, then you shall by my own possession among all the peoples" (Exo 19:5; *cf* Deut 7:6–7; 14:2; 26:18; Mal 3:17). Again, that foreshadowed the truth of Peter's statement that Christians are now a people for God's own possession. The Greek term rendered possession (*peripoiēsis*) means "to purchase," "to acquire for a price" (*cf* Eph. 1:14). Believers belong to God because he bought them at the ultimate price (1:18–19; *cf* 1 Cor. 6:20; 7:23; Heb 13:12; Rev 5:9). As Paul reminded Titus, that price was "Christ Jesus, who gave himself for us [Christians] to redeem us from every lawless deed, and to purify for himself a people for his own possession" (Titus 2:13–14; *cf* Acts 20:28; 1 Cor 6:20).[62] You belong to God. You are his purchased treasure. Do whatever he wants you to do. Know that he has you in his hand and no one can pluck you out of his hand!

A People Praising God

1 Peter 2:9e | That you may proclaim the excellencies of him who called you out of darkness into his marvelous light.

We are chosen and treasured that we might praise God and proclaim his excellencies. This is something we must choose to do intentionally. Life must be lived from the heart. Praise comes when we consider all the good that God is doing even in the worst circumstances. Anyone can complain, but when life is hard, we remember that he

---

[62] Ibid., 130.

called us out of the darkest night of sin into his marvelous light. Even if all goes wrong in the earthly realm, we lose nothing in the heavenly realm for our reward has always been the Lord. Indeed, he is our "exceeding great reward" (Gen 15:1, KJV). Praise him! Praise him! You have Christ! You are an heir of God and a joint-heir with Christ. God who graciously gave you his Son will freely give you all things (Rom 8:32). You have every spiritual blessing in Christ (Eph 1:3). Proclaim his excellencies!

Brothers and sisters, we have no reason to complain. Philippians 2:14 (CSB), "Do everything without grumbling and arguing." No complaining, no crabbiness! That's not allowed because you are a chosen race. You are a treasured possession of your heavenly Father.

A People Adopted by God

We go from worthless to worthy. We have gone from abandoned to adopted. Peter ends by referencing Hosea 1:6–10. Remember Israel had gone astray and lost their identity. They had spiritual amnesia. They had forgotten the deep love of God. Remember the prophet Hosea was commanded by God to marry a prostitute. She had children with other lovers, illegitimate children. God gave names to the children, and two of them are mentioned here. He called them, "Not-my-people" and "No-mercy". Can you imagine? Peter says: those nicknames described your life before you knew Christ.

> **1 Peter 2:10** | Once you were not a people, but now you are God's people; once you had not received mercy, but now you have received mercy.

No longer are you estranged from God with your mother (the world) as a prostitute. You've left that life and been adopted by God. You once were a person without a spiritual family. You were an orphan, but now you are adopted into the family of God. God is your Father and you have received his mercy.

Conclusion

Remember the day you came to know Christ? He turned your complaining into conviction and your worry into worship. We are a people of praise! This summer I've had the opportunity to go camping out in nature. When we camp, if you are quiet, you can hear the praise of all creation. The loud cicadas. The birds whistle and chirp. The coyotes howl. All creation is praising the Lord. Listen, if we do not praise him, then the rocks will cry out! Let us "proclaim the excellencies of him who called you out of darkness into his marvelous light."

10 | 1 PETER 2:11-12
WINNING OVER THE FLESH

Beloved, I urge you as sojourners and exiles to abstain from the passions of the flesh, which wage war against your soul.
1 PETER 2:11

My grandfather Charles Cunningham Black enlisted in the Scottish army during World War I when he was 15 years old in 1914. His sister lied and said he was of age. Intense training followed. They had to be ready for action. They had to keep their ears open. They had to have their clothing and their weapons in order. They couldn't allow themselves to be distracted.

As Christians we are also at war, and it's easy to get tangled up in the things of this life. If you are in a battle, you can't get tangled up in earthly pursuits. Paul said that in 2 Timothy 2:4, "No soldier gets entangled in civilian pursuits, since his aim is to please the one who enlisted him." Peter said it in 1 Peter 1:13, "Therefore, preparing your minds for action, and being sober-minded, set your hope fully on the grace that will be brought to you at the revelation of Jesus Christ."

This world is not our home any longer. We pray, "Your will be done on earth as it is in heaven" because God's realm is our home. We could never be at home on this rebellious earth. How do we stay preserved for heaven? Peter tells us how in 1 Peter 2:11-12.

> **1 Peter 2:11-12** | Beloved, I urge you as sojourners and exiles to abstain from the passions of the flesh, which wage war against your soul. ¹² Keep your conduct among the Gentiles honorable, so that when they speak against you as evildoers, they may see your good deeds and glorify God on the day of visitation.

How do we stay preserved for heaven? First, remember where you are from. Your homeland is where God dwells.

REMEMBER YOUR HOMELAND (2:11A)

> **1 Peter 2:11a** | Beloved, I urge you as sojourners and exiles to abstain from the passions of the flesh.

The Bible tells us we are sojourners and exiles on this earth. We are not buying what the world is peddling. The Bible tells you what you are, and that's what you are indeed. Martin Luther once said, "The word of a human being is a little thing. It flies up into the air and is gone. But the word of God is heavier than heaven and earth." [63] The word of God tells us what we are.

The Bible says, "Heaven and earth will pass away, but my words will never pass away." Jesus says, "... one jot or one tittle shall in no wise pass from the law ..."[64] There are so many places that testify to your identity in the Scriptures. You are in Christ. You are an overcomer over the world. You will persevere to the end. You have the righteousness of Christ placed upon your account. Your sins have been placed upon Christ's account and can never be held against you. For you there is no condemnation. You have been predestined to be conformed to God's Son. No weapon formed against you shall prosper. All things, both good and bad, will work together for your good and God's glory. You are now citizens of heaven. You don't fit into this world.

We are Sojourners and Exiles

We are sojourners. That means we are citizens of another country. We are immigrants. Brothers and sisters, we are sojourners and exiles when it comes to this world. Peter has already told us that we are "elect

---

[63] Martin Luther. "On the True Nature of Faith," *Sermon on John 4:46-54* (Wittenberg, Germany: Church Postil, 1526), paragraph 34, http://www.go-drules.net/library/luther/129luther_e17.htm.

[64] Timothy J. Keller, (2013). *The Timothy Keller Sermon Archive.* New York City: Redeemer Presbyterian Church, "Practicing Faith in a Pagan World, Part 2."

exiles." We don't fit in here. We belong to another place. We don't fit in because we are "citizens of heaven" (Phil 3:20). You should be living your life not as citizens of this earth, but citizens of heaven. The Christian is "a temporary resident in a world that is not his home, for his true homeland is in heaven."[65]

What does it mean to be a sojourner? It means you are a foreigner in this world, on your way to another world. It means the moment you become a Christian your citizenship is transferred from this world to the next. You're living in the future. You now have rights and privileges that belong to the citizen of heaven.[66] As citizens of heaven, we don't belong here. By faith, we are entitled to all the rights and privileges of Christ. He won them for us on the cross. He changed our allegiance to him. Because you believe that Jesus is the Christ, the King of kings, the Son of God, then you long for his rule on this earth. The rebellion of this present age is offensive. If you are a true citizen of heaven, then you can no longer feel comfortable breathing the aroma of sin of this sin-sick world.

We are Exiles

We are exiles. That means because we are from somewhere else, we don't fit into this world system or paradigm anymore. It's like in the Lord of the Rings trilogy. We are kind of like the little, tiny elves. They are not originally the most glorious creatures. But they align themselves with these angelic warriors, called the holy ones. They go, and they fight tremendous battles. They win honor and glory on the battlefield. They go through tremendous difficulties and adventures. And when they come back to their own homeland, they become leaders, because they have a new perspective. They see things that the people who stayed there never can see. They laugh louder now. They sing better. They cry more. They're just bigger people. They're greater people. They have depths that their fellow citizens of their old homeland don't understand. They sing their elven song:

We still remember, we who dwell
In this far land beneath the trees

---

[65] Grudem, *1 Peter*, 122.
[66] Keller, Sermon Archive, "Practicing Faith, Part 2."

The starlight on the Western Seas. [67]

That's how we are as Christians. We still remember. We touch the eternal continually through his eternal Spirit who dwells within us. We are seated in the heavenly realm. We've seen things with our spiritual eyes that lost people can never see. We love our homeland – our family, our culture. But this land is so dry, and dead compared to the land we travel to when we are with our Christian brothers and sisters.

We realize we really don't belong here anymore. We have this complex relationship. We love our homeland, and yet our homeland can't understand us because they realize our true land is in heaven. Jesus Christ tells his disciples, "I'm sending you into the world, and yet the world will hate you because you're not of the world anymore, but I have chosen you out of the world.... As the Father has sent me into the world, so send I you." (Jn 15:29; 20:21).

Your lost friends and family can't understand the eternal perspective you now have as an exile of heaven. "The person without the Spirit does not accept the things that come from the Spirit of God but considers them foolishness and cannot understand them because they are discerned only through the Spirit" (1 Cor 2:14, NIV). By the Spirit, you have a new heart and mind. You have seen another universe. You have seen Christ's universe of love and mercy and joy that is not from this world. You have known infinite forgiveness. You have been made holy. The Almighty God, the living God has made himself at home in your heart.

We are like Moses in the Old Testament who knew God in such an intimate way that he had to cover his face because of the glory of God showing from his face. This was so uncomfortable for the people around him that they asked him to veil his face. That's what we've undergone. We have the same living God that appeared to Moses. We are now exiles here. We've seen too much. We know too much. The glory of God shines out of our lives. Paul says, we have that same glory of in us that Moses experienced with God, and we see Christ with an unveiled face. "And we all, with unveiled face, beholding the glory of the Lord, are being transformed into the same image from one degree of glory to another. For this comes from the Lord who is the Spirit" (2 Cor 3:18).

---

[67] Ibid.

REMEMBER YOUR VICTORY (2:11B)

We are called to win against those things that wage war against our soul. No sin should have dominion over the Christian (*cf* Rom 6:14).

Understanding Controlling Desires

1 Peter 2:11 | Beloved, I urge you as sojourners and exiles to abstain from the passions of the flesh, which wage war against your soul.

Peter is later going to tell us to have one passion that should control us: to glorify God. That ought to be our controlling passion. In order to do that, Peter tells us to abstain from the "passions of the flesh." What is that? Literally translated it is an "over-desire" or a "desire that controls you" – something that absorbs you. It's an idolatrous passion. It's something you want to put in the place of God, and it wars to have possession of your soul. There is something about the sinful heart that wants to take other things instead of God and put them in the center. That's a controlling passion. The reason you're so excited sometimes and so depressed sometimes and you get so bitter, the reason you're all over the map emotionally is because of over-desires, good things that have become too important. Inordinate desires is another way to put it.

This isn't just sex, money and power. It could be those things, but it's often more subtle than that. It's anything that is an "over-desire" – a controlling thing in your mind. What is it that you feel you must have to be happy? These controlling passions have the potential to dominate you.

Examples of Controlling Desires

Paul says the exact same thing in 1 Corinthians 6:12, "All things are lawful for me... but I will not be dominated by anything." John says it this way in 1 John 5:21, "Little children, keep yourselves from idols. Amen." A controlling passion is anything I'm willing to *sin* in order to get or to get rid of. It could be emotions, relationship, fashion, social media, control. A controlling passion is any expectation that you have which if you don't get them you willing to punish the other party, or if you didn't get what you want you exalt them.

And this happens something either is your master or your savior. A controlling passion could be emotions, relationships, fashion, social media, or control and manipulation to get your way. It could be a thousand other things. John Calvin said, "The heart is an idol making factory." [68] A controlling desire is any expectation that you have which if you don't get them you are willing to punish the other party. It's something if you don't get you get bitter. This often is true in close relationships or marriage. You have certain expectations. They get dashed. You are looking to something or someone and it doesn't deliver. An idol is something that takes over your heart. Don't depend that way on anything or anyone in this world. Anything or anyone outside of Jesus will always let you down. Jesus is the only Savior. Let me give you a few more examples of controlling desires. You are not to be a slave to any of these.

Fear / Negative Emotions / Depression

Fear can be one of these controlling passions. I want the fear gone. I want the fear gone. I'll do anything to get the fear gone. There's nothing wrong with wanting to live in peace. But if you are willing to sin to have peace, then you have a controlling passion.

Marriage / Relationships

Marriage can be a controlling passion. I need a spouse to be happy. Or perhaps you are married, and you say, "I need a certain kind of spouse to be happy." That's all hogwash. Your spouse is not your savior. You need Jesus to be happy. God often calls us to live happily in marriage with someone who is very different than us. Our problem is we think real love is to be served. That's not love. You like being treated well. Real love is laying your life down for your spouse. You can do that for whoever you are married to.

There are those who think, "Well I married the wrong person." I hear this all the time. But do you realize there is no one out there that can be Jesus. Only Jesus can do that. No spouse can be just what you need. Your one controlling passion must be to please Jesus. That person you are looking for to make you happy. His name is Jesus! What is dominating you right now?

Acceptance / Reputation

Does acceptance dominate you? Are you co-dependent? Do you need people to affirm your worth? Are you living as a people pleaser?

---

[68] John Calvin, *Institutes of the Christian Religion*, Ch XI, Para 8.

That's a controlling desire. If you have such high expectations of a person that it takes away your joy when they fail you, you may be looking to that person as a false savior. When our happiness is caught up in whether or not another person accepts me, I am looking to a fallen human being instead of Christ. My acceptance is in Christ alone. Reputation can be a great idol in our lives. "What will people think?" It doesn't matter. What matters is what God thinks. In Christ I am accepted. In Christ all my sins have been washed away. Because of Christ, my reputation before God the Father is perfect. There is no condemnation (Rom 8:1).

Materialism

Does materialism dominate you? It's not wrong to have material things, but perhaps the reason you are in debt today or you don't give to your local church is because you are afraid to be without. Or you need to have this or that. Don't fool yourself. Materialism may have its grip around your neck. It's killing your relationship with God. It's not wrong to have stuff. How do you know if it's an idol? If I love it too much. Someone confronts you about it and you get mad.

Pleasure

Porn is a controlling desire for some who fall into it. And it wages war against their soul. God created sex. But if you are going and looking at another human being in an intimate situation, you are killing your soul. You are sinning against the person you are looking at. You are killing your relationship with God. God created pleasure. He says it's so precious you need to guard it for marriage. You may be a young person, and you may be tempted to throw your purity away. Don't do it. Don't kill your soul. Don't throw your relationship with God away.

Let Jesus be your joy. Let Jesus give you the strength to be pure and clean for the one he's preserving for you. This isn't just for singles. Married people – God invented pleasure. But your spouse is never going to be able to satisfy your needs. Are you thinking you could be happier with someone else? Stop right there. You are putting marriage in the place where only God should be. God is the only one that can fulfill your needs.

Even "Good" Things

Anything can be an enslaving passion. It could be a good thing, like a certain philosophy of child-rearing. You have to have it "this" way or "that" way. It could be that you that you are convinced of a certain kind of schooling: home-schooling or Christian schooling or public school. Let me say that none of those things is the Savior. It could be that natural medicine or traditional medicine. Look live free in Christ, but don't think that any of those things is the Savior. It could be food! I love food. Food is a great thing to serve to show your love to people. We need food to live, but food can't be our savior. I'm preaching to myself now! As believers we are to be free from all these passions and to have one guiding passion: Jesus Christ.

By way of review, let's ask again, what is a controlling desire? It's slavery to anything but God. "Anything you feel like you have to have has your soul in its grip. It's trying to dominate the soul. It's waging war against the soul. It wants to be your salvation. It wants to capture your soul. That's why it's warring against it. It's trying to capture it. It's trying to storm it. It's trying to take it."[69]

There is a war going on in your soul. Don't be controlled by your passions. This could be translated, "controlling passions." Paul says it similarly, "All things are lawful for me," but not all things are helpful. "All things are lawful for me, but I will not be dominated by anything" (1 Cor 6:12). Peter says something similar in 1 Peter 2:16, "Live as people who are free, not using your freedom as a cover-up for evil, but living as servants of God." Brothers and sisters, we are not servants of the flesh, but servants of God.

Victory Over Controlling Desires

Now let us consider the pathway to victory. As Christians, we were made to serve God with a holy and infinite passion. You cannot love him too much. And all our sin and idolatry is simply revealing a lack of love for God. God tells us we are to love him wholly and completely—with everything we've got. You have been freed from controlling passions. You have no other goal, no other passion than to glorify God. You are victorious over sin. You have the power already over sin, but will you use it?

---

[69] Keller, ibid. "Passions, Pt 2."

God guards us from sin. Jude 24-25, "Now to him who is able to keep you from stumbling and to present you blameless before the presence of his glory with great joy, ²⁵ to the only God, our Savior, through Jesus Christ our Lord, be glory, majesty, dominion, and authority, before all time and now and forever. Amen."

Jesus protects us from sin. 1 John 5:18, "We know that everyone who has been born of God does not keep on sinning, but he who was born of God protects him, and the evil one does not touch him."

The Spirit leads us into righteousness. Galatians 5:16, "walk by the Spirit, and you will not gratify the desires of the flesh." Ezekiel 36:26-27, "And I will give you a new heart, and a new spirit I will put within you. And I will remove the heart of stone from your flesh and give you a heart of flesh. ²⁷ And I will put my Spirit within you, and cause you to walk in my statutes and keep my judgments."

The word keeps us from sin and helps us walk in the light. Psalm 119:11, "Your word have I treasured in my heart, that I might not sin against You." Psalm 119:105, "Your word is a lamp to my feet and a light to my path."

Brothers and sisters encourage us. Ephesians 5:18-19, "And do not get drunk with wine, for that is debauchery, but be filled with the Spirit, ¹⁹ addressing one another in psalms and hymns and spiritual songs, singing and making melody to the Lord with your heart…"

God always gives a way of escape. 1 Corinthians 10:13, "No temptation has overtaken you that is not common to man. God is faithful, and he will not let you be tempted beyond your ability, but with the temptation he will also provide the way of escape, that you may be able to endure it."

Don't get tangled up in the mess of controlling and enslaving passions. Don't do it. Hebrews 12:1-2, "since we are surrounded by so great a cloud of witnesses, let us lay aside every weight, and the sin which so easily ensnares us, and let us run with endurance the race that is set before us, ² looking unto Jesus, the author and finisher of our faith, who for the joy that was set before Him endured the cross, despising the shame, and has sat down at the right hand of the throne of God."

REMEMBER YOUR MISSION (2:12)

1 Peter 2:12 | Keep your conduct among the Gentiles honorable, so that when they speak against you as evildoers, they may see your good deeds and glorify God on the day of visitation.

Peter tells us our mission is to live such a Christlike life that unbelievers who persecute us will turn from their wicked life and glorify God.

A Mission to Walk Honorably

1 Peter 2:12a | Keep your conduct among the Gentiles honorable...

How vital it is to be careful in our thoughts, words, and deeds. People are watching. Angels are watching (1:12). God may use your honorable walk to rescue a lost sinner from hell.

What is this "day of visitation"? This phrase is often used as a way of talking about Christ's second coming or of judgment day. But commentators have said this phrase could be translated both "the day" or "a day." Interesting. Many commentators believe this is referring to the day when God saves the lost people that are persecuting you or speaking evil of you. Through your honorable walk, God may visit those who persecute you and actually save their soul. Unbelievers are examining our lives. They may speak loudly that they do not believe in God, but God is always working through your heart and life to shine the light of Christ.

So then, our mission is clear. It is to glorify God by living in a way that is honorable before the lost world. We are to bring glory to God in every area of our conduct. Why? Because we are being watched. God has saved us to give the lost a reason to look to him. You are to be God's mirror. Are you a mirror of his love? You can't be a mirror if you are all tangled up with enslaving desires. Your mission is to live in such a way that people see your life and glorify God.

A Mission to Walk Eschatologically

1 Peter 2:12b | So that when they speak against you as evildoers, they may see your good deeds and glorify God on the day of visitation.

Our worthy walk has eschatological effects. Eschatology refers to the study of "last things" when Jesus returns and judges the world.

When unbelievers slander and hurt you in this present time, you must not take it personally. Instead, set your heart to the final eschaton, when Christ will judge all people. This mindset will increase mercy in your heart, so that you might love your enemy and those who persecute and slander you and love them with God's everlasting love.

We need to be careful of your conduct, because through it, we are preparing the lost for judgment day. We need to be living examples of citizens from another world. God will use it to get at their heart. You want the lost world to "see your good deeds and glorify God on the day of visitation" (1:12). Jesus said, Matthew 5:16, "Let your light so shine before men, that they may see your good works, and glorify your Father which is in heaven."

The picture of *aliens and strangers* found in 1:1, 17, comes originally from Abraham's confession in Genesis 23:4. Abraham lived by faith, not following his sinful desires, but living in a way that made the pagan world wonder and glorify the God he served. Follow the flow of Peter's argument with that in mind. If we are truly to live as exiles, we are to refuse *sinful desires*, as they wage war against God's purpose of Christlikeness for us (*cf* Gal 5:19–21). *Pagans* describes those who are outside the relationship to God enjoyed by the church as the true Israel. We can live in such a way as to bring these pagans into the church so that when the day he visits us, i.e. to judge the world, there will be those who are saved from his wrath as a result of seeing our faith lived out.[70]

Conclusion

I am a distracted person by nature. I've often been taken off course with the simplest distraction. Driving is a big example. Twice I was driving friend from the airport in Bilbao, Spain, and we ended up in France because of I was so immersed in our conversation. Once we were headed to Indiana as a family, and we ended up in Michigan (where 90 and 94 split).

Let's not be distracted. Our mission is to glorify God and to point people to Christ. Don't let anything distract you or control you and enslave you, in order to keep you from your mission and your destination.

---

[70] Wheaton, 1 Peter, 1377.

11 | 1 PETER 1:13-17
HONORING PAGAN GOVERNMENT

> *Be subject for the Lord's sake to every human institution, whether it be to the emperor as supreme, or to governors as sent by him to punish those who do evil and to praise those who do good. ... Honor everyone. Love the brotherhood. Fear God. Honor the emperor.*
>
> 1 PETER 2:13-14, 17

The entire book of 1 Peter is about living as lights in a pagan world. 1 Peter 2:9 – "We are called out of darkness into his marvelous light." How can we be lights in the most extreme situations in this world, especially when the government is hostile toward Christians? What is our responsibility toward pagan government?

I can remember so many times when my sister and I and our friends would walk down our road at night. We lived a mile into the bayou near Lake Ponchatrain in Louisiana. When it was cloudy, you couldn't see your hand in front of your face. There were no streetlights. This was the day before everyone had a flashlight on their cell phones. There were no cell phones. We didn't usually carry flashlights, so it was always interesting. But on a clear night there was the light of the moon and the stars out in the middle of nowhere was so brilliant, so fantastically bright. The moon is a reflector of the sun. The moon could shine its light into the darkest place on earth and light it up.

So it is with Christians. Peter says in 1 Peter 2:9, you are to "proclaim the excellencies of him who called you out of darkness into his marvelous light." The entire book is about how to do this. The theme of this book is that we are elect exiles from a foreign, glorious place shining the light of Christ into this dark place.

Peter tells us how to shine our light in every venue of life: civil government, the home, the church, and the world. He begins with how we relate to a government that is hostile toward Christians. He says: submit to every human institution (lit. "creature").

> **1 Peter 2:13-17** | Be subject for the Lord's sake to every human institution, whether it be to the emperor as supreme, **14** or to governors as sent by him to punish those who do evil and to praise those who do good. **15** For this is the will of God, that by doing good you should put to silence the ignorance of foolish people. **16** Live as people who are free, not using your freedom as a cover-up for evil, but living as servants of God. **17** Honor everyone. Love the brotherhood. Fear God. Honor the emperor.

How should we live as citizens of heaven and yet be governed by a very pagan world? The first major thing Peter says is that we are to "be subject for the Lord's sake to every human institution." Literally every human authority or creature put there by God. How can we shine our lights in darkness? How can we proclaim the excellencies of him who called us out of darkness, into his marvelous light? By exalting our Master. We need to call attention to our Master.

OUR MASTER (2:13-14A)

> **1 Peter 2:13-14a, 17** | Be subject for the Lord's sake to every human institution, whether it be to the emperor as supreme, **14** or to governors. **17** ...Honor the emperor.

It is quite shocking to Christians when they read Peter tells us to be subject to pagan, and sometimes tyrannical governing authorities. The vast majority of human authorities and institutions are wicked in some way, so this is at first a perplexing command. But it is in honor of the one Master over everything: our Lord Jesus Christ. It is for his sake that we submit to human government.

The Meaning of Submission

1 Peter 2:13a | Be subject...

We are under the authority of Christ. And Jesus says: Submit. What does that mean? The word "submit" is a military term that literally means to "get in line." Even if we don't like the rules, we are to "get in line" anyway. Note how specific he is. We are not only to obey "the king," but also any "governors" (referring to all the various levels of authority) sent by him. And there are no exceptions. That's the part that gives us trouble. What in the world is Peter saying? He's saying trust that even the most wicked of governments cannot thwart the Lord's good purposes for his people. Daniel explained this concept to one of the greatest kings of the ancient world, Nebuchadnezzar. Daniel said: "Blessed be the name of God forever and ever, to whom belong wisdom and might. 21 He changes times and seasons; he removes kings and sets up kings..." (Dan 2:20-21). And again, "The Most High rules the kingdom of men and gives it to whom he will and sets over it the lowliest of men" (Dan 4:17). Paul says it this way in Romans 13:1, "Let every person be subject to the governing authorities. For there is no authority except from God, and those that exist have been instituted by God."

The Motive of Submission

1 Peter 2:13-14, 17 | Be subject for the Lord's sake to every human institution, whether it be to the emperor as supreme, 14 or to governors as sent by him to punish those who do evil and to praise those who do good. 17 ...Honor the emperor.

What is Peter saying? "Be subject." Notice the qualification, "for the Lord's sake..." even so much as honoring the emperor Nero who would eventually put Peter to death by crucifying him upside down. Here is a ruler, Nero, who murdered his mother and many of his officers. He would actually disguise himself and go into Rome and murder people for sport. We are to submit for one supreme motive—for the Lord Jesus Christ's sake.

To make more contemporary: *"Submit yourselves to the President and to the Supreme Court, and to the federal judiciary system, and to the Congress, and to the Governor, and the state legislature, and to the state police and the local police, and to the principal at the school your children attend, and to your local mayor and board of trustees."*

That list could be greatly extended. The truth is, we all live under multiple layers of authority, and it's very likely that we won't care for some of those people and for the laws they pass and the rules they make. There will always be leaders we don't trust, laws we don't like and taxes we don't want to pay. What do we do then? Peter's answer is very clear. We are to submit for the Lord's sake. Brothers and sisters, we have one Master, and his name is Jesus. We are elect exiles from another place. Yet Christ is in control of the entire human governmental system. He will use even tyrants to fulfill his will (consider everyone from Nebuchadnezzar to Nero).

The Manner of Submission

1 Peter 2:13c | Be subject ... to every human institution.

We are commanded to submit, but to who? And how? We are to submit to civil authority, regardless of its nature. Even unreasonable, evil, harsh rulers and oppressive systems are far better than anarchy. And all forms of government, from dictatorships to democracies, are filled with evil because they are led by fallen sinners. Still, civil authority is from God, though the individual rulers may be godless.[71]

We are citizens of heaven. If a ruler were to call us before him and command us to do something, we could say, "I have one master Jesus Christ. He is my only king and sovereign. But he has commanded me to obey you in all ways that are righteous. I therefore gladly obey. A good example of this is Daniel and his three friends. They were commanded to eat things that were not in accordance to the Mosaic Law. They very respectfully presented another option.

The Mystery of Submission

1 Peter 2:13-14, 17 | Be subject for the Lord's sake to every human institution, whether it be to the emperor as supreme, **14** or to governors as sent by him to punish those who do evil and to praise those who do good. **17** ...Honor the emperor.

In his day, the Roman emperor—the authority—was an object of worship. But Peter is clear: the emperor isn't divine, so he's not to be worshiped. No human ruler is to be worshiped. But we are to submit to

---

[71] MacArthur, *1 Peter*, 146.

the emperor. Peter is clear. How do we understand this "mystery" that confounds us?

Our leaders are mere human creatures like us, but as human creatures they bear God's image. They are to enjoy our submission (1 Pet 2:13) and our respect (1 Pet 2:17), but not our worship. Yes, at that time this was written, Nero was in power. He was quite insane. Why would Peter say to "honor the emperor"? Peter and Paul both lived in the openly sinful, decadent Roman Empire run by insane emperors who were worshipped as gods. Rome was a society infamous for heinous evil (homosexuality, infanticide, government corruption, abuse of women, immorality, violence), and yet both apostles said to obey civil authority. Paul says that "whoever rebels against the authority is rebelling against what God has instituted" (Rom 13:2). Jesus himself had commanded, "Render to Caesar the things that are Caesar's" (Mt 22:21).

OUR MISSION (2:15-16)

1 Peter 2:15-17 | For this is the will of God, that by doing good you should put to silence the ignorance of foolish people. **16** Live as people who are free, not using your freedom as a cover-up for evil, but living as servants of God. **17** Honor everyone. Love the brotherhood. Fear God. Honor the emperor.

The Integrity of Our Mission

1 Peter 2:15 | For this is the will of God, that by doing good you should put to silence the ignorance of foolish people.

There are many slanders against Christians, some of which are more plausible. For example, "Christians are hypocrites." Surely Jesus said there would be many pretenders and fakers, so this is plausible, but true Christians by their integrity silence the critics. True Christianity has nothing to fear from impartial observation. In belief and practice, true Christians "adorn the doctrine," as Paul puts it (Titus 2:10). Then, let our enemies examine us. Slanders will die when they are exposed fairly and honestly to the truth.[72]

God's will is that Christians do good and have a life of good works. Christians evidence their faith by living a life that displays the love of

---

[72] Phillips, *Epistles of Peter*, 1 Pe 2:15.

Christ and the conviction of truth. True believers not only know the word, they walk in it (Jas 1:22-25).

The Tension of Our Mission

1 Peter 2:16 | Live as people who are free, not using your freedom as a cover-up for evil, but living as servants of God.

There is a tension here. We are to "submit." But then he says we are to live in freedom. Which is it? First, we are free! We have one master. In a sense we are subject to the laws of another realm above this realm. We are free. Jesus is our Lord. It's not the president or the supreme court or the mayor. It's not the laws of this land. Our Master is Jesus.

Some people might say, "Well then, I don't have to obey the speed limit, pay taxes, or get a construction permit for the church or home when we remodel. What I'm doing is more important. I'm free to do this." No, don't use your freedom as a cover-up for evil. As a citizen of heaven, you need to be a good citizen on earth. We obey the speed limit. We submit to the permit laws, and property tax laws. We pay our bills on time.

In other words, God says, you are totally free in Jesus. So how should you use that freedom? By serving others. By submitting to the government as long as they are not asking you to break God's law. We are free to do the will of God. We submit to God in everything.

The Order of Our Mission

1 Peter 2:17 | Honor everyone. Love the brotherhood. Fear God. Honor the emperor.

Honor Everyone

Everyone should have honor. Since Jesus is our master, we should follow his example. He taught us that he did not come into the world to "be served, but to serve and give his life a ransom for many." Everyone we meet, we are to look at them as higher than us. We are to "honor" them. We are to be their servant. So perhaps you are rich and well-educated and articulate – you are to see all people whether they are like you or the exact opposite of you as higher than you. You are to have the mindset of a servant for them, a mindset of humility.

We are to give honor to all men regardless of color, class, or creed. God has no partiality. The ground is level at the cross. He sends his beneficial rain upon the just and the unjust. We see people who are steeped in superstition, or sodden with sin, or slaves to terrible lusts occupying high positions in the land. We wonder how we can honor such people. God loves all of us. We are all precious to him. Man was made in the image and likeness of God. The image is often terribly defaced and barely discernible anymore, but the eye of God can still see it. No one is beyond the reach of His redemption and his transforming grace.[73]

Love Your Forever Family

Paul refers to the church here as the "brotherhood," or we could call it God's "forever family." Love is displayed first and foremost by just being present with the brothers. We are to be hospitable, enjoying fellowship not only on the Lord's Day, but in each other's homes in the regular circumstances of life, bearing each other's burdens, and encouraging each other in our brief time on earth.

Fear God

We are called to obey God rather than men, so there is a hierarchy in how we as Christians are to comport ourselves. If we are not being asked to compromise our morality, then we are to obey the government. But if we are called to violate our worship of God or the holiness of life that we are called to, then we must lovingly and respectfully disobey. God must be feared above all. It is helpful to remember that there is always a separation of church and state. The state can never control the government of the church, for the church is governed by her head, Jesus Christ. We must obey and fear him above all kings and presidents and governments on the earth.

Honor Government Leaders

Notice what Peter says: honor everyone... honor the emperor. The emperor is just a man. He is not to be worshiped. Fear God. Worship God. But honor the emperor. That means we are to honor even tyrannical government leaders. Certainly, it would not be honorable to sin or to worship them (as the Roman emperor commanded). How then do we honor tyrants? Pray for them. Respect their laws as long as they are not asking you to sin. Obey the speed limit, traffic laws. Pay your taxes.

---

[73] Ibid., 1 Pe 2:17a.

File for renovation permits. Pay your property taxes. Be honest in all you do. Our goodness will be our greatest apologetic for the gospel. Good works silence false accusations. We ought to be throwing ourselves into good things. Submission is the great apologetic for the gospel.

Learning this lesson didn't come overnight for Peter. Do you remember the night Jesus was betrayed in the garden? Peter brought a sword that night. He thought this was the hour for action, and he cut off the ear of one who had come to arrest his Lord. But now, decades later, as an older and wiser man, Peter says to us in essence, "I have put that sword away." God has given a sword to the state, but except for the word of God, "the sword of the Spirit" (Eph 6:17), the church is to keep hers sheathed. For Peter, preaching from the Bible was enough. It cut to the bone and marrow of the harshest in authority. Peter has learned his lesson. He is now free to submit.[74]

OUR MESSAGE

To understand why we are to obey tyrants, except when they ask us to sin, we must go back to verse 9.

> **1 Peter 2:9** | But you are a chosen race, a royal priesthood, a holy nation, a people for his own possession, that you may proclaim the excellencies of him who called you out of darkness into his marvelous light.

We are not to use our freedom as a cover-up for evil. We are to use our freedom to bring glory and honor to Jesus Christ, so we can silence (and save) those who are now in the dark ignorance and foolishness of this world.

Proclaim the Message

Let's proclaim the message. Jesus is Lord! Jesus is our governor. Just as Isaiah 9:6 says, "For to us a child is born, to us a son is given; and the government shall be upon his shoulder, and his name shall be called Wonderful Counselor, Mighty God, Everlasting Father [*Father of the world to come*], Prince of Peace." Realize that that our great God and King, Jesus "works all things after the counsel of his own will" (Eph 1:11). Nothing and no one is going to thwart the plan of Jesus. He is

---

[74] Helm, *1 & 2 Peter and Jude*, 93.

almighty. Our message to the authorities and powers in this world is simple: Jesus is Lord! Obey him. We are to be "proclaiming the excellencies of him who called you out of darkness into his marvelous light" (1 Pet 2:9). What are these excellencies? He is an excellent governor not only of the earth, but of the universe. He's an excellent Savior and Redeemer. This is what Paul says in Colossians 1:15-20. Turn there.

There's coming a time when Christ returns and renews this earth, and heaven and earth are one. And Christ will rule as King of kings and Lord of lords! Knowing that Christ is our Master, Savior and Redeemer, Christians should promote the welfare of their society and government while waiting for their eternal home (*cf* Jn 14:2–3; Heb 4:9–10; 11:13–16; Rev 21:1–4).

Live Out the Message

We are to live out the message by praying for those in power and living a godly life. This is what Peter just told us, and Paul agrees, as this is exactly how he instructed Timothy.

> Pray for kings and others in power, so that we may live quiet and peaceful lives as we worship and honor God. —*1 Timothy 2:2*

This raises the question is it ever right to disobey the government? Granted that the authority of rulers is derived from God, but what happens if they abuse it, if they reverse their God given duty, commending those who do evil and punishing those who do good? What is the right thing to do in those situations? The answer is that we should obey the authorities in all that is moral and right, but obedience to God, always comes before obedience to the state. If the state commanded us to do something that God forbids, or forbids what God commands, then our Christian duty is to resist, not to submit, to disobey the state in order to obey God. Our moral duty is always to put God's will first, and so whenever laws are enacted that contradicts God's law, civil disobedience becomes a Christian duty. We see a number of examples of this in Scripture.

When Pharaoh ordered the Hebrew midwives to kill the newborn boys, they refused to obey. "The midwives feared God and did not do as the king of Egypt commanded them, but let the male children live" (Exo 1:17). When King Nebuchadnezzar issued an edict that all his subjects must fall down and worship his golden image, Shadrach, Meshach and Abednego refused to obey (Dan 3). When King Darius made a decree that for thirty days nobody should pray 'to any god or man' except himself, Daniel refused to obey (Dan 6). And when the Sanhedrin banned preaching in the name of Jesus, the apostles refused to obey saying "We must obey God rather than men" (Acts 5:29). This is the strict meaning of civil disobedience, disobeying a particular human law because it is contrary to God's law.

Today there are Christians who face imprisonment and persecution in many different countries around the world because the civil laws of the country where they live are in conflict with the laws of God. For example, Bonhoeffer, in defiance to the Nazi Government, helped smuggle Jews out of Germany and into safety. Corrie Ten Boom did the same thing in World War II and was imprisoned because of it. In situations like this, there is often great personal risk involved, but the primary concern of the people involved is to demonstrate their submissiveness to God, *not their defiance of the government.*

And so we say no to government sponsored abortion. We stand against it. We support pregnancy centers, and we work to change the laws of our land so that one day, the safest place on earth will truly be the womb of a mother. We say no to promoting a transgender agenda. We stand against it. God made people male and female. You can't just choose to be something you are not. Transgenderism is mental illness. It's like saying "I feel like I'm a bird" or "I feel like I'm a fish." Well, look if God made you male, then you are male. By the way, it is cruel to encourage anyone to have reassignment surgery. That is self-injury. We say no to promoting the homosexual agenda. That's asking for the destruction of our society. God told married people to "be fruitful and multiply." Look at the plumbing and you'll realize that homosexual marriage is absurd and hurtful. For those with same sex attraction, you can renew your mind and your heart. You may need to live as single for your life and be a eunuch for the kingdom. There is hope in Christ!

In these areas where our government is wrong, we are not trying to defy our government. We are instead submitting to a higher authority: Jesus Christ. In these situations, we say: "We must obey God rather than men" (Acts 5:29), demonstrating our submissiveness to God. Even though the government is often hostile toward the church, we must submit as much as we can, in all things. The only exception is if we are told to sin.

Conclusion

What a joy to remember in this dark world that Jesus is King of kings and Lord of lords! Let us trust that he is working all things "after the counsel of his own will" (Eph 1:11). Despite the world's hostility against the church, Jesus will come in glory and power. He says, "I make all things new" (Rev 21:5). You may look around and feel discouraged. Don't be discouraged. The story is not finished yet. There's coming a day when "every knee will bow, and every tongue confess... that Jesus Christ is Lord to the glory of God the Father" (Phil 2:10-11).

12 | 1 PETER 2:18-21

SLAVES OF JESUS

Servants, be subject to your masters with all respect, not only to the good and gentle but also to the unjust. For this is a gracious thing, when, mindful of God, one endures sorrows while suffering unjustly.

1 PETER 2:18-19

When our children are young, we wonder, what will they be when they grow up. We dream about it. In modern America, it's usually whatever the child chooses. In our passage, Peter addresses the issue of slavery in his day. Many people in that time did not have a choice regarding slavery. Some were born into it. Many were forced into it by defeat of war. Others actually wanted to become slaves because it was a legitimate pathway to Roman citizenship. After serving as a slave, many people would gain their freedom by the age of 30.

There is a popular story about Christian Missions which describes how two young Moravian Brethren from Herrnhut, Germany were called in 1732 to minister to the African slaves on the Caribbean islands of St. Thomas and St. Croix. When they were told that they would not be allowed to do such a thing, the young men sold themselves to a slave owner and boarded a ship bound for the West Indies. As the ship pulled away from the docks, it is said that they called out to their loved ones

12 | 1 Peter 2:18-21
Slaves of Jesus

on shore, "May the Lamb that was slain receive the reward of His suffering!"

What do we you do when you are in a life situation that is unjust? When someone slanders our reputation, gossips behind our back, or threatens our livelihood, things can get pretty nasty. In my experience, our knee-jerk reactions to unfair treatment generally fall into one of three categories. First, we may adopt the aggressive pattern of blaming and bitterness, focusing on the person who did us wrong and doing whatever it takes to exact revenge. Other times we can turn to self-pity and complaining. Or, a second way perhaps, we pretend everything is ok, but we are dying inside and seething beneath a calm surface. I'm probably most like that. Hiding and acting like everything is ok. Those are all our natural and human responses.

Peter gives us here in 1 Peter 2:18-21, a supernatural response to being treated unjustly. He calls on slaves to remember that they belong to Jesus, and they are to follow in his steps. And remember this morning that we are more than slaves and servants of Christ. We are that, but we are much more than that. We are sons and daughters of the living God. Indeed, "there is neither Jew nor Greek, there is neither slave nor free, there is no male and female, for you are all one in Christ Jesus" (Gal 3:28).

> **1 Peter 2:18-21** | Servants, be subject to your masters with all respect, not only to the good and gentle but also to the unjust. [19] For this is a gracious thing, when, mindful of God, one endures sorrows while suffering unjustly. [20] For what credit is it if, when you sin and are beaten for it, you endure? But if when you do good and suffer for it you endure, this is a gracious thing in the sight of God. [21] For to this you have been called, because Christ also suffered for you, leaving you an example, so that you might follow in his steps.

Peter says, household servants, fall in line with what your master says. Treat him respectfully, regardless or not if he deserves it. Why, because "it is a gracious thing" (vs. 19, 20) for you to endure unjust suffering. Why, because you are following in the steps of Jesus. Peter addresses slaves, and we are going to find out that whatever low position you are in, God is calling us out of the slavery of sin and into sonship and adoption with him.

But first let's consider what Peter says to servants in verse 18.

A CALL TO SUBMIT (2:18-19)

1 Peter 2:18-19 | Servants, be subject to your masters with all respect, not only to the good and gentle but also to the unjust. ⁱ⁹ For this is a gracious thing, when, mindful of God, one endures sorrows while suffering unjustly.

The Instruction to Slaves

Why does Peter address slavery? Why doesn't he just say: "Slavery is wrong – do away with it" and have a slave result? He does something even more radical. He asks them to serve their masters with grace.

The word for "servants" is *oiketēs*, the word for a household servant. This is not the usual New Testament word for a servant, which is doulos, the word for a slave. The word *oiketēs* occurs in only three other places in the New Testament (Lk 16:13; Acts 10:7; Rom 14:4).[75] He addresses household slaves (sometimes this was hired help and sometimes it was servitude).

He asks household servants to do "a gracious thing." Peter asks slaves to be subject to their masters (i.e. employers) for the sake of Christ, and that's his grace might work in and through them. Peter says, "It's a gracious thing." This is a vital passage in the book of 1 Peter, because slaves made up around half of the Roman empire at the time this was written. Slaves, through their gracious attitude could look with eyes on eternity. Their masters, if they didn't know Christ, were in a far greater enslavement than earthly slaves who knew Jesus.

The History of Slavery

The slavery in Rome was different from the modern slave trade that occurred in the United States and England and many other places around the world. In actual fact the Bible does condemn, and in no uncertain terms, the slavery practiced in North America. In 1 Timothy 1:8–11 the Apostle Paul makes a list of activities that are "contrary to sound doctrine" (1:10)—behavior that is against the glorious gospel. One activity in the list is the noun translated "enslavers." This word refers to those who would take a person captive in order to sell him or her

---

[75] Phillips, *Epistles of Peter*, 1 Pe 2:18.

into slavery.[76] The Bible condemns "enslavers" in 1 Timothy 1:10, "The law is not laid down for the just but for the lawless and disobedient, for the ungodly and sinners, for... enslavers, liars, perjurers..."

Half the population of the Roman empire were slaves: 60 million out of 120 million. Our passage is addressed to slaves. There were millions of slaves in Romans society. In fact, many of the churches that Paul planted throughout the Roman Empire were made up of slaves. If half of Roman society were slaves, that means that one half of the entire society was enslaved to the other half! We look back at that and can see the depravity of man's heart.

Modern Slavery

The horrible degradation of slaves in 19th-century America gives the word "slave" a far worse connotation than is accurate for most of the society to which Peter was writing.[77] "Most persons in slavery were treated well; they had been born in the house of their owner and they had been trained to perform important domestic, industrial, business, or public tasks."[78]

There is a contrast between Greco-Roman slavery and the American slave trade. The American and British slave trade was essentially kidnapping people from their homeland and forcing human slavery in the most wretched conditions and circumstances. There was extensive Roman legislation regulating the treatment of slaves. They were normally paid for their services and could expect eventually to purchase their freedom.[79]

Slavery in Israel

There was servitude in Israel, but it was completely different. There was to be no kidnapping. Servitude in Israel was very different than the African slave trade that went on in this country. A person could not be forced to go into slavery. He would enter because of his debts. It was a way for him to legitimately pay back anything he owed.

Every seventh year, regardless if your debt was paid, something wonderful occurred. If you were a Jew, in the seventh year, you were

---

[76] Helm, *1 & 2 Peter and Jude*, 94.
[77] Grudem, *1 Peter*, 131.
[78] Scott Bartchy, *Mallon Chrésai: First-century Slavery and the Interpretation of 1 Corinthians 7:21*, SBL Dissertation Series 11 (Missoula, MT: SBL, 1971) 174.
[79] Grudem, *1 Peter*, 132.

set free, and every fiftieth year, both Jews and Gentile slaves were set free. This also likely occurred for Romans if the person was a slave because of debt.

Slavery in Rome

Greco-Roman slavery was also quite different. By the time of the Christian era and the writing of the letter to Ephesians, sweeping changes had been introduced which radically improved the treatment of slaves. Slaves under Roman law in the first century could generally count on eventually being set free. Very few ever reached old age as slaves. Slave owners were releasing slaves at such a rate that Augustus Caesar introduced legal restrictions to curb the trend. Almost fifty percent of slaves were freed before the age of thirty.[80]

In the Roman Empire a person might become a slave if he had a great amount debt, so he would sell himself into slavery to pay the debt. Most slaves though came from the territories Rome conquered, through defeat in war. A person might be a doctor, a teacher, or a merchant, and suddenly, if Rome conquered his land, he could be a slave. Slavery gave the person a safe place to exist in the Roman Empire. You would have food, clothing, a warm bed. Slaves could own property and even own other slaves. It is true that when a person became a slave, he or she would lose all of his rights, but there were laws passed in the days of Paul that allowed for slaves to purchase themselves out of slavery and become citizens. The only ones that could never become free were slaves that became criminals. They were branded, and they could never have freedom. Here's something very interesting. According to R. Kent Hughes:

> Being a slave did not indicate one's social class. Slaves regularly were accorded the social status of their owners. Regarding outward appearance, it was usually impossible to distinguish a slave from free persons. A slave could be a custodian, a salesman, or a CEO. Many slaves lived separately from their owners. In fact, selling oneself into slavery was commonly used as a means of obtaining Roman citizenship and gaining an entrance into society. If you worked hard, there was a possibility of adoption into the family by the time you were 30, which meant the coveted Roman citizenship. Shockingly, Roman slavery in the first century was far more humane and civilized than

---

[80] R. Kent Hughes, *Ephesians: The Mystery of the Body of Christ*. Preaching the Word (Wheaton, IL: Crossway Books, 1990), 206.

the American/African slavery practiced in this country much later. This is a sobering and humbling fact![81]

There were various distinctions in Roman society that segregated people. We'll look into these more in depth later but let me say there were differences between men and women. Women couldn't own property or vote. There were differences between Jews and Gentiles. They hated each other. There were different classes of society. That difference was no more apparent than between slaves and masters.

Paul taught something amazing in his writings. It is especially seen here: he elevated all people. The ground is level at the cross. There is no male or female superiority. No difference between Jews or Gentiles. No superiority between slaves and free people.

Of course, the cross brings all groups to level ground. We are all equally deserving of hell, and all equally in desperate need for a Savior. It is only Jesus Christ that can take these distinctions and erase them by the Cross. Slaves, which were despised in Roman society, are now made equal to their masters. And masters are brought down to be slaves of Jesus Christ. In fact, it was not uncommon for slaves to be the pastors of churches. In the body of Christ, it is not social status that is important – it is surrender to Christ!

The Attitude of a Slave

What do you do if you are a slave in the first century? Unrest among slaves was widespread at this time, and undoubtedly some Christian slaves believed that, having been "bought" by Christ, they had been set free from their earthly masters.[82] But Peter, in the midst of possible abuse, says that it is a gracious thing to endure unjust treatment in employment.

> **1 Peter 2:19** | For this is a gracious thing, when, mindful of God, one endures sorrows while suffering unjustly.

We are called to be mindful of God and endure unjust suffering with grace. We know who is in charge when we are wronged. We understand we are to be gentle and do good when we are wronged. This was Paul's attitude among the brothers, "We were gentle among you,

---

[81] Hughes, *Ephesians*, 206.
[82] Stephen Motyer, *1 Peter* in *Evangelical Commentary on the Bible*, Vol. 3 (Grand Rapids, MI: Baker Book House, 1995), 1167.

like a mother caring for her little children" (1 Thess 2:7). "By the meekness and gentleness of Christ, I appeal to you" (2 Cor 10:1). Paul says "this is a gracious thing" to submit and do a good job when you are unjustly treated. How about you? Are you at times unjustly treated at work? Remember the command of Paul in Ephesians 6:5, "Slaves, obey your earthly masters with deep respect and fear. Serve them sincerely as you would serve Christ."

A CALL TO SANCTIFICATION (2:20-21)

> **1 Peter 2:20-21** | For what credit is it if, when you sin and are beaten for it, you endure? But if when you do good and suffer for it you endure, this is a gracious thing in the sight of God. ²¹ For to this you have been called, because Christ also suffered for you, leaving you an example, so that you might follow in his steps.

Growing in Endurance

The word for "endure" is *hupopherō*, meaning "to bear up." It is not easy to take wrongful abuse. Peter doubtless remembered the Lord's teaching in the Sermon on the Mount: "But I say unto you, that ye resist not evil: but whosoever shall smite thee on thy right cheek, turn to him the other also" (Mt 5:39). Such a standard of behavior is supernatural and calls for the moment-by-moment ministry of the Holy Spirit in the heart.[83]

It's not enough, Peter says, to endure merely when we sin and suffer bad consequences. The world without the power of Christ can do that. No, it takes supernatural power from Christ to endure unjust suffering.

Growing in Imitation

In 1 Peter 2:21, Peter calls us to use our mistreatment as an opportunity to grow in sanctification, conformed to Christ's image. We've been given a calling to follow the example of Christ in suffering. Peter's solution for unjust treatment is simple to understand but so difficult to live: "Follow in his steps." Go to the cross. Suffer unjustly. Commit yourself to the providence and sovereignty of God. And here in verses 22-25, Peter begins quoting Isaiah 53, with Christ as our example. The key to it all, Peter says, is that the crucifixion of the Messiah was the

---

[83] Phillips, *Epistles of Peter*, 1 Pe 2:19.

most unjust and wicked act the world had ever seen. Here was the one man who deserved nothing but praise and gratitude, and they rejected him, beat him up, and killed him.[84]

> **1 Peter 2:22-25** | He committed no sin, neither was deceit found in his mouth. **23** When he was reviled, he did not revile in return; when he suffered, he did not threaten, but continued entrusting himself to him who judges justly. **24** He himself bore our sins in his body on the tree, that we might die to sin and live to righteousness. By his wounds you have been healed. **25** For you were straying like sheep, but have now returned to the Shepherd and Overseer of your souls.

This is one of the clearest statements in the whole New Testament of the fact that Jesus, the Messiah, took upon himself the punishment that his people deserved.[85] We are called to suffer, to be like our Lord Jesus Christ. You will suffer unjustly often in this life. And it is a "gracious thing" when you endure it. For this "you have been called" to "follow in his steps." We are called in suffering to follow in the steps of Christ!

We are to "follow in his steps." Upwardly and outwardly we are the body of Christ on this earth. Paul says, "I press on to reach the end of the race and receive the heavenly prize for which God, through Christ Jesus, is calling us" (Phil 3:14). We are called to follow in the steps of Jesus! He went from the highest heights of praise by the angels to the lowest depths in his crucifixion. He took on the nature of a servant, though he was God. We are to have this very mind among ourselves (Phil 2:5-8).

A CALL TO SONSHIP (2:21B)

> **1 Peter 2:21** | For to this you have been called, because Christ also suffered for you, leaving you an example, so that you might follow in his steps.

We are called to be a slave to God, but simultaneously, we are his precious children. A Christian may be a slave on earth, but he is a son of heaven. The marvelous doctrine of adoption assures us that, as believers in Jesus Christ, we are now and forever full-fledged members of

---

[84] Wright, *James, Peter, John and Judah*, 70–71.
[85] Ibid., 71.

God's family. Think of it. The only begotten Son of God took on the form of a slave (Phil 2:7), so that the slaves of sin might become both slaves of righteousness and sons of God. We are adopted into God's family as sons and daughters of the living God (Rom 8:14-17). Yet we must always remember that any state of slavery on earth is temporary. Full freedom will one day be obtained for every child of God. Believers in the eternal state will serve the Lord not as unknown slaves, but as sons and daughters forever, "and his name will be on their foreheads" (Rev 22:4). Peter tells us, if we keep Christ at the center of our lives, we will be able to do a "gracious thing" – to bring honor to God on earth even in unjust situations, thereby demonstrating we are sons and daughters of our gracious God.

God's Ownership

We are owned by God because we've been purchased by the blood of Christ. Roman law considered slaves to be "property in the absolute control of an owner." Hired servants, like modern employees, could choose their masters and quit if they wanted to do so, but slaves had no such choice. Peter had reminded us of God's claim on us. "Knowing that you were ransomed from the futile ways inherited from your forefathers, not with perishable things such as silver or gold, [19] but with the precious blood of Christ, like that of a lamb without blemish or spot" (1 Pet 1:18-19). "Or do you not know that your body is a temple of the Holy Spirit within you, whom you have from God? You are not your own, [20] for you were bought with a price. So glorify God in your body" (1 Cor 6:19-20).

Though we were born as slaves of sin, having inherited an enslaved state from Adam, we were purchased by Christ through his death on the cross. We were bought with a price; therefore, we are no longer under the authority of sin. Instead, we are under the exclusive ownership of God. Christ is our new Master. As Paul told the Romans, "Thanks be to God that though you were slaves of sin, you became obedient from the heart to that form of teaching to which you were committed, and having been freed from sin, you became slaves of righteousness" (Rom 6:17–18). As Christians, we are part of "a people for his own possession" (Titus 2:14).

Complete Obedience

Christ submitted himself in every way to the Father, and so should we. Being a slave not only meant belonging to someone else; it also meant being always available to obey that person in every way. The slave's sole duty was to carry out the master's wishes, and the faithful slave was eager to do so without hesitation or complaint. After all, "slaves know no law but their master's word; they have no rights of their own; they are absolute possessions of their master; and they are bound to give their master unquestioning obedience." First John 2: 3 is explicit in this regard: "By this we know that we have come to know him, if we keep his commandments." As his slaves, we are expected "to obey Jesus Christ" (1 Pet 1: 2). Paul says: "Whether, then, you eat or drink or whatever you do, do all to the glory of God" (1 Cor 10:31).

It's interesting, in the Bible whenever you see our obedience mentioned, we are often called to be like slaves – i.e., we are to obey God whether we feel like it or not. When it comes to life on this earth, we are called to deny the flesh and obey Jesus Christ. We are called to be "instruments" or "tools" for God. That's what a slave is. He is property. He is a human tool. When it comes to our flesh, we are to die to our desires and be an instrument of righteousness for God. Paul had instructed slave owners in Colossians 4. "Masters, treat your bondservants justly and fairly, knowing that you also have a Master in heaven" (Col 4:1).

Singular Devotion

In Old Testament days, poverty-stricken Jews would occasionally be forced to sell themselves into service to their fellow Jews. The Law required that all servants were to be treated with justice and that they were to be freed at the end of six years. But in Exodus 21, we find an unusual option for a person who was due to be released from servitude. Exodus 21:5-6, "But if the slave plainly says, 'I love my master, my wife, and my children; I will not go out free,' ⁶ then his master shall bring him to God, and he shall bring him to the door or the doorpost. And his master shall bore his ear through with an awl, and he shall be his slave forever." This wasn't another six-year stint, but it was permanent, and it meant the servant would be there now for life, belonging to his master. He does it because he loves his master.

Almost all the Apostles open up some of their letters with, "Paul, a slave of Jesus Christ" (Rom 1:1), "Simon Peter, a slave and apostle of Jesus" (2 Pet. 1:1), "James, a slave of God and of the Lord Jesus Christ" (Jms 1:1), and Jude does the same thing (Jude 1:1). I have come to believe that there is no greater calling than to be marked as Christ's slave—to give my life in the service of the Master I have grown to know and love and trust. Let us pray to the Lord as Charles Spurgeon suggests: "Make me a child of God with a hole in my ear. Make me obedient in all things regardless of the circumstances." [86] As those who have willingly become slaves of Jesus Christ, what are the distinctions of our slavery to Christ.

Christ's one calling was to do the will of the Father, and so should our call be. The life of a slave in New Testament times may have been difficult, but it was relatively simple. Slaves had only one primary concern: to carry out the will of the master. In areas where they were given direct commands, they were required to obey. In areas where no direct command was given, they were to find ways to please the master as best they could. Our greatest concern is summed up in the words of Christ: "You shall love the Lord your God with all your heart, with all your soul, with all your mind, and with all your strength" (Mk 12:30, NKJV). We have one "ambition, whether at home or absent, to be pleasing to Him" (2 Cor 5:9).

Total Dependence

As part of the master's household, slaves were completely dependent on their owners for the basic necessities of life, including food and shelter. Unlike free persons, slaves did not have to worry about finding something to eat or somewhere to sleep. Because their needs were met, they could focus entirely on serving the master. Again, the parallels to the Christian life are striking. As believers, we can focus on the things God has called us to do, trusting Him to meet our needs. "Do not worry then, saying, 'What will we eat?' or 'What will we drink?' or 'What will we wear for clothing?'" Jesus told his followers. "Your heavenly Father knows that you need all these things. But seek first the kingdom of God and his righteousness, and all these things will be added unto you" (Mt 6:30-33). But we are more than slaves. We are sons of God!

---

[86] Charles Spurgeon. *Metropolitan Tabernacle Pulpit,* Vol 20, Sermon 1174, "The Ear Bored with an Awl" (London: Passmore & Alabaster, 1874), 289.

Simultaneously Slaves and Sons

The marvelous doctrine of adoption assures us that, as believers in Jesus Christ, we are now and forever full-fledged members of God's family. Think of it! The only begotten Son of God took on the form of a slave (Phil. 2:7), so that the slaves of sin might become both slaves of righteousness and sons of God! But please, do not stop there. That would be awful. Jesus Christ is our master. Amen! But he is much more than that. We are adopted into God's family as sons and daughters of the living God.

Conclusion

Just as first-century slaves would receive new names from their earthly masters, so will we each be given a new name from Christ. He himself promised in Revelation 3:12, to the one who overcomes, "I will write on him the name of my God, and the name of the city of my God, the new Jerusalem, which comes down out of heaven from my God, and my new name." Believers in the eternal state will serve the Lord not as mere slaves, but as sons and daughters forever, "and his name will be on their foreheads" (Rev 22:4).

13 | 1 PETER 2:21-25
FOLLOW IN HIS STEPS

For to this you have been called, because Christ also suffered for you, leaving you an example, so that you might follow in his steps.

1 PETER 2:21

I have five siblings. I am 14 years younger than my oldest brother, Scott. When I was young, we used to take walks together. My brother is six feet, six inches tall. I used to try and keep up with Scott. I wanted to be like him, and I would literally try and follow him around. I would have to take two steps for his one step. I love going on walks with my

Today I am on a different walk. I am following my Lord Jesus Christ. Peter, in our text, calls us to Christlikeness and "follow in his steps."

The One Way We Cannot Follow Jesus

> **1 Peter 2:21-25** | For to this you have been called, because Christ also suffered for you, leaving you an example, so that you might follow in his steps. ²² He committed no sin, neither was deceit found in his mouth. ²³ When he was reviled, he did not revile in return; when he suffered, he did not threaten, but continued entrusting himself to him who judges justly. ²⁴ He himself bore our sins in his body on the tree, that we might die to sin and live to righteous-

ness. By his wounds you have been healed. **²⁵** For you were straying like sheep, but have now returned to the Shepherd and Overseer of your souls.

There is a sense in which we cannot follow in Christ's steps, because Christ's death was unique. Christ atoned for sin so that the unrighteous might become righteous in God's sight. In that way we cannot follow Jesus, because he alone can do that. We cannot atone for our sins. You cannot atone for another's sins. We must get that guilt-ridden, performance focused mindset far away from us. From Tim Keller: "At one time, and at one time only, God treated someone who was righteous as if he were unrighteous. The words *righteous* and *unrighteous* have a legal meaning in the Greek. One is *dikaios*. One is *adikos*. What it means is to be right with the law or not right with the law. If you're right with the law, there are no claims against you. You're free to come and go and do what you wish."[87]

"For Christ died ... once for all, the righteous for the unrighteous, to bring us to God" (1 Pet 3:18). This is identical to what Paul says in 2 Corinthians 5:21, where he says, "God made him who [knew] no sin to be sin ... that in him we might become the righteousness of God." This is the identical concept, but it's just stated a little bit differently. At the central moment of the central day of history, at the triumphant moment, there was a transfer.

If you want a rough analogy of it, it would be something like this. Imagine the IRS is coming to shut you down because what you owe is twice what you have. What if a friend of yours came and she walked in at the last minute and said, "I'll tell you what. I am worth exactly what you owe. Therefore, I will pay it"? The IRS people say, "Fine. If that's how you like it, great. That's fine." Over they go to her place, and of course, she's worth exactly what you owe, which means she's ruined. They take the paintings off her walls. They take the jewelry off from around her neck. They take the furniture out of her house. They throw her out in the street. She's worth exactly what you owe. In a sense, you have this metaphor. She's righteous tax-wise, but she's treated as if she's unrighteous. Your liabilities have been transferred to her, and she

---

[87] Timothy J. Keller, "The Death of Jesus Christ, 1 Peter 2:23-25," *The Timothy Keller Sermon Archive* (New York City: Redeemer Presbyterian Church, March 27, 1994).

is gutted. She's been gutted. This is what the Scripture says on at the fullness of time as the perfect and prophetic moment on that day happened. There was a legal transfer. [88]

THE CONCEPT OF FOLLOWING CHRIST (2:21)

> **1 Peter 2:21** | For to this you have been called, because Christ also suffered for you, leaving you an example, so that you might follow in his steps.

We are called to follow Jesus, to be like him, to imitate him. The Bible calls this progressive sanctification.

The Call to Christlikeness

We are called to Christlikeness, Peter says. Paul says that we are actually "predestined" to be conformed to the image of God's dear Son (Rom 8:29). It means that through your life, if you are born again, you will most definitely, though not perfectly, follow in the steps of Jesus. Charles Haddon Spurgeon trumpeted the Scriptures' promise of progressive sanctification for every believer. He said, "Those whom free grace chooses, free grace cleanses. We are not chosen because we are holy, but chosen to be holy: and being chosen, the purpose is no dead letter, but we are made alive in Christ and made to seek after holiness."[89]

Discipleship, according to the *Lexham Theological Dictionary* is, "the process of learning the teachings of Jesus and following after his example in obedience through the power of the Holy Spirit. Discipleship not only involves the process of becoming a disciple but of making other disciples through teaching and evangelism."[90] Disciple means "learner." Discipleship is the relationship between a teacher (discipler) and student (disciple). As in the life of Jesus, discipleship takes place in the soil of our Christian relationships, with the water of the word and the sunlight of ministry. In other words, discipleship is not just learning the word, but learning it in committed relationship with other

---

[88] Ibid.

[89] Charles Spurgeon. *Exploring the Mind and Heart of the Prince of Preachers* (Oswego, IL: Fox River Press, 2005), 228.

[90] C. Byrley, D. Mangum, D. R. Brown, R. Klippenstein, & R. Hurst (Eds.), *Lexham Theological Wordbook*. (Bellingham, WA: Lexham Press, 2014), *Discipleship*.

Christians in the context of ministry. Discipleship means you are afraid to jump in the deep in. It's intensely practical.

What does it mean to "follow in his steps"? It means to be willing to suffer for humanity. Not, of course in the way he did. His was vicarious and substitutionary. Our suffering is one of discipleship. We are to give up all and follow Jesus. God calls us to slowly progress into the image of Jesus. Peter tells us to "follow in his steps." Christians are to follow in the path of discipleship with Jesus. We are his followers. We are called to be disciples and to "make disciples" (Mt 28:18-20).

Two thousand years ago, Jesus approached a handful of men and called them to be imitators of him. He said: "Follow me." The call of the first disciples is no different than ours. A disciple is a follower – an imitator. We are called to stop following everything else and follow only one person – the Lord Jesus Christ.

Think about Jesus command to his apostles. He went to Matthew at the seat of customs and taxes and basically told him, "Follow me." And Matthew left his self-focused life and followed Jesus into all kinds of suffering. Peter and James and John were commanded as well, "Follow me." They left their fishing businesses and followed Christ.

Charles Sheldon, who wrote, "In His Steps," and asked the famous question, "What would Jesus do?" declared, "The call of this dying century and of the new one soon to be, is a call for a new discipleship, a new following of Jesus, more like the early, simple, apostolic Christianity, when the disciples left all and literally followed the Master."[91]

Jesus described what it means to follow him in Luke 9:23-24, "And he said to all, "If anyone would come after me, let him deny himself and take up his cross daily and follow me. 24 For whoever would save his life will lose it, but whoever loses his life for my sake will save it."

The Process of Christlikeness

Someone described discipleship with the acronym F.A.T.E. The fate of every believer is to be conformed to the image of Christ (Rom 8:28-30). F-Faithful: Christ obeyed the Father in all things. He was fully committed to everything he put his heart to! A-Available: Christ gave himself completely to pay for our sins with his own blood on the cross. We must give ourselves to God and to each other. It is hard to

---

[91] Charles M. Sheldon. *In His Steps* (Chicago: Advance Publishing Co., 1899), 277.

disciple someone who is not around. Therefore, a potential disciple must show a willingness to be around the brothers and sisters. He or she must model commitment. T-Teachable: John 15:15, "all things that I have heard of my Father I have made known unto you." It is impossible to teach someone who thinks they know everything and are not receptive to instruction or rebuke. Just as Jesus modeled, we are not to waste the stewardship of our lives with know-it-alls. E-Educating/Evangelizing Others: Jesus Christ trained twelve who went out and made disciples of all nations across the Roman Empire and then all paid dearly with suffering for their obedience.

Examples of Christlikeness

D. L. Moody was an unknown shoe salesman in Chicago when he started his own Sunday School in an abandoned freight car. D.L. Moody simply made himself available. The school became so large teaching 1500 children a week that the Mayor of Chicago gave him the hall over the city's North Market for his meetings, rent free.

During his first trip to England while Moody was recovering from a spiritual depression and fatigue, he heard these words, "The world has yet to see what God will do with and for and through and in and by the man who is fully and wholly consecrated to Him." D.L. Moody again, made himself available. Moody said, "The world has yet to see a man fully consecrated to God—he did not say a great man, nor a learned man, nor a rich man, nor a wise man, nor an eloquent man, nor a smart man, but simply a man. I am a man, and it lies with the man himself whether he will or will not make that entire and full consecration." [92] "By the grace of God, I'll be that man." D.L. Moody made himself available.

C. H. Spurgeon was an unknown young preacher at age 17. At only 17 years of age, two years after his conversion, he took the pastorate of a very small church, Waterbeach Baptist Chapel. Then at age 19, he took the New Park Street Church in London. (With a new building it later became known as the Metropolitan Tabernacle). Spurgeon was an unknown, but he made himself available. There were 232 members then. During his pastorate, 14,692 were baptized and joined the Tabernacle. Spurgeon made himself available.

---

[92] William R. Moody, *The Life of Dwight L. Moody*, (Sword of the Lord Publishers: Murfreesboro, TN; 1900), 134.

Susana Wesley was a mother of 18 children, and she made herself available as a "keeper of the home" and changed the world through her love for God.

Jim Elliot and the other four martyrs to the Auca Indians were not extraordinary people. They just made themselves available to God! And what about Rachel Saint along with Elizabeth Elliot who went in after her husband's death to live among the savage Indians who killed her husband to point them to Christ? These were not amazing people. They were regular people with an amazing God. They made themselves available.

My dear wife is a wonderful example of a disciple. She follows Jesus when exhausted and when filled with energy. Whatever state she is in she follows Jesus. She points the children to Jesus. She points me to Jesus. You say OK, I want to be a disciple. I want to follow in Jesus' steps. How do I do that? Peter spells it out for us.

THE PRACTICE OF FOLLOWING CHRIST (2:21-23)

> **1 Peter 2:21-23** | For to this you have been called, because Christ also suffered for you, leaving you an example, so that you might follow in his steps. [22] He committed no sin, neither was deceit found in his mouth. [23] When he was reviled, he did not revile in return; when he suffered, he did not threaten, but continued entrusting himself to him who judges justly.

In this passage Peter draws extensively on the language and theology of the fourth Servant Song in Isaiah (Isa 52:13–53:12). The particular form of the Servant Song used by Peter may have already been circulating among the early church as a type of hymn.

Suffering with Christ

> **1 Peter 2:21** | For to this you have been called, because Christ also suffered for you, leaving you an example, so that you might follow in his steps.

Oh, how Jesus suffered. He abused and bloodied by the cat-o-nine-tails whip that included shards of glass and metal in the whip. Yes, his back was ripped to shreds, with muscles hanging loose and pulsating and blood spurting. And yes, he was hung on a cross, fastened with spikes that cut through nerves in his hands and feet that made every moment a physical hell for him. In order to breathe, he had to push up on the burning excruciating nerves in his feet. Every moment was torment. And that was only the physical suffering. Then he received the full wrath of God, separated from his Father. He would cry out with a prophetic cry, "My God, my God, why have you forsaken me?" (Mt 27:46; *cf* Psa 22:1). Why? Because he so loved sinful humanity. He exchanged his righteousness for our sin (2 Cor 5:21). He rescued us from hell and gave us heaven.

God's Son stood upon the rim of the universe, and seeing our need for a Savior, he said to the Father, "I will go." So the eternal Word of God took on flesh. And this one, Jesus, the one who possesses all authority and all power—humbled himself and rescued us from sin and death and hell. Peter, knowing just how difficult our sojourning in this world is, says in essence, "I have an example for you to imitate. I have an exile for you to follow. The one who flung the stars into space—this one shall lead you!"[93] How did Christ set an example for us? He redeemed the world.

We must follow Christ's example in order to be a true disciple. The Greek for "example" is ὑπογραμμός—a word which occurs nowhere else in the New Testament. It means "a copy set by a writing or drawing master, which was to be exactly reproduced by his students."[94] We are to copy Christ in his suffering and selfless love toward sinners. Christians evidence Christ's indwelling presence by his Spirit in us when we choose to love those who hurt us. Remember in Christ's dying moments, there was a thief on the cross who had just been mocking him, but now he was asking for Christ to remember him when he rules in his kingdom. Jesus, in his infinite love, forgave that thief and made him in that moment of faith, a child of God.

This is what we do as Christians. We go into the burning building. People are perishing, and we risk ourselves, our rights, our comforts, and we are willing to suffer for those for whom Christ died. We will do the work of our good Shepherd, and we will go after the lost sheep; we will find those who are stranded in the crags and crevices. We will risk our own lives to save them. That's what followers of Christ do.

---

[93] Helm, *1 & 2 Peter and Jude*, 96.
[94] Spence-Jones, *1 Peter*, 75.

Denying Sin with Christ

1 Peter 2:22 | He committed no sin, neither was deceit found in his mouth.

The world around him are rebels, but Christ is obedient – "He committed no sin" (2:22a). Everywhere are deceitful words and crooked, gossipy people, but Christ is truthful – "neither was deceit found in his mouth" (2:22b). Deception wasn't a tactic of Christ's. He didn't slander people. He didn't try to lie about people to get them back. He didn't gossip. He spoke the truth with love.

While the Christian is not sinless, there is a transformation of character that comes from a new heart that rejects sin. Truly, "sin shall have no dominion" over the born-again believer (Rom 6:14). When Christ died to sin, we died with him, and now we live unto God in righteousness (Rom 6:9).

Gentle with Christ

1 Peter 2:23 | When he was reviled, he did not revile in return; when he suffered, he did not threaten, but continued entrusting himself to him who judges justly.

When we are treated badly, it often brings out what's really in our hearts. There can be pride and resentment, returning evil for evil, but not so with Christ. Instead of vengeance, he was gentle and loving, crying out from the cross on behalf of his killers. "Father forgive them for they know not what they do" (Lk 23:34). The Jews were raging with lies against him, and all the while he was gentle. "Like a sheep that before its shearers is silent, so he opened not his mouth" (Isa 53:7). They were killing him, but he was "healing them" (Augustine).[95] Anger and vengeance is usually the first human reaction when we are wronged. Christ did not "get even" with anyone. He took the pain with a gentle spirit. He suffered, and he did not make threats.

In America, we are all kind of personal vigilantes. In other words, we believe in a just society which is a good thing. It's our way of life here. It's the best place in the world to live because of this. If we are wronged, we use force to make it right. There are certainly times when

---

[95] St. Augustine. In J. E. Rotelle, ed. *Works of St. Augustine: A Translation for the Twenty-First Century, Volume 6 (*Hyde Park, N.Y.: New City Press, 1995) 284.

we need to do that, especially for the vulnerable. But when Christ is personally injured, he is gentle. He is love. He is forgiving. Can we as Christians be gentle in the face of injustice? This was the mark of Christ and is the mark of those who follow him. We love our enemies and leave vengeance to God.

Trusting with Christ

> **1 Peter 2:23b** | He did not threaten, but continued entrusting himself to him who judges justly.

When Christ was unjustly treated, he could have called ten thousand angels to destroy the world. But he didn't. Instead, he "continued entrusting himself" to his Father. God would just and work things out in a just way. Just not today. But that day would come. Christ did that. The greatest sin ever committed in humanity was committed against him. There is nothing more unjust than the Creator of the universe being crucified by his own creation. Yet Christ, at his crucifixion, was not bound by the present horror, but looked forward to God's final justice, entrusting himself to his Father. Each believer also needs to entrust himself to our gracious and sovereign Father who will judge justly.

Obedient with Christ

> **1 Peter 2:21-23b** | When he suffered, he did not threaten, but continued entrusting himself to him who judges justly.

On the earth, Christ is doing his own imitating. He's revealing the Father to us. To understand Christ's example, you must know that he is "the Son is the radiance of the glory of God and the exact imprint of his nature, and he upholds the universe by the word of his power" (Heb 1:3). John 1:18, "No one has ever seen God; the only God, who is at the Father's side, he has made him known." Literally it says, "He has revealed God to us." To "make known" is the word *exēgéomai* which means to "reveal," to "dig it out, to "explain," or to "recount." Christ is digging out the treasures of the Father and showing them to us. He's revealing and explaining and recounting the glories of the Father to us because he's "full of grace and truth" (Jn 1:14).

How does Christ reveal the Father's glory to us? The King of glory enters into a state of suffering. All the while he is expressing the Father's love to a rebellious world. We can almost see him standing before the earthly governor, Pilate, and, out of love, not reviling in return. When he suffers at the hands of the officer who flogged him and tore his flesh to pieces, he did not threaten in return. Why? Because he loves them. He wants them to "die to sin and live to righteousness" (1:24). How did he do it? He entrusted himself to the one who judges justly.[96] We are prone to take that in a negative, vengeful way, but don't. God is actually going to judge the rebels as righteous because of Christ's sacrifice. Remember his cry, "Father forgive them for they know not what they do" (Lk 23:24). Here we see Christ's example. Peter sums it up in chapter 3:18, "Christ also suffered once for sins, the righteous for the unrighteous, that he might bring us to God" (1 Pet 3:18).

Application

Peter is telling to follow Christ in his life of suffering that ended in his death for unworthy sinners. We should love sinners like he did. We should be gentle to those who hate us like they hated him. We should be willing to be treated unjustly in order to see Christ redeem sinful humanity.

THE BENEFITS OF FOLLOWING CHRIST (2:24-25)

1 Peter 2:24-25 | He himself bore our sins in his body on the tree, that we might die to sin and live to righteousness. By his wounds you have been healed. **25** For you were straying like sheep, but have now returned to the Shepherd and Overseer of your souls.

What are the benefits of following Christ? We entrust ourselves to a perfect loving Father. We have a good, good Father indeed. We can entrust ourselves "to him who judges justly" (1:23). He's going to judge us righteous because of Christ. He will repay if he must, but he is "not willing that any should perish, but that all should come to repentance" (2 Pet 3:9, KJV).

New Life in Jesus

1 Peter 2:24a | He himself bore our sins in his body on the tree, that we might die to sin and live to righteousness

Christ gives us new life! By the indwelling Spirit through faith that comes by the word of Christ (Rom 10:17), we are born again and now

---

[96] Helm, *1 & 2 Peter and Jude*, 97-98.

dead to sin! Through new life in Christ, our old life is put to death. Because of the death of Christ, by faith we receive Christ's life into us and we now live to righteousness. We die to sin by living in Christ. Our new life puts the old life to death. All of this is a gift because Christ died in our place.

Healing in Jesus

1 Peter 2:24b | By his wounds you have been healed.

All of us are wounded by sin – wounded by our old nature. Anger. Lust. Pride. Being controlled by toxic emotions. We need healing. In Christ our righteousness, we have healing. We will never be that person that we once were because Jesus has healed us! He's transformed our heart, given us his Spirit, implanted his word in our heart and mind. We are healed. Now we still struggle with sin, but now we have the victory! Daily now we need to apply the word like a salve to our heart!

Shepherding by Jesus

1 Peter 2:25 | For you were straying like sheep, but have now returned to the Shepherd and Overseer of your souls.

When I was a kid, we used to play kick the can every Saturday night in the summers. And we always had our lookouts. Someone had to keep their eye on the one guarding the can. But we are all human, and though we would always try to kick the can, sometimes our lookout would get distracted. If you are a Christian, you have a lookout and a Shepherd for your soul who never fails or gets distracted. The Shepherd of Israel never sleeps or slumbers. He cares! "Casting all your care upon him for he cares for you" (1 Pet 5:7). Now realize that the Shepherd and Overseer of your soul is bringing you to a place of perfect peace in him. He tells us in the 23rd Psalm that his goodness and mercy (i.e. unrelenting love, Heb. *hesed*) are going to follow you like sheepdogs all the days of your life. His love and kindness are with you at all times, and he's guiding your steps to come closer and closer to him.

Conclusion

As followers of Christ, we are forever connected to him. He's our head, and we are his body. Romans 6 tells us that when we were baptized, we dramatized our union with his death and resurrection. When we went under the water, we showed that we died with Christ, and we died to sin. And then coming out of the water, we showed that we were resurrected with Christ, and that we are alive to God. We follow Christ to death and resurrection every day. We are dead to sin and are now alive to him. We do this by closely walking in the footsteps of Jesus.

There is a book by Scott Walker entitled *Life Rails*. Walker tells the story of his older friend, James Pearson, who fought in World War II. On one occasion Pearson was a part of a reconnaissance team sent out to scout German troop positions. The patrol left very early on this winter morning.

As they departed the relative security of their own front lines, the patrol had to cross an American minefield. The mines had been clearly marked for their safe passage, and, therefore, very cautiously they made their way around the explosives. On the other side of the field they entered the woods and tensely approached the German positions. They had not advanced very far when a machine gun nest opened up on them, pinning them to the ground. For hours they lay unable to advance or retreat. As time marched by ever so slowly, the blue sky became slate gray and snow clouds began to form. By mid-afternoon a virtual blizzard had descended on the land, and visibility became very limited. As the snow came down heavier, the platoon leader decided they had to risk a retreat under cover of the storm. By a saving act of nature, they were able to furtively slip away from the deadly German crossfire and return to the American lines.

However, when they reached the edge of the woods and looked out across the pastureland containing the minefield, a new and especially dangerous problem confronted them. The deep snow had completely covered all the markings that had indicated where the mines had been planted. As the sky grew darker a decision had to be made.

The platoon leader sensed that a German offensive was imminent. If his patrol waited until the next day to cross the minefield, they could easily be wiped out by a German advance at dawn. Although it was very risky, they really had only one option. They had to take their chances and cross the minefield before darkness totally enveloped them. The lieutenant called the men together. He informed them he was going to lead them single file across the meadow. He sternly ordered them to walk thirty yards behind each other and, most important, to place their boots exactly in the imprints left by his boots. In this way, if a mine exploded, only he would detonate it, and he alone would be killed.

Slowly the reconnaissance team advanced across the meadow. Only one set of boot prints was left by the entire platoon. Miraculously, they all made it safely to the American lines. The next day as the men awoke, they found that their boot prints could still be seen in the snow. Several hours later as the engineers again marked the mines, they discovered that the entire platoon had neatly stepped over a mine, miraculously avoiding detonating its deadly explosive power. They had followed in their leader's footsteps, and they reached home safely.

There is a theological illustration from Ephesians 2 that illuminates what Peter is saying. We follow in Christ's steps, and Ephesians says that those steps are predestined.

> For we are his workmanship, created in Christ Jesus for good works, which God prepared beforehand, that we should walk in them. —*Ephesians 2:10*

The idea is that you are God's masterpiece, and he has not only created you anew through the new birth, but he's God predestined your "good works" before the foundation of the world. He chose everything in your life that you might be "conformed to the image of his Son" (Rom 8:29). Way before you were born, Christ planned salvation for you. He chose you. He even chose your good works. He called you to holiness and service in all the steps of your life. And so imagine in your life there are footprints to follow, footprints that the Lord put in your life before you were even born. And you are to follow those footprints. Walk where Christ has walked. Christ walks before you, child of God. He loves you, and he wants you to look to him. Listen to his voice. Hear his words as he bids you, "Follow me." Follow Christ, and you will never be disappointed.

14 | 1 PETER 3:1-6
THE WIFE OF INNER BEAUTY

Let your adorning be the hidden person of the heart with the imperishable beauty of a gentle and quiet spirit, which in God's sight is very precious.
1 PETER 3:4

My wife and I are planning on growing old together. She is beautiful. The world's beauty fades and is so ugly. How ugly it is that as men age many will toss out their wives for some younger woman and abandon his vows to satisfy his own ego. That's not beauty, that's narcissism. True beauty is the countenance of a woman who fears the Lord. My wife Jill and I are planning on turning into raisins together. We plan on displaying the imperishable beauty that we have in Christ to our children and our grandchildren if the Lord will allow us.

God help us reject the idea of the world's beauty that requires a woman to put all her focus on her outward appearance. Paul says, "Though the outward man perish, the inward man is being renewed day by day" (2 Cor 4:16). I want to grow old with my beautiful wife. She understands what true beauty is.

> **1 Peter 3:1-6** | Likewise, wives, be subject to your own husbands, so that even if some do not obey the word, they may be won without a word by the conduct of their wives, **2** when they see your re-

14 | 1 Peter 3:1-6
The Wife of Inner Beauty

> spectful and pure conduct. **³** Do not let your adorning be external—the braiding of hair and the putting on of gold jewelry, or the clothing you wear— **⁴** but let your adorning be the hidden person of the heart with the imperishable beauty of a gentle and quiet spirit, which in God's sight is very precious. **⁵** For this is how the holy women who hoped in God used to adorn themselves, by submitting to their own husbands, **⁶** as Sarah obeyed Abraham, calling him lord. And you are her children, if you do good and do not fear anything that is frightening.

The book of 1 Peter is all about suffering. Why does Peter address marriage in this context? No matter how good your marriage, there are issues where you don't see things the same way. You take a man, and you take a woman, and you put them together, you're going to have differences, and you're going to have challenges and opportunity for suffering. Peter is addressing a very painful situation in the churches – young ladies who are new believers, and they are married to unsaved husbands. What could be more difficult? In the very polytheistic Roman culture, it was expected that whatever gods the woman had would be forsaken upon marriage, and she would submit to worshipping the husband's gods. Can you imagine how painful it would be to live contrary to your husbands wishes? It was for this reason Peter is telling the wives, be subject in everything else. Does your husband need to change? Yes. What's the best way to serve him? Submit to him with a gentle and quiet attitude.

Now Peter is not saying it's ok to be unequally yoked together in marriage. Believers must always marry other believers. But these women had come to know Christ after being married. And as it is in our day, so it was in Peter's time, there were unsaved husbands who were ridiculing their Christian wives. It was a very painful thing. So what does Peter say you have to do? Suffer. Specifically, he says, "Be subject. Be submissive. Come under God's authority. And coming under God's authority means coming under the authority of that mate and doing it with a spirit of meekness and a gentle, quiet spirit." This is what Jesus did. He came into a hostile world with a gentle and meek spirit. Jesus says, "Come to me, all who labor and are heavy laden, and I will give you rest. ²⁹ Take my yoke upon you, and learn from me, for I am gentle and lowly in heart" (Mt 11:28-29).

THE IMPERISHABLE BEAUTY OF CHRIST (3:1)

We read about the imperishable beauty of the wife, but truly all are to seek this beauty, because it comes from Christ. The wife is not the only one who is to put on the beauty of a submissive spirit. Christ is submissive to the Father.

The Beauty of Christ's Submission

> **1 Peter 3:1** | Likewise, wives, be subject to your own husbands, so that even if some do not obey the word, they may be won without a word by the conduct of their wives.

Peter says, "Likewise...be subject." Like who? The greatest example of submission is Christ. We read in 1 Peter 2:21, "For to this you have been called, because Christ also suffered for you, leaving you an example, so that you might follow in his steps." We are called to submit and suffer, just like Christ.

He came to do the Father's will. He said, "I have come down from heaven, not to do my own will, but the will of him who sent me" (Jn 6:38). "Not my will, but yours be done." Christians are to present themselves before a watching world as people who emulate Jesus. We are to pattern our lives on his example. For in doing so we present the world fresh and vibrant pictures of living hope.

The Beauty of Submission in All Realms

Peter says, "Likewise...be subject." The idea is that everyone in society is to be submissive. Human society should be like an orchestra, everyone giving way to everyone else. Because of the fall, there is great disharmony, but God created humanity to be first and foremost in submission to him. We are all to fall in line with authorities in our lives and be accountable. Peter says if you got into debt and you needed to become a slave, then you were to submit to your master. We are to "be subject" to the governing authorities. Children are to submit to their parents. Church members are to be subject to the elders. All are first and foremost to be subject to God.

Submitted to God's Word

We must first be submitted to God's word. We firmly hold to the word of God and receive it as authoritative over our lives. Submission in the home comes from our submission to the Bible. This passage addresses married women and married men. Wife, do you receive this as God's word? Husband do you receive it as straight from Jesus? Our society is wayward because they have rejected God's word. This teaching is abhorred and mocked in our society, but it ought to be celebrated in the congregations of Jesus.

If we live according to this passage, we are planting seeds of peace for marriage. And singles need to receive this passage as well. We all came from a family. We all need to know how the home should operate. This passage is for all of us here today. You don't have to be married to appreciate the truth of this passage. At the very least, all of us need to pray for the married people they might live according to the word of the Lord.

THE WIFE'S IMPERISHABLE BEAUTY DESCRIBED (3:1-2)

1 Peter 3:1-2 | Likewise, wives, be subject to your own husbands, so that even if some do not obey the word, they may be won without a word by the conduct of their wives, **²** when they see your respectful and pure conduct.

This text tells us that all wives have the power to change bring transformation to their husbands. The text is clear that Peter's words apply to all Christian wives, not just those who are married to unbelieving husbands, for the text says, "even if some do not obey the word." So the emphasis is that this text is intended for all Christian wives.

The Power of a Submitted Life

Imperishable beauty is powerful. The sweet and godly character of a woman can transform a man. Yes, men need to change, and there is something so powerful that most married women have difficulty tapping into. Peter says something that I find surprising. He says to the ladies, if you have a husband that needs a radical transformation in his life, stay quiet! This is extremely difficult because a woman has a deep desire to communicate and connect with her husband. That's a good thing. But Peter says if you want to win your husband, he must be won "without a word by the conduct" of the wife's life, not her words (3:1).

There is a beautiful example of this in church history. In the year 397 A.D. an aging saint in the Christian faith wrote what would become one of the most compelling autobiographies ever published. When the book was finally finished, he titled his own tale The Confessions of Saint Augustine. Buried in this celebrated narrative is the moving tribute Augustine gave his mother, Monica, on the influence she had in bringing her unbelieving husband, Patricius, to personal faith in Jesus. Augustine described his mother's role with these words:

> She served her husband as her master and did all she could to win him for You, speaking to him of You by her conduct, by which You made her beautiful.... Finally, when her husband was at the end of his earthly span, she gained him for You."[97]

A wife is not to be subject to all men, but to their "own husband." The goal is that those who "do not obey the word...may be won without a word by the conduct of their wives." It doesn't mean the unsaved husband will definitely come to Christ in this manner, but if there is any hope of him hearing the message, he must first "be won without a word" by the wife's submissive conduct.

Intrinsic to this text is that husbands need to change. We all need to change. If you have a saved husband, he needs to change. If you have a lost husband, he needs to be converted. God tells us they proper and effective way to change your husband is through submission. He describes this submissive spirit as: "respectful and pure conduct" (3:2). The focus is not mainly to be on outward fashion (3:3) but on the inward adorning of the heart. This passage is primarily dealing with unsaved husbands. But can we all agree that all married men need to change. No one knows it better than our wives.

The Preoccupied Husband

Maybe you're a *preoccupied* husband. You're home physically, but your mind is always someplace else. You come home from work, but you bring work with you. Or maybe you are just preoccupied with something else – your phone, the newspaper, your thoughts. You are home but you are not home. Have you ever had one of those conversations with your wife She's talking and this is important to her. But she get's the sense that the husband is zoned out. And the wife says, "Well don't you agree?" And he says, "Huh?" And she says, "Well you know, do you agree with what I've just said?" And he says, "Oh absolutely!" So she says, "Well, what did I just say?" And he knows it. He's busted. He

---

[97] Aurelius Augustine, quoted in Helm, *1 & 2 Peter and Jude*, 101.

says, "I don't know exactly, but I agree with it whatever it was." Husbands need to change wouldn't you agree? When husbands are there at home, it's important to be all there. Men can get so focused on one thing that he's able to block everything (and everyone else) out. Did you know the average man in America has an average of four minutes of meaningful conversation with his wife each day? Some of you ladies are thinking, "I dream of four minutes!" But those of you who are mature in Christ know that a godly husband shepherds his wife.

The Hobby Husband

Then there is the *hobby* husband. He works all week but doesn't care about his job. He works just so he can do what he really wants to do, which is drive cars or play video games or build stuff in the garage. And he's so consumed with that at the expense of what is really important. His family secretly hates dad's hobbies because it's robbing them of a husband and a father. And yet there are some immature men in the church that love worthless things more than their family.

The Angry Husband

What about the *angry* husband? Be careful he could go off at any moment. The whole family is walking on eggshells. We don't know when it's going to happen. But it will happen eventually. Everyone is so afraid of the next blow up.

The Neglectful Husband

What about the *neglectful* husband? Work, sports, friends. He even has some mystery time. Little contact with his family. He's made his wife a work widow or a sports widow. He has time for his friends, but he's rather escape somewhere else than deal with a real living family who needs his love and leadership.

The Dangerous Husband

Then there is the dangerous husband. Where's my husband tonight? We don't know exactly. We don't know where he is or when he's coming back. He seems to have work appointments and trips at the strangest times. He's not transparent. He's hiding something. Twenty-two percent of men admit to committing adultery during their marriage. Twenty-nine percent of women report they've been physically abused by their husbands. Thirty-five percent report emotional abuse.

And yet I've seen God through the years change even the dangerous and unfaithful husband into a faithful husband through a faithful, gentle wife.

All Husbands Need Christ

Husbands, if we asked your wife if you need to change I'm sure she'd say "Give me a pen." These are the things that need to change in our marriage, with our children, with your walk with God. Men, we need to change, and our wives are well aware of it. The point is all husbands need Christ, and the Christian wives know it. She desperately wants to change her husband. And there is a time for communication, don't get me wrong. But the first thing a wife must do is to let God change her. The husband needs to see Christ lived out before him. You let God change you, and you need to trust God to change your husband.

The Picture of a Submitted Life

Peter is laying out the proper order of the home. Submit means to *yield to another*. There is a command to "be subject."

What Submission Means

We know what submission means. You come to a four-way stop at the same time as another car, and you yield to that car. Or even better, in traffic when you see the "merge" sign, you know that someone has to go first, and someone has to go behind. Too often the "I'm-going-to-go-first" battle causes frustration. Everyone knows that sooner or later there is only going to be room for a single file of cars. That's what this means. Wives need to allow their husbands to lead. "*Well, what if my husband isn't following Christ?*" That's exactly what Peter is talking about. Especially if your husband is not following Christ, you need to show him Christ by a life submitted to Christ and to your husband.

What Submission Does Not Mean

Submission has nothing to do with equality. The Son is not pouting around heaven going, "Why can't I be the Father?" The Son is in submission to the Father and the Spirit to the Father and the Son. Yet Scripture teaches they are equal. Headship has nothing to do with equality. Men and women are equal under God in every way.

Submission also has nothing to do with worth. I love Proverbs 31:10, "Who can find a virtuous wife? For her worth is far above rubies."

It's not about gifts. In certain areas, my wife has gifts that far exceed mine. It's about God's design for the order in the home. Changed women help God change husbands by being submissive to their own husband.

There are a few qualifications that we need to add about submission. Christian women, regardless of their marital status, have too often been subjected to degrading explanations and abusive applications from this very text. Given the pain that can be evoked by this text, it is important to mention a few things about what Peter's call to submission does *not* mean for Christian wives. It does not mean that if your husband asks you to abandon your faith in Christ, you should do so. It does not mean that if your husband asks you to sin, you should do so. It does not mean that you must always agree with him and never present a differing view. It does not mean that if he is unfaithful to you, you are left without Biblical recourse. It does not mean that if he abuses you physically or abandons you through incessant verbal humiliation, you must remain quietly in the home and accept the daily cruelty of that relationship at all costs.

In other words, no wife should allow their husband to use this text for sin or abuse of any kind. If your husband is abusing you or your children, you should call the police. It also does not mean that the woman has no voice in the marriage. Wives naturally want to communicate with their husbands – sometimes with anger and fierceness. That's not right. "Well, if I have to submit, then he can do whatever he wants." That's not true. Look at 1 Peter 3:7. The husband is to be understanding and considerate. He is to consider you in all of his decisions that affect you. It is right that a man should consult with his wife and consider her. That means he can't boss you around. He has to ask you before making decisions that affect you. That's the law of love. He's to be "considerate."

The Quietness of a Submitted Life

1 Peter 3:1b-2 | They may be won without a word by the conduct of their wives, **²** when they see your respectful and pure conduct.

The context of 1 Peter 3 is that there were wives that were likely new Christians. They wanted to see their husbands change, and their solution was to talk to them. Talk, talk, talk. That's noble. You want to be clear. But Peter says something very surprising. "Likewise, wives, be subject to your own husbands, so that even if some do not obey the word, they may be won without a word by the conduct of their wives" (3:1). Even if your husband has the greatest, most important need for change in his life: the salvation of his soul, wives should approach them "without a word" win them "by the conduct" of their lifestyle and choices and attitudes.

The Natural Inclination of a Wife

The natural inclination of a wife, her predisposition is to bring the need for change to the forefront by verbal communication. But God says through Peter what she needs is to win him "without a word" by "her conduct." She's to have a gentle and quiet spirit. God says, "Be still and know that I am God" (Psa 46:10).

How can you as a wife produce the desired change your husband needs? Ladies – your natural inclination to may be the very thing that kills the change you desire. We need to consult what God's word says from 1 Peter 3 – you need a gentle and quiet spirit. And the whole of Scripture agrees with Peter. Proverbs 14:1, "A wise woman builds her home, but a foolish woman tears it down with her own hands." A woman who follows her natural inclination instead of the word of God is a foolish woman who instead of building her house up, she does the exact opposite: she tears it down. Proverbs 25:24, "It is better to live in a corner of the housetop than in a house shared with a quarrelsome wife." When a woman sees something in her husband that needs to change, she wants to communicate about it, and it often leads to quarrels.

Peter says that's not the way to change your husband. The wife is inclined to give a speech, to point out what needs to change. If necessary, she's willing to give that speech repeatedly. She's very willing to remind him every day if that's what it takes. She's thinking the problem is somehow he forgot. However *that is not the problem.* God's way to change a husband is found here in 1 Peter 3:1, "Likewise, wives, be subject to your own husbands, so that even if some do not obey the word, they may be won without a word by the conduct of their wives" (3:1).

God's wants your husband to change. If he needs the most supernatural change in his life, that of being born again by the word of God and the touch of God, then the way to go about that change is not primarily verbal communication. It's by your character and your conduct and your gentle and quiet spirit.

The Most Powerful Tool of the Wife

1 Peter 3:1b-2 | they may be won without a word by the conduct of their wives, ² when they see your respectful and pure conduct.

Respectful conduct. The changed woman is respectful in her conduct. The word respectful means "Fear, reverence, respect, or honor."[98] That means she puts his needs over her needs. Now it's interesting that the husband is commanded to do the same thing in Ephesians 5:25, "Husbands, love your wives, as Christ loved the church and gave himself up for her." Love and respect have the same outcome: you put your spouse's needs above your own. The husband is to lead in this. But married ladies, you are called to respect the leadership of your husband. He is often going to make mistakes, but he is going to give an account for his leadership in your marriage, rather than you. You are not the leader. That doesn't mean you have no say in the marriage. The Bible says that the wife is a "helper fit" for her husband (Gen 2). The husband leads, but you help guide him with your wisdom and your intuition and your gifts. You are called to be the biggest influencer of your husband. Respect and submission does not mean that you are silent when it comes to matters of your home.

Pure conduct. The changed woman is pure in her conduct. Your husband is going to be impacted when he observes "when they see your respectful and pure conduct" (3:2). This describes the effect of what you do in the kitchen, the car, the backyard, and in the bedroom—every activity in every place. Pure means holy, righteous, or chaste. Pure means having godly responses to conflict, being pure in your dress, your language, your choices of entertainment and being righteous in decisions. It means you are sincere and not manipulative. You are without guile. Pure does not mean self-righteous or judgmental; not uppity or prudish—just pure. A wife's purity is a powerful tool God uses for change in the life of her husband.

THE WIFE'S IMPERISHABLE BEAUTY ADORNED (3:3-4)

Peter says, don't be so worried about outward fashions but inner, imperishable beauty.

---

[98] Spiros Zodhiates, *The Complete Word Study Dictionary: New Testament* (Chattanooga, TN: AMG Publishers, 2000).

Our Temptation with External Adorning

So, what does this soul-winning conduct look like in Christian wives? Peter begins his answer by way of contrast.

> **1 Peter 3:3** | Do not let your adorning be external—the braiding of hair and the putting on of gold jewelry, or the clothing you wear.

Peter's culture, like our own, had an obsession with external adornment. Women were under enormous pressure to look beautiful. They were fixated on their hair, the wearing of jewelry, and clothing. In response, Peter wants Christian women not to be overly concerned about external beauty.

Amelia Bedelia. Only the famed children's book character Amelia Bedelia could misunderstand the meaning of this verse. Amelia took everything she was told to do literally—in a wooden way. So she would put real sponges in the sponge cake she was baking or pitch a tent by throwing it into the woods. An Amelia Bedelia interpretation of this verse would leave women without *any* braiding of hair, wearing of jewelry, or wearing of clothing. Peter is not advocating any such thing. His concern is one of emphasis, as any discerning reader will understand. It's fine to dress appropriately, but your emphasis ought not be on outward fashion, but on inward beauty. "Charm is deceitful, and beauty is fading, but a woman who fears the Lord is to be praised" (Pro 31:30). Christian ladies need to put the emphasis on the imperishable beauty of the heart.

The pressures placed on Christian women by today's culture are nothing short of oppressive. Women today can't walk into a store without being bombarded with shelves devoted to hair products. They can't walk down the street without being overwhelmed by the need for more jewelry. Women cannot open a magazine without being assaulted by the sense that their own closets are threadbare of anything worth wearing.

Inward Adorning

Peter tells us instead of an emphasis on the external, we should be concerned with adorning "the hidden person of the heart." What does inward adorning look like?

The Hidden Person of the Heart

> **1 Peter 3:4a** | But let your adorning be the hidden person of the heart...

We can all put on an act on the outside, but what are we really like on the inside. God wants us to be more concerned with inward adorning of our hearts with the fruit of the Spirit than adorning our physical bodies.

Inward modesty is seen when we open our mouths and talk. Jesus said it is "out of the abundance of the heart the mouth speaks" (Mt 12:34). There is a modesty to a godly woman's spirit where she doesn't have to say everything that impulsively comes to her mind. The godly woman has a "gentle and quiet spirit." This is the kind of inward adornment you need as a wife for your spirit – a spirit that is respectful, pure, gentle and quiet. This is the beauty that never fades. This is the fashion that never perishes. Clothes cost money. Spend more time and resources on your inner beauty than your outward beauty, on "the hidden person of the heart." Ladies, do you want to know how to do that?

A Gentle, Quiet Spirit

1 Peter 3:4 | Let your adorning be the hidden person of the heart with the imperishable beauty of a gentle and quiet spirit, which in God's sight is very precious.

Peter says is, "Be subject. Be submissive. Come under God's authority. And coming under God's authority means coming under the authority of that mate and doing it with a spirit of meekness and a gentle, quiet spirit."

Well, what's a gentle, quiet spirit? It's a spirit that trusts God. It trusts that God is bigger, God is greater, God is more real, God is in control. "The king's heart is in the Lord's hand." (Pro 21:1) Your husband is not the ultimate king of the universe, even if he thinks he is. And neither are you. Peter says, "Be subject to the Lord," and then, because you're subject to the Lord, you can be subject to your mate. And you can do it with a spirit of meekness—that is, you're not mouthing back, you're not returning to him his way of talking or dealing with situations.

This is what he gave his Son for. Not only is this beauty valuable and attractive to your husband, but it is precious to God. It demonstrates the beauty of Christ in you through regeneration. It's precious because it costs you much. It takes much self-control. But it cost God more than it cost you. It cost him his own dear Son.

THE WIFE'S IMPERISHABLE BEAUTY EXEMPLIFIED (3:5-6)

Peter doesn't stop at simply giving women instruction and motivation. He goes on in this text to provide an illustration, an example, for every woman to follow.

The Example of the Holy Women

> **1 Peter 3:5** | For this is how the holy women who hoped in God used to adorn themselves, by submitting to their own husbands.

Peter says when we think of submission, we should think of the holy women of old. It takes courage to be submissive. They trusted God, not mainly their husbands. Think of Rahab and Ruth and Hannah. Think of even Bathsheba. These were strong women who had to trust God. But God calls our attention to one particular woman: Sarah

The Example of Sarah

> **1 Peter 3:6a** | As Sarah obeyed Abraham, calling him lord.

When Peter went looking for a woman whose life modeled good works, he chose Sarah, the wife of Abraham. When he wanted to put forward someone with "a gentle and quiet spirit," he selected Sarah. And we can all thank Peter for doing so. After all, Sarah wasn't a wallflower woman. Sarah wasn't weak. She was real. And the Scriptures portray her faith and life as precious and beautiful.

Sarah is the perfect choice. When Christian women hear preachers call upon them to put on "a gentle and quiet spirit," the culture will bombard their minds in an effort to convince them that God's word is asking them to be weak. Our culture is constantly trying to make women think that applying this principle will in the end be a setback to women everywhere. But Peter says, "No. No. No. Look at Sarah!" Sarah was a woman who got into her husband's face a time or two—and he needed it a time or three more.

Remember Sarah is called to follow her husband out of Ur of the Chaldees. He was to literally leave the area of what would later be Babylon and Iraq and go to the Promised Land. Sarah followed but remember how they got to the Promised Land and there was no land flowing with milk and honey. There was a drought. There was a famine. So Abraham led the way. He went all the way to Egypt. He didn't lead in a godly way. He lied and gave Sarah over to Pharaoh's harem.

But God protected Sarah. Sarah trusted God, and God protected Sarah. He gave Pharaoh a dream and inflicted pain on Pharaoh for almost harming Sarah. They came out of Egypt with great riches. God blessed Abraham and Sarah not because of Abraham's great leadership but in some ways because of Sarah's great faith.

An Example that May Be Frightening

Submission is a scary thing. Is says the women of the Old Testament had this inner beauty of submission and specifically names Sarah. Submission was a beautiful thing to them, but it wasn't easy. In fact it was a scary thing. That's what Peter says.

> **1 Peter 3:6b** | You are her [*Sarah's*] children, if you do good and do not fear anything that is frightening.

Married ladies you are submit to your husband in everything unless he is asking you to sin. So if he's abusive – that's not only sinful, it's illegal and you should call the police. If he tells you not to go to church, that's sinful. You are commanded by a higher authority to "not forsake the assembling of yourselves together" (Heb 10:24-25). So submission never means you are to take abuse or you are to carry out the sinful desires of your husband, whatever they are. You are to be courageous and "do not fear anything that is frightening." We wrestle not against flesh and blood. Stand strong in Christ ladies. Be courageous!

Conclusion

The imperishable beauty of a woman is something that does not fade. The beauty that a godly man looks for is inward. Look at her character. Look at her countenance. She's beautiful. God help us to shed the thoughts of the world where a woman feels worthlessness as she gets older in her life – so attached to the world's version of what beauty is. God help us to take out our minds and wash them in the word so that we can embrace and encourage and exhort the girls and ladies at Living Hope to have an imperishable beauty in Christ that never fades!

15 | 1 PETER 3:7
THE LISTENING HUSBAND

Likewise, husbands, live with your wives in an understanding way, showing honor to the woman as the weaker vessel, since they are heirs with you of the grace of life, so that your prayers may not be hindered.

1 PETER 3:7

There are few things more satisfying in marriage than knowing you what you say and how you feel about a matter is valued by your spouse. There is also nothing more devastating than barriers to communication in marriage. So often I have seen couples who love the Lord dead-locked with each other. Pride or panic has set into the heart and neither wants to listen.

The wife: "He just won't listen to me. I've tried to communicate the importance of many things – even with tears – but it seems to just make him harder toward me. What can I do?"

The husband: "All she does is manipulate. Those tears are just passive anger. She doesn't want me to listen to her. She just wants her way." Can you see the pride on both sides? Both are convinced the other won't change. This study of one verse in Scripture (1 Pet 3:7) is all about how to break that kind of typical deadlock in marriage through listening.

We just heard Peter tell us that wives are to submit to their husbands by supporting them, listening to them, and allowing their husbands to lead the way. Yet I believe the husband has to submit himself in a greater, more profound way. He must submit himself to God, and lay down his life for his wife. I would propose that a man's submission to God is a call for greater sacrifice for the woman than the woman's sacrifice of submission to the man. He is called to be crucified for his wife, to love her, listen to her, and lead her (Eph 5:25). The call is impossible with the help of Jesus (Jn 15:5). So a man is to sacrificially love his life. Now Peter says, a man is also to carefully listen to his wife and learn all about her.

> **1 Peter 3:7** | Likewise, husbands, live with your wives in an understanding way, showing honor to the woman as the weaker vessel, since they are heirs with you of the grace of life, so that your prayers may not be hindered.

This is one of the Bible's primary passages for men on marriage. You know what I love about it? It's just one verse. God knows men. Most men need the bottom-line. However, that one verse for men packs six actions that, if a man will do consistently, it will totally, radically change his wife, his marriage—and himself. Let's look at them briefly, one by one.

SPEND TIME WITH HER

> **1 Peter 3:7a** | Likewise, husbands, live with your wives…

That word "live" could mean "to cohabit" and possibly refer to the sexual relationship, but most commentators agree that the intention is deeper than just physical intimacy. It encompasses all that married life involves. The nearest English equivalent to the word "live" is the idea of "to make a home with." It is all about spending time together.

Every man understands the concept. If you want to lower your handicap or raise your bowling average or grow the best lawn or shrink your waistline or demolish the competition at work—it takes time! Get this in your head: you don't get a great marriage by riding around in the same car, or by sleeping in the same bed or eating at the same table. A good marriage is not contagious—you can't catch it. You have to invest in it. Pour time into your relationship or you're not going to have a great marriage. That is what it means to dwell with her.

STUDY HER

1 Peter 3:7b | Likewise, husbands, live with your wives in an understanding way.

The text says you are to live with your wife in an understanding way. We are to gain knowledge about her. Knowledge means every piece of information you can get your hands on. Become a student of your wife. Know what she loves and hates. Discover what fires her up and what discourages her. Identify when the good time and the bad time is to approach her. Understand what makes her tick. You will bless her if you do. Wives appreciate being understood. They love it when they don't have to explain stuff to you; they love it when you just know.

A wife is called to show honor to her husband by submitting (Eph 5:22-23). This is a highly offensive word in the twenty-first century, but it is nonetheless a vital concept upon which our culture and society are hinged. For instance, if a boss tells his employees that they need to obey and submit, that would be very offensive. But if he says to them, "*You need to listen to me. You need to follow instructions.*" That is not only perfectly acceptable, but it is vital for a prosperous company culture.

Is it semantics? Perhaps. We all know there are a thousand ways a husband can ask his wife to submit, that while technically biblical, are attitudinally sinful to the core. For instance, a husband wants to win an argument, and he throws the trump card on the table, and with a demanding tone commands his wife: "*the Bible says you must submit, so stop arguing with me.*" The husband by doing this has disrespected his wife and cornered her, not to mention he's chosen to be domineering in his attitude. He could make a similar statement with love and compassion and be within the guidelines he has from God to "love" his wife "as Christ loved the church and gave himself up for her" (Eph 5:25).

He might say with a loving, patient tone: "Honey, we need to listen to each other. I'm willing to listen to you. Forgive me if I've been a bad listener. One day I'm going to give an account to God for you. I need your support. I want to lead our family in the right way. I want to listen to you, and I need you listen to me."

God calls us to understand our wives. "Few motives in human experience are as powerful as the yearning to be understood. Being listened to means that we are taken seriously, that our ideas and feelings are recognized, and, ultimately, that what we have to say matters."[99] Unless you are a mind reader, the only way a husband can understand is by listening to her express her heart to him.

The Intimacy of Listening

God stated this principle in the form of a command. What word or phrase from this verse teaches us that this is a command? The command to "live with your wives in an understanding way" implies more than sharing the same address. Peter reinforces God's original plan for marriage which states: "the two shall become one flesh" (Gen 2:24). Therefore, living with your wife in an understanding, listening way fulfills, in part, the one flesh relationship of the husband to the wife. What would you say to a husband who viewed this as optional?

This is a command to understand. The word "understanding" actually comes from a Greek word which is also translated "knowledge." This particular word means a knowledge based on personal experience. That is, because of what you've done with that person, because of interaction with them, because of heartfelt listening to them, you understand or know them. This is the same word that Paul used in Philippians 3:10 when he said, "...that I may know Him, and the power of his resurrection and the fellowship of his sufferings, being conformed to his death." There is deep intimacy and understanding here. Our culture says, "You just can't understand a woman." But God says to the husbands, you must understand your wife and you must learn to "live with them in an understanding way." Jay Adams writes:

> To be understanding, he must try to enter into her situation and see as much as he can what she is facing from the woman's viewpoint. That is difficult to do, but that is what it means to be understanding of another person: to try to get into her shoes."[100]

The Effort of Listening

Understanding involves more than knowing. A husband can know his wife's favorite color, sweater, restaurant, etc., and still not understand her. Understanding involves learning your wife's communication style. Women, for example, tend to speak indirectly. What your wife

---

[99] Michael P. Nichols, *The Lost Art of Listening, Second Edition: How Learning to Listen Can Improve Relationships* (New York: Guilford Publications, 2009), 9.

[100] Jay Adams, *Christian Living in the Home* (Phillipsburg, NJ: Presbyterian and Reformed Publishing, 1972), 97.

may frame as a question ("Does the trash can look full to you?") may actually be a request, an order, or an expectation ("Take out the trash!").

Understanding involves grasping your wife's communication perspective. Women tend to see communication as the glue of a relationship, whereas men tend to see it as something you do when there's a problem. For women, self-revealing conversations are valued because they make them feel close to another. Accordingly, a wife can be extremely hurt when her husband gives her the silent treatment, or she feels he is keeping secrets from her.

Understanding involves appreciating your wife's communication rituals. For instance, when women discuss a problem, they're often looking for concern, not a solution. When a decision needs to be made, they typically want to negotiate a consensus (unilateral decisions by husbands invite resentment and are asking for trouble). Understanding your wife requires cracking her communication code.

Of course, there are exceptions to every rule. What may be true of women in general may not be true of your wife in particular. If you want to understand your wife, study her, pay attention to what she pays attention to. There is no shortcut to comprehending your wife's heart.

To live with her in an understanding way takes effort. It means that a wise husband controls his own needs and desires so that hers are met. He places her needs above his own, just as Christ did. He does not belittle her, minimize her contributions to the family, or expect her to do what God has given him to do. He makes the study of one woman, his wife, a lifelong endeavor, and he wants to be an expert at it. It's amazing how we as men can be sometimes, to the detriment of our marriage. We spend a lot of time becoming expert at things that contribute absolutely nothing to the spiritual wellbeing of our marriage. We spend a lot of time learning about sports teams and their players, we learn about all the latest technology i.e., computer software programs, cell phone apps, electronic games, and gadgets, etc.

We can become so obsessed with our jobs that we don't know how to leave work at work. We often come home disgruntle, distracted or depleted of the emotional energy required to lovingly engage our wife. We can become so preoccupied worrying about a particular problem or problem person, we lie in bed tossing and turning, starring at the ceiling unable to sleep. Rather than worrying, it would be far better to cuddle with our wife at night which is something that all wives love to do. It's a wonderful way to end the day and begin the next one. Worrying solves nothing. (Mt 6:34).

We study politics and can give all the pros and cons about one political viewpoint vs another. But we invest very little time in studying the one person who can have the most profound impact on our life and the lives of our children, i.e., our wife.

The Areas of Listening

Marriage is the place for men and women to find expression and fulfillment for their important relational needs. Some of the most important needs are family commitment,[101] affection,[102] sexual needs,[103] companionship,[104] admiration/respect,[105] and financial support,[106] among many other areas. Husbands and wives have all these relational needs. But personality, temperament, and gender-differences account for differences in how important each need may be for each spouse.

HONOR HER

1 Peter 3:7c | Showing honor to the woman...

What's honor? The idea is to value who she is, what she does, and to reward her with every means available to you. The primary focus here, however, is verbal. Honor her in public, in front of people, and not just in private.

The responsibility here is on the husband to give the honor to his wife. Therefore, a husband cannot use the excuse that "she doesn't deserve it." The husband must give honor to his wife by being a learner regardless of his wife's imperfections. When a husband knows his wife, treats her with respect, loves her, provides for her, as the marriage covenant requires, he then honors her.

Being a learner means giving honor to the wife. Sometimes a husband does not want to honor his wife by being a learner. A wife often

---

[101] Eph 6:1-4; Col 3:20-21; 1 Tim 3:4-5; 5:10, 14; Titus 2:4
[102] Eph 5:33; Col 3:19; 1 Pet 3:7
[103] 1 Cor 7:2-5; Heb 13:4
[104] Gen 2:20; 1 Cor 9:5
[105] Eph 5:33; 1 Pet 3:1-2
[106] Eph 5:29; 1 Tim 5:8

needs to "decompress" and share her thoughts with her husband. Let her decompress. A husband should tenderly listen to his wife and not think she is mad at him even if she sounds completely stressed out. It is often the case that she is trusting him with her heart. She doesn't want you to fix her. She wants you to care about what she is saying. Husbands, here are some ways you can honor your wife:

1. **Be sensitive to her needs**. If you ask what it is she needs, then listen carefully, she will reveal her needs to you. Then ask God to help you meet as many of those needs as you can.

2. **Let your actions, as well as your words, show her respect**. Don't sit in front of the TV while she washes the dishes, picks up after the kids and gets them to bed. She's more than mommy, maid, cook and nurse - she's your fragile vase, remember?

3. **Pay attention to her when she talks with you**. Put down the paper, look her in the eyes, and respond in more than monosyllables.

4. **Do not speak harshly to her and never tear her down, especially in public**. You can deeply wound her spirit by a harsh, discounting word. It's bad enough when you do this in private, but it's devastating when done in public. Remember, a wounded heart finds it hard to give love.

5. **Accept her feelings**. You may not understand them, but you must respect them as real and viable. Never tell her, "There's no reason to feel that way, Honey." The worst thing to tell a hurting wife who's emotions are out of control is: "control yourself!" Instead care for her as a priceless, fragile vase.

6. **Do not compare her unfavorably to someone else and never try to change her**. When you criticize, you are saying, *I don't like you the way you are. Be different or I won't love you.* On the other hand, if you show her you love and accept her just the way she is, she may change simply because she doesn't feel pressured to do so. Regardless, you must commit yourself to allowing her to be all that she can be, not all you want her to be.

7. **Never do anything to betray her trust.** Unfaithfulness is the ultimate dishonor to your wife. Before God, commit yourself to be a faithful husband. Accept her for who she is and love her as the woman God made for you and planned to be your wife before the world began.

PROTECT HER

1 Peter 3:7d | Showing honor to the woman as the weaker vessel.

A husband gives "honor" to his wife "as the weaker vessel"– as he would handle a precious, priceless, fragile vase. Women are not lesser, but like an expensive vase, they are more fragile than men. They are to be honored, cared for, and protected.

The term "weaker vessel" has often been misunderstood. It does not imply inferiority, since the verse continues by stating that a woman is a co-heir with her husband. Within the context of this verse, "weaker" means that a woman is not to be treated as "one of the guys." She is created differently, in both body and spirit. She is a precious delicate vessel God has entrusted to your care.

In other words, husbands, treat with respect and sensitivity this fragile creature God has made, called woman. She is not fragile only because you are physically stronger, but because you can crush her spirit with brutish words and actions of disrespect. All through Scripture, the human body is compared to a vessel (Jer 18, Acts 9, Rom 9, 2 Tim 2.) The word "vessel" communicates the idea that the human body is a like a piece of pottery or a clay jar. Honor is protective. Here are some ways husbands can practice wise protectiveness.

With Patience

Men can protect their wives physically by showing patience when things seem dangerous. We can be impatient with our wives' fearfulness. When she reaches across the front seat and puts her hand on your leg and says, "Could you slow down, please?" she's not feeling safe with you. Women get no adrenaline rush from danger. Men can protect their wives physically by showing patience.

With Care

Men can protect their wives physically with oversight and care by insuring her safety in your absence. When you need to be out of town overnight, you can go a long way to sit down with your wife and just make sure she knows she's safe. "I've talked to the neighbors. Someone is going to check in on you. I'll be calling to make sure you're safe."

With Gentleness

Men can protect their wives physically by managing our aggression during conflict. I'm guessing I'm not the only person who knows what it is like to have an argument with his wife. I don't think men realize the damage they can do. Men don't bully her. Don't use a deeper voice to power over her in an argument and suppress her opinion into silence through fear. Don't throw things. Don't punch the wall. Conscientiously back away, men. Have the fight but keep it fair. Make sure she feels safe. Ask yourself, "Does my wife feel safe with me?" Does she feel covered by my strength? Does she feel protected by my God-given presence? Does she feel secure because of my sensitivity to her given need for protection?

With Accountability

Men can protect their wives emotionally by giving their wives a way to hold them accountable. The wife and children should always have the cell number of a pastor, elder, or leader in the church. The husband should give his wife and children permission to reach out for help without having to ask beforehand. I recommend sending a spiritual "9-1-1" text that will indicate the leader needs to call the husband. I've done this for my own family, and it allows the shepherds to care for the husband and protect the wife. Once, when my father died, I really just wanted to be alone. I told my wife and kids I just wanted to get away for a few days to grieve. This unsettled one of my daughters, and she remembered that she could call an elder. Within a minute, my dear elder was on the phone with me. How compassionate he was! He told me how he had lost his father, and how hard it was, but that we are the gatekeepers of our homes. This was a time to be strong, he said. And I needed to be there and be strong for my family. Wow. I needed that. That kind of loving accountability keeps the wife protected and the husband cared for.

With a Good Example

Christian wives desire godly leadership, not dictatorship. However, a man cannot lead where he has not been. A leader goes first, forging the way, wrestling through spiritual issues and then presenting God's instruction to his family. An ongoing personal relationship with Jesus Christ is crucial in order to lead a family spiritually. God holds men responsible for the spiritual and physical well-being of their families according to 1 Timothy 5:8, "But if anyone does not provide for his relatives, and especially for members of his household, he has denied the faith and is worse than an unbeliever."

Even though the wife may be better at teaching and leading, the husband is still to be involved in teaching their children. He must lead by example in church attendance, Bible reading, prayer, and spiritual disciplines. It is difficult for a Christian wife to respect her husband in other areas when he has not been consistent in providing her the spiritual leadership she needs and desires.

OPEN UP TO HER

1 Peter 3:7e | Since they are heirs with you of the grace of life...

Open up to her. The "grace of life" encompasses all of the blessings that God pours into our lives—all his goodness that we don't deserve. The grace of life is everything from the joy of the honeymoon to the children, to the children's marriages, to all of the joyful, happy things that happen in married life. *"With you"* is the operative phrase. It's not my right to hoard the blessings of life on myself. God's design is that we would share life together. If you're going to have a relationship with your wife, that is going to mean you must open yourself up to her, disclose yourself to her, share yourself with her.

Women's number one complaint as it relates to their husbands—Christian or otherwise—is "Why won't he open up to me?" Your wife can't know you just by watching you. The only way she can get to know you is if you tell her about yourself. Your wife wants a husband who will call her during the day, listen to her, take her advice, and see her as your very best friend. Be open with her. She wants to be "number one" in your life.

PRAY WITH HER

1 Peter 3:7f | So that your prayers may not be hindered.

Pray with her. The wife needs tenderness in listening, but she needs you to lead her in prayer. The word *hindered* means *to cut off*.

It's the idea of throwing an obstacle in the way of an intended path. If you're not listening to and learning about your wife, your prayer life is being blocked. It doesn't say failure will hinder your prayer life in some specific way. It will hinder your prayer life in every way. Do you struggle with in prayer? "God doesn't answer me." "I practically never pray with my wife." "My prayers are cut off somewhere." All that describes the word hindered. This is a negative promise of Scripture: If you don't dwell with your wife in an understanding way, giving honor to the wife as to the weaker vessel, as heirs together of the grace of life, your prayers will be cut off, hindered, made difficult in every way.

This clear warning is sounded here. You want God to listen to your prayers? Then take heed to this command. A husband's prayer life is affected by the kind of learner he is of his wife's heart. In other words, marriage is a measure of your walk with God. If a couple is not right with each other, they are not right with God. Consider some implications to a husband's marriage and family if his prayer life is being hindered by his disobedience to 1 Peter 3:7. According to Psalm 66:18, what are the results of harboring unconfessed sin in our hearts? David says: "If I regard wickedness in my heart, the Lord will not hear."

"Hindered" (*ekkopto*) is in the present tense and passive. Failure to give due honor to the wife will result in the cutting off of the efficacy of prayer. In other words, a couple that is not in matrimonial harmony will find it difficult to pray together and for one another. A couple's domestic relationship has a profound impact on their spiritual fellowship with God. Our relationship with God can never be right if our relationships with our fellow human being are wrong.

Conclusion

So those are six actions that practiced consistently will absolutely transform your marriage, your wife and you personally. You've got God's word on it. God has a perfect design in marriage making you male and female. This means God intends you and your spouse to work in harmony in marriage. It may be a little clumsy at times, but if you work at it, you can be like a beautiful orchestra. You may be wondering: how can we work together when we are so different? Mark Gungor explains:

> Once you understand why your husband acts that way, or why your wife thinks that way, it will change how you feel about him or her, though nothing has really changed. Compassion will come with an

accompanying perseverance—all because you now understand. I cannot overstate the importance of understanding." Compassion will help you to be a better listener.[107]

Dear man of God, you are called to love your life and lay your life down for her. The very best way to do that is by listening to her. So many men "talk at" their wives instead of cherishing them by listening. Your dear wife is not looking for perfection. Most wives appreciate that their husband is trying. Let her know you want to listen to her and do what it takes to get to that place where she indeed feels listened to. If you are not able to do this on your own, enlist the help of a loving pastor or elder or biblical counselor. You will not regret it!

Men often measure themselves by externals, which are outside their control. Money, fame, popularity, physical ability, and power are fleeting and temporary. However, a husband can choose to define success by how well he has followed God's command to cherish his wife and lead his family.

---

[107] Mark Gungor, *Laugh Your Way to a Better Marriage: Unlocking the Secrets to Life, Love and Marriage* (New York: Simon and Schuster, 2008), 20.

16 | 1 PETER 3:8

THE HARD WORK OF CHRISTIAN FELLOWSHIP

Finally, all of you, have unity of mind, sympathy, brotherly love, a tender heart, and a humble mind.

1 PETER 3:8

Isn't it amazing that God has made us his temple? He dwells in us. The Spirit has made our heart his home. As a result, we are brought into a fellowship with the Spirit and with each other. Peter talks about how we have this fellowship, but we have to work hard to maintain it.

1 Peter 3:8 | Finally, all of you, have unity of mind, sympathy, brotherly love, a tender heart, and a humble mind.

Maybe you've experienced it. You walked into a room filled with people looking at their phones. You are not alone, but you are totally alone. MIT professor Sherry Turkle makes the following observation in her book *Alone Together: Why We Expect More from Technology and Less from Each Other.*

> We are changed as technology offers substitutes for connecting with each other face to face. As we instant message, text and twitter, technology redraws the boundaries between intimacy and solitude. Teenagers would rather text than talk. Things that happen in 'real time'

take too much time. Tethered to technology, we are shaken when that world "unplugged" ... does not satisfy. Adults too choose keyboards over the human voice. We build a following on Facebook, but wonder to what degree our followers are truly friends. We recreate ourselves as online personas, yet suddenly, in the half light of virtual community, we may feel utterly alone.[108]

Relationships take work with real face-to-face experiences. Real Christian fellowship takes a lot of face-to-face investment that cannot be achieved by social media. Don't get me wrong. There are benefits from the use of technology, but technology is no substitute for face-to-face interaction. Technology can serve in a limited way when rightly used, but it is not a replacement for the power of God's use of real people to transform broken humanity. Don't ever let technology fool you into a false substitute for fellowship.

I've known people that have listened to sermons online but have not seen God work in a meaningful way until a real human was there to care and listen and respond. God has created the living church of Christ, where real human beings are meant to connect with each other face to face. The keyboard was never meant to replace the human voice or the human face.

Saint Peter never heard of an iPhone, but he tells us how God brings his people together in the hard work of fellowship. These words of Peter are so relevant and needful for us as a church. He says: "Finally, all of you, have unity of mind, sympathy, brotherly love, a tender heart, and a humble mind" (1 Pet 3:8). These are the elements and components of true fellowship with each other. Peter is describing the relational richness that is to characterize the church's fellowship *in a world that wants to limit so much of its communication to 140 characters of text*. The Christian life requires so much more! Christian fellowship is hard work.

We could call these the five virtues, five muscles of fellowship. Fellowship is sharing the life of God together. You share his presence, his glory, his life in you. I've started to work out. Can you tell? Not yet huh! Well, whether you work your body out, you need to work your soul out and stretch these five muscles of Christian fellowship. These five vir-

---

[108] Sherry Turkle. *Alone Together: Why We Expect More from Technology and Less from Each Other* (New York: Basic Books, 2011), 11.

tues of fellowship distinguish the church from the culture. Peter's original readers are objects of slander and insults and hostility and persecution. Life is hard! Christians need a refuge from persecution. Their new faith is a threat to the Greco-Roman culture. The church is meant to be a relational refuge of support for these original Christians.

We need to grow in these virtues. This list is how Christians are supposed to relate with each other in the local church. This is what we are to experience and contribute to in the church. Peter wants us to be a genuine friend, not just a Facebook friend. He shows us how to build meaningful and lasting relationships in the local church.

The problem is that the world is hostile to the church. But have you noticed that sometimes church isn't a safe place? It ought not to be that way. The church should be a refuge from the world. How can we be that refuge? In 1 Peter 3:8, we are looking at a description of a healthy and mature church. As our culture becomes increasingly hostile to the gospel, we need a refuge. Living Hope, I want us to be that refuge. This list of virtues makes the relational healthy church more and more relevant and important in an increasingly disaffected, lonely and cynical world. So here's the first virtue of fellowship. This morning our attention will be devoted to just one verse. And it's a verse that is easy to overlook. So Christians now display five virtues that brings them together in Christ. These marks display the transformational power of the gospel. The gospel transforms how we relate with one another.

The Final Application

Peter says, "Finally" (3:8). This is not a reference to the impending conclusion of the letter. It's a reference to the final application of the exhortation he issued in 2:12, "Keep your conduct among the Gentiles honorable, so that when they speak against you as evildoers, they may see your good deeds and glorify God on the day of visitation." How do I get lost people ready for the final day, the Lamb's day of wrath? I can be submissive to ungodly government as long as I am not sinning. I can be submissive to unjust employers so long as I am not sinning. Ladies can be submissive in their marriage so long as they are not sinning. Finally, church, this application is for you: be a refuge for Christian fellowship. Display these virtues. This is how you can silence the slander against you because of the gospel. Be a refuge for fellowship. How? By flexing these virtues. By exercising these virtues. "Finally, all of you..." (3:8). All Christians needs to consider this. No one is exempt. As you flex these virtues, the church will be strengthened and protected. It will build a refuge.

These exercises must take place face-to-face. They accent the importance of community not independence. We are inter-dependent as Christians. We are a body. We are not much good on our own. We need to have a care and concern for others, not a pre-occupation with oneself. They express a love for the church that Jesus died to create.

The false prosperity gospel says: improve yourself, focus on yourself. The true gospel says, "Deny yourself. Die to yourself. Live for others. Love others. Serve others." These virtues are all a way to cultivate self-denial. You cannot cultivate these virtues apart from or isolated from the local church. We need each other. You can't do this stuff by text. You can't do this stuff by skipping real fellowship and gathering on Sunday morning. You need to be face-to-face. These virtues assume an involvement in the local church. You can't do this from home. You can't be isolated from God's church and expect to grow. You need to be together with your forever family for these virtues to be expressed.

WORK HARD FOR UNITY

1 Peter 3:8a | Finally, all of you, have unity of mind.

Unity Begins with Union with Christ

The first fellowship mark or muscle is: unity. Peter says: "Finally, all of you, have unity of mind..." (3:8a). We need to flex and exercise this muscle. This is a supernatural union with Christ created by the Holy Spirit. All true Christians here at Living Hope are supernaturally joined together by the Spirit. We've been joined because we believed when the gospel was proclaimed to us. This is not an arbitrary mark, but an essential mark for the growth of the Church. If you are not united with Christ by the Spirit, then you are not a Christian and you have no fellowship and no refuge.

The world's culture divides us by ethnicity: "black and white and Asian, Indian, Middle Eastern." In Christ there is no ethnic barrier. We are all one in Christ. This is a call to live in harmony with each other. We may have nothing else in common, but we have Christ! All Christians have a new culture, a new kingdom, a new nature in Christ! We are united in Christ. We die to self and live to Christ by laying down our lives for our forever family.

Jesus is our all-sufficient substitute for sin. I am one with all who love him. Therefore, to be a Christian is to be in union with Jesus. We are "in Christ." Peter says, "1 Peter 3:8, "Finally, all of you, have unity of mind..." Jesus prayed in John 17:21, "that they may all be one, just as you, Father, are in me, and I in you, that they also may be in us, so that the world may believe that you have sent me." God brings us into union with himself through regeneration. I was dead in sins, but the Spirit brought me to life. I was in the valley of dry bones, and the word was prophesied to me, and I became part of God's living army! I am a new creation in Christ.

Unity Requires Hard Work

Peter says: "Finally, all of you, have unity of mind..." (3:8). Peter says, it's something you have, but it's also something you maintain. The other apostles say the same thing. St. Paul commands: "walk in a manner worthy of the calling to which you have been called... eager to maintain the unity of the Spirit in the bond of peace" (Eph 4:1, 3). It's something you have supernaturally, but it is something you need to work hard to maintain. All Christians are brought into union with Christ by the Holy Spirit. We have unity as a miracle gift from God. It's a gift of the Spirit in the new birth. But Paul says, be "eager" or "work hard" to "maintain the unity of the Spirit." Work hard to maintain your unity in Christ.

Work hard for this amazing blessing of unity! Guard it! Psalm 133 describes the joy of unity. "Behold, how good and pleasant it is when brothers dwell in unity! 2 It is like the precious oil on the head, running down on the beard, on the beard of Aaron, running down on the collar of his robes! 3 It is like the dew of Hermon, which falls on the mountains of Zion! For there the LORD has commanded the blessing, life forevermore" (Psa 133). Unity in our church creates a place that is life sustaining.

Unity Requires Death to Self

We must promote unity. We must also protect it. How? If unity is given to us by God by the Spirit that dwells within us, how must I work hard to maintain it and defend it and guard against dissension and division? I must die to my old nature. Actually, the Bible teaches that I am already dead and crucified to it (Gal 2:20). We all have the ghost of our old fleshly selfish nature. We have died to it, but the ghost of it is still with us to harass us. The old nature can never be satisfied. "The desires of the flesh are against the Spirit" (Gal 5:17). The flesh is always hungry and selfish and can never be satisfied. The flesh according to Romans 7:23 is a slave master that brings you into slavery to sin. "In my flesh dwells nothing good" (Rom 7:18). 2 Peter 2:14 says the flesh's "desire for sin is never satisfied" (Berean Study Bible Version). It's "insatiable." It always wants more and more. Unity, then, is hard work because we always have to die to our desire to nurse our hurts. We have to cover with love and deny ourselves constantly.

Unity Requires Love

If we are to have unity, we need love. Love helps us to cover those matters of conscience we may not agree on. So we are to be alert to anything personal, relational, or even doctrinal that would divide us. Be patient in teaching sound doctrine. Don't be quick to give up on someone. Help them through it. If there is a doctrine of secondary importance, like the timing of the second coming or a system of theology, then love one another because of Christ. Someone speaks in tongues, and someone doesn't speak in tongues. Don't divide over that. Love one another. Be alert to anything that would weaken your unity of mind. Work hard to serve God in harmony with one another. Don't let a disputable matter divide you. Romans 14 says that we should love one another by giving up our rights if your freedom offends another, even if it is not sinful. Let the Spirit of God rule and reign in you. Work hard to submit in love to one another. Cover with love if you have to. Let us deal with the indwelling sin in ourselves by thinking the best of our brothers and sisters. That's not just a platitude. That's a command. We are to think the best of one another. We are to be suspect of ourselves. "The heart is deceitful and desperately wicked, who can know it?" (Jer 17:9). I am to "not lean to my own understanding" or perception of things (Pro 3:5b).

Unity Requires Tolerance

Unity is hard work, because we are all porcupines. We are to bear with one another and put up with one another. We are all porcupines. We all have quirks and idiosyncrasies. We all have hang-ups that make us look uncaring. We can easily offend and easily be offended. We need to guard the unity of the Spirit. We are not called to nurse our hurts, but instead to bear personal injuries and hurts. We are called to return good for evil. Do not dismiss this. There are no "buts" to Peter's argument. Be like Christ. He did not return evil for evil, but when he was insulted, he did not insult back. "He was oppressed, and he was afflicted, yet he opened not his mouth; like a lamb that is led to the slaughter, and like a sheep that before its shearers is silent, so he opened not his mouth" (Isa 53:7). What do we do when we are oppressed and afflicted? We often act more like citizens of the USA than citizens of heaven.

Unity Requires Forgiveness

If we are to have unity, we must be quick to forgive. We don't hold grudges. Holding grudges invites Satan to have an opportunity to harass us and counsel us with his toxic counsel of hatred (Eph 4:26-27). We are to be non-resistant. Jesus said in the Sermon on the Mount, "Do not resist the one who is evil. But if anyone slaps you on the right cheek, turn to him the other also" (Mt 5:39). This is not a verse encouraging abuse, but a verse not to retaliate when you are personally injured. In other words, your defensiveness is the opposite of unity. Be quick to give up your rights. Leave vengeance with the Lord. Holding a grudge is the opposite of unity. Be quick to forgive. Try to move on quickly from personal offences. Work hard to guard the unity in this church. Work hard to guard unity in your home.

Unity is Not Uniformity but Harmony

Unity is not the same as uniformity. In other words, we don't all have to see things the exact same way. We are to live in harmony and unity. This does not mean the church will never have any differences of opinion. Believers should live and minister together so that the differences do not divide the church but serve to enrich its life and work.[109] Personally injuries should be carefully and lovingly worked out.

Unity isn't the same as *uniformity*—where everybody looks and acts exactly the same. Nor is it the same as *unanimity*—when everybody agrees 100 percent on everything. Peter isn't calling us to sing together in *unison*, but in *harmony*—which means we all contribute our unique notes in a beautiful chorus that far surpasses any single note.[110]

---

[109] Walls, *I & II Peter, I, II & III John, Jude*, 51.
[110] Swindoll, *Insights on James and 1 & 2 Peter*, 195.

Most of our personal injuries occur because of misunderstandings. We all different ways of communicating and different preferences and gifts in the way we serve God. We ought to respect each other's differences and seek to live in harmony. It's not uniformity but harmony where we each respect and think the best of each other. But of course, this kind of harmony is hard work!

Unity is a Testimony to the Gospel

So how do you explain the unity of such a diverse people group here at Living Hope? It's because our love for Jesus Christ is greater than all our differences. And what really matters is not all our preferences and personalities, but the character and culture of Christ that unites us in the Spirit of God. Let us praise God for the unity we have in Christ. It's a miracle. The only thing most of us have in common is that the love of God has been poured out into our hearts. Hallelujah!

I love to see the diversity in this room. The diversity of ethnicity, the diversity of education, of background, of financial standing, the great diversity of culture. Whether you are from the north, south, east, or west, whether you are rich or poor, whether you went to college or you work a trade, the only thing that matters is this: are you united to Christ? If you are united to Christ, you are my brother and my sister and my mother and my father. Jesus said, "whoever does the will of God, he is my brother and sister and mother" (Mk 3:35). Are you united to Christ? Then we are united forever!

Let's put our phones down. Let's shut our computers down. Let's get together, face-to-face and edify each other with Christian unity. Let's get together and rejoice in the cross of Christ! Let's rejoice that the blood of Christ cleanses us from all sin. Let's get together and rejoice that the love of Christ has been poured into our hearts. Hey, brothers and sisters, we are not going to hell today or tomorrow or ever! Let's rejoice in the power of the Cross and the work of Christ. Let's rejoice that God's grace and love is greater than all our sin. Because of what Christ has done there is a "unity of mind," a harmony of heart created by the gospel. And we need to protect it and promote it in the church.

This unity is meant to protect the church from dissention and division. Let the healing power of the cross overshadow us and protect us from division. The love of Christ in our hearts is the basis of Christian unity.

WORK HARD FOR SYMPATHY

Here's a second virtue to grow in fellowship. Work hard for Christian sympathy.

1 Peter 3:8b | Finally, all of you, have... sympathy.

Because of Christ, we have a harmony of feeling for and with each other. The original Greek word means, literally, "to feel with" someone. Because of the work of Christ that unites us, we "rejoice with those who rejoice, and weep with those who weep" (Rom 12:15).[111]

The Adoption of Sympathy

Sympathy involves an eagerness to engage with the emotions of fellow believers. We are to enter into their feelings so that their feelings become our feelings. We are to adopt and experience what our brothers and sisters in Christ are feeling as your own feeling and experience. To have sympathy with someone you must interact with them face to face. You need to be with them. This includes looking into their eyes, looking into their face, praying with them, connecting with them, talk with them. I must in an unhurried way draw them out. Why? So that their feelings become our feelings. This is how God has constructed the church to be a unique refuge in a hostile world.

You may think, does anyone care? If the Spirit of God is here, then yes! We care for you. We may not know you needs. Have patience with us. We want to love you. We want to know your deep-down needs. We want to know your struggles. We care! We love you. Why do we care for one another? Why do we enter into each other's feelings and struggles? Because we are a church that has been transformed by the gospel. Doing this is not complicated. I'm a hugger, but you don't have to be a hugger to do this. You do have to care to do this. Ask sincere questions that show you are interested in your brother or sister in Christ. Listen carefully. A husband is to dwell with his wife in an understanding way. The whole church should be dwelling with each other in understanding. Don't jump to conclusions.

The Actions of Sympathy

How does sympathy act? The key to sympathy is to let the person you are talking open up to you and share their heart. Avoid interrupting

---

[111] Ibid.

them. Avoid thinking you know what their problem is. Avoid inserting your experience in a way that suddenly the conversation becomes about "me." Don't do that. Let it be about them. Laugh with them. Cry with them. Pray with them. Let it be about them. Take time and listen and let your hearts be knit together. Feel what they feel. Draw that person out if they are struggling. Make their feelings your feelings. This is not complicated. I love to see circles and huddles of prayer after the service. That's sympathy. I love to see meals brought to families that are hurting and sometimes devastated by live. That's sympathy.

Work hard to feel what others feel. Work hard to celebrate with them without making it about you. Work hard in mourning with those who mourn. To sympathize with someone demonstrates the power of the gospel. Sympathy is the opposite to selfishness and narcissism. The flesh is never concerned about others, but self. So this sympathy is really a distinctive of the new birth. We celebrate that we have the power to get our eyes off our selves. Are you that person in marriage that is always sad and discontent and complaining? That's the opposite of sympathy. Snap out of it! You are born again. Get your eyes off of self and onto your brother and sister in Christ. This distinguishes the church from the culture. It takes place in face-to-face meetings. This is one of the reasons God commands us to gather together. Twitter doesn't cut it.

WORK HARD FOR FAMILY

1 Peter 3:8c | Finally, all of you, have... brotherly love.

We are to have brotherly love – a love for each other as members of God's forever family. You are part of the family of God. This love is possible because of the redemptive love of Jesus and the adoptive love of God the Father. The original readers had lost their families. They had lost their jobs. You couldn't be a Christian and be a member of the trade guilds throughout Asia Minor. Some had lost their marriages. Some had been ostracized by their families. Our true family is God's family. This is not just a theological reality, but a practical reality. For the Asia Minor Christians, the church was their forever family.

The Joy of God's Forever Family

These churches in Asia Minor was not just a new church, but a new family. The new love they have for each other transcends the love that they had in their lost families. We now have a new family! I'm so glad I have a new family. I've been adopted into the family of God. There is a family language: prayer. There is a family likeness: conformed to Christ's image. There is the family location: I'm seated in the heavenly realm with Christ. There is a family love: God's love is poured into my heart by the Spirit. There is a family lineage: I'm bought by the blood of Jesus! That's my bloodline. Born by the Spirit, washed in the blood! Because of the new birth, I have a new family and a new love for my brothers and sisters in Christ. Real agape love means I put your needs above my own needs. I serve you. I think the best of you. You are my forever family.

Membership in God's Forever Family

How do we get into God's forever family? Membership in the family of God does not depend on any earthly relationship. It does not come by your physical, or natural birth, but by a supernatural birth—a new birth. Preachers cannot impart it to their hearers. Parents cannot give it to their children. You may be born in the godliest family in America and grow up under the strongest preaching any church can supply, and yet never belong to the family of God. You see, Jesus said, "Unless a man is born again, he cannot see the kingdom of God" (Jn 3:3). Only the Holy Spirit can make you a living member of this family. It is his special function and prerogative to bring into the true church all those who will be saved. Those who are born again are born, "not of blood, nor of the will of the flesh, nor of the will of man, but of God" (Jn 1:13).

When Jill and I lived in a small Basque town in Spain on the border of France, we noticed everyone was kind to each other. In the big city people would honk. People were rude. Not in the small town. They had to live with each other, so there was a great deal of patience. There was one main road through town, and people would stop in their cars and talk. They would block traffic just talking to each other as if the world was standing still. The Chicago boy in me wanted to honk my horn and remind them that other people are living their lives, but I dared not do that. Why? Because we were such a small town we were like family. I'd see those men who were talking later in the evening when we were pushing our kids around main street or playing with our kids in the park. We were like a family.

Listen, if you are in God's family you are my true family. I can't treat you rudely. You are my forever brother and my forever sister. I was raised without a father and my mother died when I was 15. But in the church, I have a hundred mothers and a hundred fathers. You are my family.

You and I need to work hard to remember we are family. You husbands and wives need to remember you are forever family. The church is my new family. It's like no other family. God's family is an infinitely large family. Do not measure the God's family by what you see with your eyes. You may see only a small body of believers in your city or town or local church. But we all need to remember that a great host of believers has already made it safely to heaven, and when we are all together on the last day, there will be "a great multitude, which no man could number, of all nations, and kindreds, and people, and tongues" (Rev 7:9).

The church should be (as Charles Spurgeon put it) "the dearest place on earth." Spurgeon said there is no perfect church. All churches have their flaws. He said if he had found a perfect church he could not have joined it, because once he joined it, the church would be spoiled by his own imperfection. "Still," he said, "imperfect as it is, it is the dearest place on earth to us."[112] We are to work hard at expressing a brotherly affection for one another. Even though the church may not always feel like a safe place, I would rather be hurt in the church than abandoned in the world. It takes such hard work to at continually strengthening our family ties in Christ's church.

WORK HARD FOR EMPATHY

1 Peter 3:8d | Finally, all of you, have... a tender heart.

We are to have "a tender heart." It means to have empathy. Empathy is a very interesting word. The word is different from sympathy, to feel with. The Greek word is closely related to forgiveness.[113]

A Forgiving Heart

This is a heart that is deeply moved by the condition of another. The old Authorized Version translates the "bowels of compassion" or

---

[112] Charles Spurgeon, "The Best Donation," (No. 2234) an exposition of 2 Corinthians 8:5 delivered on April 5, 1891 at the Metropolitan Tabernacle in London, England.

[113] MacArthur, *1 Peter*, 188.

literally "intestines" (e.g., Acts 1:18). This word is used of Jesus to describe him being in agony over the broken and lost condition of those around him. He was "deeply moved" because they were like "sheep without a shepherd" (Mt 9:36; cf Eph 4:32; 2 Cor 7:15; 1 Thess 2:8). This is especially used of people who are in a state of disaster in their lives, who oppose themselves and oppose others. We have a saying among us – "Sheep bite." It's true. God has saved you, but sometimes you are under such darkness and satanic attack, that you are like a soldier under attack, and you might be tempted to flail and fight against even those who love you. Empathy doesn't discount the person who hurts us; instead, we persevere and keep loving them, feeling for them and forgiving them with a tender heart.

A Big Heart

To be empathetic means to have "thick skin and a big heart." This heartfelt compassion is displayed when we reach out to the hurting [114] or those who have hurt you. Jesus said, it's easy to love those who love you, but real God-sized love allows you to love those who have hurt you. "Love your enemies" so you may show you are children of the heavenly Father (Mt 5:44-45). Jesus says, lost people love those who are good to them (Mt 5:46-47). The love of the church of Jesus Christ goes beyond that earthly love. We love those who hurt us. We keep loving true believers even when they disappoint us. To be empathetic in this way means to love those who are hurting or who have hurt you.

If someone hurts you, and you keep loving them. That's a God-size love! You've got to work hard at that kind of forgiving love, that empathy. When someone hurts you, in our flesh we want to hate them. We want to say, "I'm never coming to church again. It's supposed to be a safe place, but I don't feel safe." But we can't allow our heart to become so small. We are to show that God-size love and empathy to those who are hurting and even to those who hurt us. We don't grow bitter. Instead, we as born-again people are to have a "tender heart." Keep your heart tender. We may hurt each other, but don't allow the root of bitterness to creep in.

---

[114] Swindoll, *Insights on James and 1 & 2 Peter*, 195.

A Gentle Heart

Are you in agony that the body of Christ is sometimes in shambles? Reach out in empathy. Reach out in tender compassions and mercy not simply to "set them straight" but to shepherd that person and to love them with a "tender heart." We are to be gentle and not harsh. We are to be tender and kind in our attitude and in our disposition. In this rough and relentless world, we are to live in tenderness. There is to be an absence of harshness and self-righteousness. This makes us distinct from the culture.

Work Now listen, in this text filled world where people's hearts can be so disconnected and cruel, we can often fall into the temptation of jotting out a furious email or text to really tell somebody what we feel. This is why I despise email and texting for any kind of meaningful conflict resolution. I refuse to use text or email for that. That in my opinion is lazy and not a very courageous thing to do. Sometimes sitting behind a keyboard, we have such brazen self-confidence, and sometimes self-righteousness that does not demonstrate a tender heart, but a proud, cold heart. But what about growing in the hard work of empathy by speaking any grievances face to face with brothers and sisters. It's hard I know, but it preserves our dignity and integrity. Don't lower yourself to having a loud keyboard. Don't roar with your texts. Any fool can be brazen behind a keyboard. If you have a grievance with a precious member of Christ's body, show the respect to our Lord to go to that person face to face.

I've seen Christian post things online on a Facebook or Twitter rant that they would never have the courage to say face to face. It becomes a platform for pride and a display of fleshly selfishness. I say, have the courage to have a tender heart. If someone is hurting or wayward, have the love and empathy to meet them where they are, face to face.

HARD FOR HUMILITY

1 Peter 3:8e | Finally, all of you, have... a humble mind.

Christian fellowship takes hard work. We work for unity, sympathy, family, empathy, and finally, humility.

Humility Defined

Humility is not thinking less of yourself, but it is thinking of yourself less. Self-forgetfulness is a wonderful description of humility. Humility means "to be lowly and bowed down in mind."[115] It might surprise you that humility was not viewed favorably in the Greco-Roman culture. In ancient Greek culture of Peter's time, in the Hellenistic culture of Plato and Aristotle, pride was a virtue. Humility was despised and considered a weakness. You were to put yourself first in the ancient world. This is the culture that Peter's Asia Minor hearers were living in. One scholar "In the highly competitive and stratified Greco-Roman antiquity only those of degraded social status were 'humble,' and humility was regarded as a sign of weakness and shame, an inability to defend one's honor... The high value placed on humility by... Christians is remarkable."[116]

Humility Commanded

The Bible commands us to be humble. But in the original assembly where this was read, this was radical! What? Be humble? This is not viewed as a weakness in the culture. But that which was viewed badly in the culture was to be a distinguishing characteristic of love and fellowship in the church.

The church is made up as those who have been humbled by the gospel. We are people who have met the King of kings, and all manner of boasting will be directed toward him. I have nothing to boast in but the Cross of Jesus. I boast, Paul says, "I will boast in my weakness!" "When I am weak then I am strong." This is a remarkable and radical light to the fallen culture. In an age of the humble boast of Twitter and Facebook where selfies are posted ad nauseum, Christians are to forget themselves and lift up the King and Lord of our lives!

Paul tells Christians to stand in contrast to the world's narcissistic culture. He says in Philippians 2:3, "Do nothing from selfishness or empty conceit, but with humility of mind regard one another as more important than yourselves." Years earlier Jesus demonstrated the importance of his own example of humility when he as King of kings washed the disciples' feet (Jn 13:1-17).

---

[115] Swindoll, *Insights on James and 1 & 2 Peter*, 195.
[116] Karen H. Jobes. *1 Peter: Baker Exegetical Commentary on the New Testament* (Grand Rapids, MI: Baker Academic, 2005), 215.

When Peter was painting this picture of fellowship, you know what he was thinking about, don't you? You can see it, can't you? He was describing Jesus. 1 Peter 3:8 is a portrait of Jesus. In John 17:11, Jesus prayed for unity for us: "that they may be one, even as we are one."

He displayed such sympathy with Mary and Martha. When their brother Lazarus died, even though he knew he would raise him, "Jesus wept" (Jn 11:35). He demonstrated such care for their souls by entering into their feelings.

He also demonstrated great sympathy by entering into people's joy. When tax collectors got saved, he would celebrate with them so much so that the self-righteous people pointed their long bony fingers at him and accused him of being a "drunk" and said, "Look at him! A glutton and a drunkard, a friend of tax collectors and sinners" (Lk 7:34).

What deep empathy he had! "While we were yet sinners, Christ died for us" (Rom 5:8). Oh how he loved us, even while we opposed him! He said, "Father forgive them for they know not what they do" (Lk 23:34). And how could we forget Peter himself? The Lord knew Peter was going to deny him and warned him, "Simon, Simon, behold, Satan demanded to have you, that he might sift you like wheat, 32 but I have prayed for you that your faith may not fail. And when you have turned again, strengthen your brothers" (Lk 22:31-32). Peter denied his Lord three times! And what did Jesus do? "Your finished Peter; you will never preach again. You are washed up!" Was Jesus bitter at Peter? No! He was filled with empathy and rescued Peter. Peter said, "I go a fishing" (Jn 21:3). In other words: "I'm done with preaching." Jesus rescues Peter and says, "Peter do you love me?" Three times he asks. Three times he says, "Feed my lambs" or "Feed my sheep." (Jn 21:15-17). "Peter you're not done. I want you to preach Pentecost." Jesus wasn't bitter at him. He had thick skin and a big heart!

What about our forever family? Jesus was told his mother and his brothers were here to see him. Remember what he said?

> "Who is my mother, and who are my brothers?" [49] And stretching out his hand toward his disciples, he said, "Here are my mother and my brothers! [50] For whoever does the will of my Father in heaven is my brother and sister and mother." —Matthew 12:48-50

And oh, what about the humility of Christ. Jesus, "though he was in the form of God, did not count equality with God a thing to be grasped, 7 but emptied himself, by taking the form of a servant, being born in the likeness of men. ⁸ And being found in human form, he humbled himself by becoming obedient to the point of death, even death on a cross" (Phil 2:6-8). Jesus says, if you want to be great, you've got to become the least. He who dies with the dirtiest towel wins. Put others above yourself. This kind of healing balm, that we love each other and esteem each other and think the best of each other cannot be done on Facebook and Twitter. Social media can't do it. We need to be together, face to face.

Conclusion

It's been a hard season in our culture for the church of Jesus Christ. The government in the Bible is called "the beast" for a reason. Tyranny is growing in our world. People are giving up their rights for a new secular religion. When I look at this text, I only need to look out at our congregation and see this place is a refuge for broken and bleeding sinners. Thank you for caring for the souls of people. Thank you for caring for one another and never giving up on one another. We are so far from being anything like a perfect church, but we are a church that reflects the character of Jesus. We weep with those who weep. I've seen you care for one another like try family.

There's no place I'd rather be when I am suffering than in Jesus' local congregation. There's no place I'd rather be when I am rejoicing than in Christ's church. We are not a perfect church, but Jesus is here. He has brought us together in unity, sympathy, family, empathy, and humility. Glory to his name.

17 | 1 PETER 3:9-12
BLESSED TO BE A BLESSING

Do not repay evil for evil or reviling for reviling, but on the contrary, bless, for to this you were called, that you may obtain a blessing.

1 Peter 3:9

What do you do when you are hurting? What if another Christian hurts you? It's going to happen. What do you do? Often, we can have all kinds of toxic emotions that cripple us: fear, bitterness, anger, despair. It's not God's will for us to be crippled spiritually. So how do we get out of the quicksand? Peter addresses what we should do with our hurt in in this passage.

> **1 Peter 3:9-12** | Do not repay evil for evil or reviling for reviling, but on the contrary, bless, for to this you were called, that you may obtain a blessing. [10] For "Whoever desires to love life and see good days, let him keep his tongue from evil and his lips from speaking deceit; [11] let him turn away from evil and do good; let him seek peace and pursue it. [12] For the eyes of the Lord are on the righteous, and his ears are open to their prayer. But the face of the Lord is against those who do evil."

Do you believe in the sovereignty of God? Do you really? The Christian's anchor is that the events of this life are all in God's control. And for the Christian, God is working out every single event, every second of your life, for your good and his praise and glory (Eph 1:11; 2:10). But sometimes there are some very stressful situations that play out in our lives. Knowing and loving God does not mean that he spares us from difficulties.

DON'T STRESS (3:9A)

1 Peter 3:9a | Do not repay evil for evil or reviling for reviling.

The Fact of Stress

The evil that is referred to here is an act of evil where someone has hurt you or offended you through actions or words. It implies very stressful situations caused by the sinful, selfish choices of others. No one can hide from this kind of evil. It's something we experience regularly in this broken, sin-cursed world. People are going to hurt you at times. Sadly, we have a temptation deep within us to repay evil for evil. We want justice, or more likely vengeance. Sometimes it's words, and we want to repay reviling for reviling. However you look at it, this kind of evil is a fact of life. It's easy to stress out over it.

Stress comes in waves. Sometimes life is like a calm sea, and then all the sudden it's an intense storm! Nonetheless, life can sometimes be like the wild waves of the sea. Personally, I don't do well with motion. I easily get motion sickness. When I was a teen, I was fine, but in my early twenties I went on a few carnival rides, and I realized I can get disoriented easily. Motion sickness is no fun. Once I had the opportunity to go out into the Atlantic Ocean in the Gulf of Mexico, out through Lake Ponchatrain in Louisiana. It's great to be on a boat that goes straight ahead, but have you ever been on a small boat in the ocean? When I'm on land, the waves look so orderly. I see one coming in, and a bigger one behind that. The tide comes in and goes out. It's so orderly It's peaceful. Even the gigantic waves bring you a sense of calm as the majestic billows roll. Not so in the ocean. In a small boat the waves are in no way orderly. The waves come at you from every side. Life can be like the waves that toss you back and forth. Aren't you glad that Jesus controls the waves of the sea? And when we choose to fix our eyes on him he can command the waves and the wind, "Peace be still!" (Mk 4:39).

Don't Focus on Stress

It's so easy to focus and focus and focus on our stress and get bitter and angry. But we are told not to focus on it, but rather to leave with the Lord. Someone once said that bitterness is like drinking poison hoping the other person will die. That's the wrong focus for the Christian. Don't drown in your hurt! Don't be overcome by your hurt. I don't mean that we must be the kind of people who don't feel hurt, but rather that we must not be wiped out by the hurt. We must be able to say with Paul in 2 Corinthians 4:8–9, "We are afflicted in every way, but not crushed; perplexed, but not driven to despair; persecuted, but not forsaken; struck down, but not destroyed." We will feel the pain when someone hurts us, but we will not be incapacitated by it. As Paul says in 2 Corinthians 4:16, "We do not lose heart."

BE SURE TO BLESS (3:9B).

We are not to stress and repay evil for evil. Instead, we are to bless. This is our calling as Christians.

> **1 Peter 3:9b** | But on the contrary, bless, for to this you were called, that you may obtain a blessing.

When we are reviled and hurt, and we feel attacked, it is easy to return the same evil and attack back. It's easy to give tit for tat. It's so easy when we are accused to become defensive. Instead of stressing, we need to be blessing.

The Call to Bless

Don't let the hurt that comes into your life cripple and disable you. You weren't called to be paralyzed by hurt. If hurt disables you, you will never make it as a good disciple maker. All of us should be making disciples. I've known so many Christians that are hurt by their spouse or hurt by their job or hurt by their church, and it cripples them. Don't be crippled by the hurt in your life.

Instead, bless. This is why David said, "I will bless the Lord at all times; his praise shall continually be in my mouth" (Psa 34:1). Paul said, "Rejoice in the Lord always" (Phil 4:4). Don't stress. We are to bless God and to bless others, and the Bible says, "to this you were called, that you may obtain a blessing" (3:9c). Wow, this is our calling! Bless others instead of returning evil.

The Choice to Bless

We are all good at having a defensive posture in our relationships. The Bible here is forbidding us from a defensive posture. Don't defend yourself, instead, bless the person. Let me give you some examples of defensiveness and how you can turn stressing into blessing.

The Music of Blessing

Whenever possible, be a blessing. Be harmonious with the brothers. Let God make beautiful music through you. A symphony was announced and the featured violinist was, at that time, world renowned. The advertisements announced that he would be performing his solo pieces on a rare violin – at the time, costing an unheard of $20,000. In today's economy that would be upwards of $500,000 or more. The symphony hall was packed and the people were filled with a sense of anticipation. It wasn't long before the master violinist stood and began to play, and what beautiful music it was. As he began his final piece, he suddenly took his violin and crashed it to the floor, severely damaging the instrument. And with that, he walked off stage. The audience was dumbfounded – shocked. The conductor however, who was in on it, turned and announced with a smile that the Maestro wanted them to know that he was not playing a $20,000 violin but a $20 violin. With that, the musician returned and finished his concert on the rare, expensive violin. And few people could tell any difference. The point that he had wanted to make was that the violin was certainly important, but it could only make beautiful music in the hands of a master musician.

I find that analogy to life encouraging because, like you, I'm not a rare violin; I don't know about you, but I'm more like the $20 version. In fact, the church is reflected in this analogy as an orchestra, made up of many different kinds of instruments. All from redeemed, yet common stock.[117] What makes us uncommon is the way the Master – our Lord – plays upon our lives, demonstrating to a world just what he can do. He gets the standing ovation, not us. He receives great glory when we allow him to play his tunes of grace in and through our lives.

Many tunes could be played from your life, and Peter names at least two of them: evil or blessing (3:9). When evil is done for us, we get to

---

[117] Stephen Davey. *Uncommon and Unexpected* (Cary, NC: Colonial Church, 24 Sept 2017), online article. Accessed 3 Jan 2018. https://www.colonial.org/content/htmlimages/public/documents/general/sermons/20170924-am.pdf

choose which tune we play. Are you going to let the Master play a tune of blessing, or will you lean on your selfish flesh and try to get back at your enemy? We've all thought it haven't we? "I'm going to give that person a piece of my mind." "That person needs to be put in their place." "Let's see how things play out when I stop hanging around that person." Instead, choose to play a different tune. Play a tune of grace from your life.

The Stew of Bitterness

Peter says, there is a better way to live than bitterness. You are called to be a blessing. Don't stew on the hurts of life. Move on. Now I love stew. Jill makes the best stew. You've never had that vegetable beef stew till you've had Jill's vegetable beef stew. But, Peter says, here's a different kind of stew that will ruin your life. When someone hurts you and you stew on it, you are missing a blessing. We like good stuff in our stew. It would be awful to put dirt and rocks and bugs in your stew. That would totally ruin it. How much more is our life ruined when we add anger, bitterness, and fear in our lives because we want vengeance. We are called instead to "stew" on all our blessings in Christ that we might be a blessing.

In your marriage when you are hurt by your spouse, you are called to be a blessing. I'm not talking about abuse. Abuse should never be tolerated by either spouse. You need to call someone if you are dealing with a real constant pattern of abuse. You need call a pastor. You may need to call the police. But I'm talking about everyday hurts. Misunderstandings. Harsh words. Critical attitudes. Ugliness. Don't add to the stew. Don't return ugly for ugly. Don't return hurt for hurt. Be a blessing like our Lord Jesus Christ. You are called to be a blessing to that person that hurt you so that you may obtain a blessing.

Now Peter's original hearers are suffering persecution. The government hasn't yet turned on them, but it is about to. Nero is about to come on the scene. Peter says, don't stew about it when somebody pokes you emotionally or verbally. Get over it. Move on. You may need to address it, but usually in that moment of hurt, you are ready to return hurt for hurt. Don't do that. Be a blessing.

The Covering of Blessing

When you are hurt by someone, cover it with love. Peter will later give this advice more specifically. "Above all, keep loving one another earnestly, since love covers a multitude of sins" (4:8). Bless your those who cause you hurt and pain. Hold your tongue. Give them to the Lord. Choose blessing over stressing and bitterness. Speak kindly. This goes in all areas of your life. You need to apply this to your spouse and children if you are married. You need to apply this to any argument you are currently having. If someone has hurt you at church, you need to bless them. That doesn't mean you don't follow Matthew 18, where it instructs us to get things right and bring up the hurt in order to solve it. But if you bring up the hurt, be ready to forgive and cover it with love and grace.

MAKE SURE YOU PROGRESS (3:10-11)

1 Peter 3:10-11 | For "Whoever desires to love life and see good days, let him keep his tongue from evil and his lips from speaking deceit; **11** let him turn away from evil and do good; let him seek peace and pursue it."

Peter is quoting one of the most beloved Psalms, the 34th, which tells us that we can measure our progress by how we speak and how we live, specifically in how we pursue peace in our relationships.

The Pathway to Progress

1 Peter 3:10 | For "Whoever desires to love life and see good days, let him keep his tongue from evil and his lips from speaking deceit.

Peter says if we want a full and rich life, we need to not let rottenness be in our mouths, but instead pursue peace. As we said, Peter is quoting from Psalm 34:12-16. This is a Psalm of David. We find that David didn't stay stuck in his hurt. He progressed. This Psalm was written when David was hiding from Psalm with King (Abimelech) Achish of Gath. Abimelech means "Father King." David was hiding in caves and had to act like a crazy person in order for Achish to have pity on him (1 Sam 21:1-15). The point is, David was experiencing great evil and hurt his own king in Israel. Someone who should have protected him was doing him harm. What do you do in that situation? What does David do with his hurt? I can tell you this, his focus wasn't on his hurt. It was on his great and powerful and glorious, majestic God! Look at what David says. This is also the Psalm Peter had already quoted in 1 Peter 3. I love Psalm 34:8, "Oh, taste and see that the Lord is good! Blessed is the man who takes refuge in him!" He says, leave your hurt behind and pursue peace.

David won't let his hurt and harm slow him down. So Peter quotes from David Peter chooses to quotes from David and says instead of turning your pain into more pain through returning evil for evil and deceit for deceit, pursued peace. Instead of pursuing the pain and the hurt, pursue peace! Do you desire to "love life" and "see good days"? Then you need to pursue peace. Seek it out. Hunt it down. How? Does Peter say, in order to really enjoy life, you need to get even. You need to tell that person how you "really feel"? Go ahead and start arguing and fussing and festering about something. How's that working for you? No! He says pursue peace. Here's the heart of the matter. He tells us what you should do when you are hurt. You need to progress. Are you progressing in your Christian life?

The Hinderance to Progress

1 Peter 3:10 | For "Whoever desires to love life and see good days, let him keep his tongue from evil and his lips from speaking deceit.

Do you "love life" and want to see good, happy, days of progress in the Christian life? Then watch your tongue. Keep it from evil, and in this context, that means slander. It means character assassination. Are you destroying that someone who has done evil to you in your mind or behind their back? Do you have a bitter spirit? It will be spiritual concrete for your life. Do you desire to be conformed into Christ's image (Rom 8:29)? Do you desire to have a full Christian life and "be filled with all the fullness of God" (Eph 3:19)? Then you need to make progress by controlling your tongue. Your tongue is capable of stirring up toxic emotions. "Keep your tongue from evil and your lips from speaking deceit" (3:10).

Those who study words tell us that words are important. But one study says how we use those words is even more important. In fact, the researchers concluded that all our communication consists of 7% words, 38% tones, and 55% non-verbal actions. Real progress and maturity in the Christian life can be measured by how you control your tongue. Remember the words of James, the half-brother of our Lord.

> We all stumble in many ways. And if anyone does not stumble in what he says, he is a perfect [mature] man, able also to bridle his whole body. —*James 3:2*

You are a mature Christian if you control your tongue. This is how you know you are fearing the Lord, living in his presence. Your words reveal your heart.

> The good person out of the good treasure of his heart produces good, and the evil person out of his evil treasure produces evil, for out of the abundance of the heart his mouth speaks. —*Luke 6:45*

Whatever is in your heart is going to come out of your mouth. The measure of your fear of God and your progress in the Christian life is really how you react to the hurts in your life. What comes out of your mouth? Blessing or cursing? We need to be progressing in the Christian life. Progress in the fruit of the Spirit. Self-control is part of the Spirit's fruit. Are you able to bless when you are hurt? That takes the unction of the Spirit. Keep "growing in grace" in your walk with Christ (2 Pet 3:18). Keep progressing.

The Measure of Our Progress

1 Peter 3:11 | "Let him turn away from evil and do good; let him seek peace and pursue it."

Peter finally says that our words and actions really determine if we really love to "live life" the way God designed it. Our pursuit of peace in difficult relationships is really the measure of our progress. We are to be pursuing God's peace even in difficult relationships. God wants to bless us with his well-being in our lives. We are to be in fierce pursuit of Christlikeness. Real peace and transformation and well-being doesn't come from our circumstances, or on just hoping things will go better when we've been wronged. No, Christians are called to be intentional. God is above the circumstances, and we need to live there, not in the midst of hurt and disappointment.

Are you progressing in the Christian life, or are you crippled by your hurts? So many Christians wonder why they are not progressing like they want with Christ. It's often because they are trying to change their circumstances or change others. Do you want to see real change in your workplace, in your church, in yourself? Then ask God to change you. Make progress in the Christian life.

You can't grow when you are crippled by wrongs and hurt. Retribution and stressing about wrongs done to you never give a good return. Whenever you throw dirt, you are losing ground. Don't do it. It will take away your progress in the Christian life.

YOU NEED TO REST (3:12)

> **1 Peter 3:12** | For the eyes of the Lord are on the righteous, and his ears are open to their prayer. But the face of the Lord is against those who do evil."

We need to rest in the Lord when we are hurting. The saying goes, "Hurting people hurt people." May that never be true of God's people. How can I rest when I am hurting? You say, ok then what exactly is Peter teaching us? That's a great question. I'm glad you asked. I think he is giving us several ways to respond when we are deeply hurting.

Rest in the Lord's Shepherding

> **1 Peter 3:12a** | For the eyes of the Lord are on the righteous.

The all-loving God's eyes are fixed on you. He's your shepherd and he never sleeps or slumbers in regard to caring for you. He's guiding and caring for your life. God's eyes are on you as you reflect the love of Christ to the world. The Bible says, you are his "masterpiece" (Eph 2:10). He wants you to love like he loves. Be like Jesus. Love those who hurt you. When Jesus was nailed to a cross by his enemies, he treated them with love. He cried out, "Father forgive them for they know not what they do" (Lk 23:34). God's eyes are on the righteous. Live out the gospel. Live out the life of God in you. He's watching and guiding your every step.

You can pursue peace with people that perhaps you do not trust completely. But you can trust the Lord is watching over your life. Pursue people that they may have peace with God. You say, "How do I seek peace and pursue it?" Show your faith and trust in God by blessing those who hurt you. Know that your testimony of love is so much more powerful than bitter or harsh words. We hear Paul saying the same thing.

> Beloved, never avenge yourselves, but leave it to the wrath of God, for it is written, 'Vengeance is mine, I will repay, says the Lord.' [20] To the contrary, 'if your enemy is hungry, feed him; if he is thirsty, give him

something to drink; for by so doing you will heap burning coals on his head.' ²¹ Do not be overcome by evil, but overcome evil with good" (Rom 12:19-21).

According to theologian F.F. Bruce, Paul is likely referring to "to an Egyptian ritual in which a man testified publicly to his penitence by carrying a pan of burning charcoal around on his head."[118] Our good and kind response to evil is a power expression of evangelism! It can bring people to repentance. Return love and goodness for evil.

Rest in the Lord's Sympathy

1 Peter 3:12b | "And his ears are open to their prayer."

God cares. Peter will later tell us: "cast all your care on him because he cares for you" (1 Pet 5:7). God says that he cares. His ears are open to your heart cries to him. So pray. When you are hurting, the first thing you need to do is pray. Ask God to give you a love for those who hurt you. Anyone can love their friends. It takes God's supernatural power to love those who hurt you. Ask God for a supernatural love for the one causing your pain. Believe that God is going to work in them. You need to rest in the reality that the Lord is compassionate, and he's not ignoring your pain. He hears you. Rest in that fact. He knows you. Our high priest, Jesus, is touched your pain and hurt. "His ears are open to your prayer." We have a high priest that is "touched with the feeling of our infirmities" in every way like us, yet without sin (Heb 4:15). Jesus was hurt. Jesus was reviled. Jesus was slandered. Jesus was hurt by men and women. He was strung up on a cross. "He came unto his own, and his own received him not" (Jn 1:11, KJV). Jesus cried with strong tears. "In the days of his flesh, Jesus offered up prayers and supplications, with loud cries and tears, to him who was able to save him from death, and he was heard because of his reverence" (Heb 5:7). If Jesus was brought to tears because off the sin of humanity, so we will also be brought to tears and hurt by people. Look over at 1 Peter 2:23. "When he was reviled, he did not revile in return; when he suffered, he did not threaten, but continued entrusting himself to him who judges justly" (1 Pet 2:23).

---

[118] F. F. Bruce, *Romans: An Introduction and Commentary*, vol. 6, Tyndale New Testament Commentaries (Downers Grove, IL: InterVarsity Press, 1985), 229.

Don't stop trusting God when you are hurt. Remember God has a purpose for every pain and hurt in your life. Don't be overcome by it. You have a compassionate high priest!!

Rest in the Lord's Sovereignty

1 Peter 3:12b | "But the face of the Lord is against those who do evil."

Do you really believe God is sovereign? It may not look right now like his face "is against those who do evil." It may look like he's blessing them. Not true. The Scriptures teach us that Christians have suffering today and joy tomorrow. The lost may have joy today, but they will have suffering tomorrow. God is a just God.

One day all of us are going to stand before a just and holy God. For Christians, there is no condemnation. Jesus will do all the talking for you on Judgment Day. You see Jesus is our Advocate, our lawyer, both now, on Judgment Day, and forever (1 Jn 2:1ff). He is our "Mediator between God and man" (2 Tim 1:5). But for the unbeliever, there's no hope. You have to be your own lawyer. Every wrong that is done will be made right. It's a hope for the Christian but a warning for those without Christ. Do you know Christ today? Come to him! He is the loving Advocate of all those who trust in him. There's no better lawyer than Christ.

Conclusion

How can I be a blessing in a jaded world? I need to be like Christ. You know I have a five-year-old daughter, and we love to play games. One of Ava's favorite games is called imitation. She makes a funny face, or a funny voice and I have to imitate her. She might say, "I love you" in a really high voice. Or she may make the silliest face you've ever seen. And in that game, it's my job to imitate everything she does and says. She loves it. Something that every Christian loves is to imitate Christ. When he was reviled and hurt, he blessed. When he was crucified, he entrusted himself to God. He was willing to turn the sin and hurt of all mankind into a blessing. We are called to do the same thing! We are blessed to be a blessing!

We are blessed with every blessing in Christ, aren't we? We are blessed with God's love and kindness. Let's generously distribute that kindness to others, especially when they hurt us.

18 | 1 PETER 3:13-22
GIVING AN ANSWER

in your hearts honor Christ the Lord as holy, always being prepared to make a defense to anyone who asks you for a reason for the hope that is in you; yet do it with gentleness and respect.

1 PETER 3:15

We find out how we can share the gospel effectively in our text. This is Peter's Noah sermon. It's really powerful because we live in a day like the days of Noah. The gospel is powerful. Jesus is mighty to save. Yet what do you do when no one wants to listen (as in Noah's day).

In the darkness of the world with hardened hearts, we are called to give an answer with "gentleness and respect."

1 Peter 3:13-22 | Now who is there to harm you if you are zealous for what is good? **14** But even if you should suffer for righteousness' sake, you will be blessed. Have no fear of them, nor be troubled, **15** but in your hearts honor Christ the Lord as holy, always being prepared to make a defense to anyone who asks you for a reason for the hope that is in you; yet do it with gentleness and respect, **16** having a good conscience, so that, when you are slandered, those who revile your good behavior in Christ may be put to shame. **17** For it is better to suffer for doing good, if that should be God's will, than for doing evil. **18** For Christ also suffered once for sins, the righteous for the unrighteous, that he might bring us to God, being put to death in the flesh but made alive in the spirit, [19] in which he went and proclaimed to the spirits in prison, [20] because they formerly did not obey, when God's patience waited in the days of Noah, while the ark was being prepared, in which a few, that is, eight persons, were brought safely through water. [21] Baptism, which corresponds to this, now saves you, not as a removal of dirt from the body but as an appeal to God for a good conscience, through the resurrection of Jesus Christ, [22] who has gone into heaven and is at the right hand of God, with angels, authorities, and powers having been subjected to him.

A healthy church has a heart for the lost. We need to always be ready to give an answer to the world around us. This passage is Peter's soul winning lesson to us. Do you love souls, and want to win them for Jesus? The Bible says, "The fruit of the righteous is a tree of life; and he who wins souls is wise" (Pro 11:30, NKJV).

Story of Ralph. You don't need to be a theologian to win souls. I can remember as a new believer of a couple of months, I had a deep burden for my best friend, Ralphie John. He was my back yard neighbor. His dad would work nights, and he would shout from his backyard deck to my backyard deck, "Hey Matt the Rat!" Ha! I've been called worse! But Ralph Sr. was a very big and loving man. One day his son, Ralph Jr. called me after I was saved and told me his dad had Leukemia. He was going to die.

I prayed day and night for his soul, but I was never able to visit him. When I found out he died, I didn't know what I would tell Ralph Jr. where his dad was in eternity if he had asked. I would have to tell him I didn't know. Had I had the opportunity I would have told his dad. At the funeral, Ralph Jr. introduced me to his Uncle Lee. I listened as Uncle Lee told me how he had given the gospel to Ralph Sr. in the last three months of his life. I jumped and shouted like a Pentecostal!

Our God is mighty to save! We just need to open our mouths. "How then will they call on him in whom they have not believed? And how are they to believe in him of whom they have never heard? And how are they to hear without someone preaching?" (Rom 10:14).

Peter is about to tell us that we need to be ready to give an answer for Christ, no matter what the cost. And there is always a cost. As we go into all the world and preach the gospel, it is not always going to be well received. Often we will suffer for the gospel's sake. Remember Peter's theme of this entire book is that we are not at home here in this world. We are "elect exiles" (1:1). We are "called" out of "darkness" to shine and reflect his "marvelous light" (2:9). If you are salt and light to this world, you need to be ready to suffer.

BE READY TO SUFFER (3:13-14)

1 Peter 3:13 | Now who is there to harm you if you are zealous for what is good?

The argument of this verse is simply this: you are suffering now because of your faith in Christ, but one day in the future [at Judgment Day] you will be blessed. No persecution can steal your ultimate blessing in Christ.

Our Foe in Suffering

What is very apparent is that Peter assumes that his Christian hearers are going to be persecuted for righteousness' sake. No foe should ever be feared, since God is in total control. God will use all suffering for the Christian to conform him to Christ. When holiness takes hold of your life, and the Spirit begins to anoint you, the world will begin to hate you. Jesus says, don't be surprised if the world hates you, "If the world hates you, know that it has hated me before it hated you" (Jn 15:18). This was a major theme in Jesus' teaching. There will always be persecution of believers.

Peter wasn't saying believers won't suffer. He was saying no eternal harm will come to any believer. Indeed suffering stalks the believer until this present evil age comes to an end.[119] Paul said, "Indeed, all who desire to live a godly life in Christ Jesus will be persecuted" (2 Tim 3:12). Of course, the world is going to be offended by the Christian's life. Christians are salt and light. The life of the Christian ought to be one that at times feels like a bright flashlight has been shined into the face of a sleeping person.

The joy we have (based on our union with Christ) is in stark contrast to the roller coaster happiness that jerks the world back and forth.

---

[119] Thomas R. Schreiner, *1, 2 Peter, Jude*, vol. 37, The New American Commentary (Nashville: Broadman & Holman Publishers, 2003), 170.

Peter's point is that the world is going to stand against you. It's offensive for the world to hear that they are in sin and need a Savior.

Our Focus in Suffering

1 Peter 3:13 | Now who is there to harm you if you are zealous for what is good?

Peter begins with this question, 1 Peter 3:13, "Now who is there to harm you if you are zealous for what is good?" He's saying, no one can ultimately harm you or condemn you. There is no reason for you to fear ultimate harm if you "zealous" in pursuit of "what is good" (3:13). Live out the Christian life. Be zealous and ardent for life in the Spirit. There's nothing better than surrender to the Spirit. Let the Spirit settle your soul about these things.

So because "there is no condemnation for those in Christ" (Rom 8:1) here's the thing: Don't fear. Don't be troubled. "Have no fear of them, nor be troubled" (3:14b). You have no need to fear because no real harm can ultimately be done to you. You are safe in Christ. "Now who is there to harm you if you are zealous for what is good?" (3;13). Peter's is quoting Isaiah 50:9, "It is the Sovereign LORD who helps me. Who will condemn me?" "Who is there to harm or ultimately damn my soul" is the idea. If you are zealous for what is good, zealous for God, a true believer, then who can ultimately harm you? No one has the power to ultimately damn you. You are forgiven in Christ. Any other suffering is superficial.

You are going to suffer, but no eternal harm will touch you. Paul said, "For I consider that the sufferings of this present time are not worth comparing with the glory that is to be revealed to us" (Rom 8:18). Paul goes on to say (Rom 8:31), "What then shall we say to these things? If God is for us, who can be against us?..." Nothing can separate us from the love of Christ (8:35). Paul concludes, "In all these things we are more than conquerors through him who loved us" (8:37).

Peter is saying, *"You are immortal until God is finished with you."* No one can hurt you if you truly have the zeal of the Spirit in you, unless they have God's permission. Peter goes on to explain that "But even if you should suffer for righteousness' sake, you will be blessed. Have no fear of them, nor be troubled" (3:14).

Our Blessing in Suffering

1 Peter 3:14a | But even if you should suffer for righteousness' sake, you will be blessed.

The idea is that you will, in the future, when Jesus comes, be blessed beyond measure. He's not saying you are going to get out of persecution. He's saying you shouldn't fear persecution. Even if you suffer in this life, don't be disturbed! Jesus wins in the end.

He was almost certainly drawing on the Jesus tradition here, for Jesus himself taught in Matthew 5:10–12 (*cf* Lk 6:22–23) that those who suffer are blessed because of the eschatological reward they will receive.[120] When you are persecuted you are to "rejoice and be glad, for your reward is great in heaven" (Mt 5:12).

None can do real harm to the Lord's people; they may persecute them, but he will make all things work together for their good.[121] You are blessed no matter what, so rejoice. Replace any fear of living in total surrender to God with zeal and joy. Even if all of hell's minions descend on you like they did with Job, God is going to work it out for good in the end. Never allow yourself to despair.

Rejoice and be zealous instead of being filled with fear. Indeed, even present suffering is not a sign of punishment but of God's blessing both now and especially in the future, in the day when he rewards his people with eternal life.[122]

Our Peace in Suffering

1 Peter 3:14b | Have no fear of them, nor be troubled.

Peter's conclusion is: "Have no fear of them, nor be troubled" (3:14). Don't be controlled by fear. Yes, we all have fear. It can cripple us at times. But don't be controlled or troubled by any persecution. Be zealous for Christ. You will "suffer for righteousness" here on earth, but at the end of the world, you will be blessed. So don't fear anyone who would stand against you because of Christ. Yet it's not enough to be

---

[120] Leonhard Goppelt. Trans, John E. Alsup and Ferdinand Hahn. *A Commentary on 1 Peter* (Grand Rapids, MI: Wm. B. Eerdmans Publishing Co, 1993), 241.
[121] Spence-Jones, *1 Peter*, 131.
[122] Schreiner. *1 Peter*, 171.

willing and ready to suffer. You need to be ready to speak the Gospel to the world around you.

BE READY TO SPEAK (3:15-18)

God has commanded us to give an answer with the right attitude to all who have a question about our faith.

> **1 Peter 3:15** | But in your hearts honor Christ the Lord as holy, always being prepared to make a defense to anyone who asks you for a reason for the hope that is in you; yet do it with gentleness and respect.

Have a Right Heart

We ought not to be afraid of giving the gospel to people. But this activity can be intimidating. How do we get the right heart attitude? The alternative to fear is to focus attention on someone else.[123] The proper way to prepare to share the gospel is to magnify and honor Christ as holy.

> **1 Peter 3:15a** | But in your hearts honor Christ the Lord as holy.

Anyone who meets the living God will have a holy dread. Peter is quoting Isaiah 8:13, "But the LORD of hosts, him you shall regard as holy; let him be your fear, and let him be your dread." Literally 1 Peter 3:15a reads, "Honor the Lord (YHWH) as holy, namely Christ." Treat Christ as the almighty, holy God that he is, set apart from all else as the covenant God of his people. Let him be your dread. This says something important. Peter believed in the deity of Christ. He's using Greek, but he's calling Jesus YHWH, Jehovah.[124] In other words, regard Christ as almighty God, the God revealed to Isaiah, where the angels cried out, "Holy, holy, holy" (Isa 6:1-3). Holy evangelistic zeal comes from a heart and life surrendered to Christ as holy Lord and God of your life. Do you want to honor him? Be done with lesser things. Be done with anything questionable. Be done with halfhearted prayers or a totally dead prayer life. You have to sanctify Christ in your heart as holy.

---

[123] Grudem, *1 Peter*, 160.

[124] Schreiner, 1 Peter, 173, says, "The move from Yahweh to Christ is common in the New Testament, reflecting the conviction that Jesus the Messiah deserves the same honor as Yahweh" because he is Yahweh.

We surrender to Christ as holy, set apart and exalted above all. Where does this take place? "In your heart." The heart is the origin of human behavior (*cf* 1:22; 3:4), and from it flows everything people do. "Guard your heart above all else, for it determines the course of your life" (Pro 4:23, NLT). God will use a clean vessel to pour out his Spirit. Are you a clean vessel? God can use a donkey, but he's not going to use a dirty vessel.

Have a Ready Answer

First-century Christians were willing and able to defend the claim that Jesus is God in human flesh who died for sinful man (Jn 14:6). After all, the truth is not clearly taught unless whatever contradicts it or whatever error stands over against it is refuted. Jude exhorted his fellow believers "to contend earnestly for the faith which was once for all delivered unto the saints" (Jude 3). Peter made it a moral imperative to be prepared to give a reasoned answer in defense of the Christian message.

> **1 Peter 3:15b** | Always being prepared to make a defense to anyone who asks you for a reason for the hope that is in you.

A normal Christian life that holds Christ as Lord will provoke questions. The ESV says, "make a defense." The word is *apologia*. We get our apologetics or debate ministries from this verse. But this is really not a verse for professional Bible debaters only. It's for every Christian. It means to give an answer often in a private setting. To make a defense of the faith. We need to prepare for this by knowing the Lord and understanding the Scriptures. Yet, no one has to be a scholar to give a defense.

When I was sixteen and a brand-new believer, I worked at Ponderosa Steakhouse in Oak Forest, Illinois. I was the grill cook. Sometimes I had a fry cook. And that little kitchen was like a little church house to me. I was so new in the faith I didn't know much of the Bible, but I knew the Roman's road to salvation. And I would "give an answer of the hope that was in me." I would tell them of Christ. I'd get one 30-minute break a day. That was my soul-winning time. My booth was like the Ponderosa Counseling booth. Remember I know almost nothing about the Bible, but I know Christ. I know a handful of verses in Romans. I would open my Bible and just start reading and almost always one or two or three people would give me an audience. I sincerely shared our need of Christ and the "hope" that was in me with gentleness and reverence.

People are going to ask us the "reason" behind our faith. Why believe in Christ? Why give your whole life to him? It doesn't make sense to the lost person. Their eyes are blinded. The word "reason" is "logos." Lost people cannot understand the logic behind the gospel without divine help. "The natural [*unregenerate*] person does not accept the things of the Spirit of God, for they are folly to him, and he is not able to understand them because they are spiritually discerned" (2 Cor 2:14). The world asks, "What's the reason, the logic behind your hope in Christ?" The "reason for the hope" that is within us is that without the lordship of Christ, there could be no intelligible reason given by the unbeliever for anything at all. God has made foolish the wisdom of this world (*cf* 1 Cor 1:20). The Bible says very pointedly and powerfully, "Professing themselves to be wise, they become fools" (Rom 1:22).[125]

Have a Radical Evangelism

1 Peter 3:15c | Make a defense to anyone who asks you for a reason for the hope that is in you

We can't just stay comfortable. We have to be radical. The people of this world are in a state of foolishness. The unbeliever proclaims a pseudo-wisdom which is in reality a destructive hatred of knowledge. Nothing can be ultimately known in a meaningful way without first inviting God into our awareness and consciousness. Man's foolishness and folly comes from his blindness to the living God. This blindness spans the entire human race, so Peter's plea that Christians be prepared to make a defense of Jesus' claims and work on the cross to "anyone" is vital. There is no one who the Christian is not responsible to give an answer to. Peter's implication is that we as Christians are called to reach anyone and everyone.

Jesus Said "Go!" Who should we talk to? "Always being prepared to make a defense to *anyone* who asks you" (3:15). The stance of Christians toward unbelievers must never be merely passive or neutral. We can't just be focused on our own lives and forget the world lost in darkness. It's not an option for a Christian. We need to be ready to answer

---

[125] Greg Bahnsen, *Always Ready: Directions for Defending the Faith* (Nacogdoches, TX: Covenant Media Press, 1996), 63.

anyone! Not every Christian will be a skilled apologist for the faith. It does mean that every believer should grasp the essentials of the faith and should have the ability to explain to others why Christ is Lord and Savior. Remember, the last command of our Lord Jesus is to "Go!" Teach and make disciples. Go to everyone! All creation. Jesus says, "Go into all the world and proclaim the gospel to the whole creation" (Mk 16:15). He said, "Go therefore and make disciples of all nations.... behold, I am with you always, to the end of the age" (Mt 28:18–20). Jesus said to those on the Emmaus Road, "Thus it is written, that the Christ should suffer and on the third day rise from the dead, and that repentance for the forgiveness of sins should be proclaimed in his name to all nations, beginning from Jerusalem.... Stay in the city until you are clothed with power from on high" (Lk 24:46–49). Again, our Lord said, "... As the Father has sent me, even so I am sending you" (Jn 20:21). He told his disciples, "You will receive power when the Holy Spirit has come upon you, and you will be my witnesses in Jerusalem and in all Judea and Samaria, and to the end of the earth" (Acts 1:8). The moment God saved you, he prepared you. He gave you his Holy Spirit. He gave you a heart to obey his command: "Go!" Be ready to give an answer to anyone who asks.

Have a Respectful Attitude

As we go, we evangelize with the message of Jesus Christ, but with what attitude should we answer the lost?

1 Peter 3:15d | Yet do it with gentleness and respect.

As we become better equipped to defend the faith, we find greater confidence and boldness to carry the message of the gospel to every dark place. No challenge shall intimidate the believer as he gently and respectfully closes the mouth of unbelief. "Do it with gentleness and respect." We ought to have "gentleness" toward the lost, and respect of literally "fear" toward God.

Toward the Lost

We approach God's people with a sweet gentleness and humility. We are to be gentle, patient, courteous, and unquarrelsome. We are to model the fruit of the Spirit, be salt and light to this dark world. I've heard Christians share the gospel in an angry, proud way. That does not befit the sweetness of the gospel message. We approach lost sinners with gentleness and respect, never trying to merely win or dominate the argument. We share the gospel like a skillful heart surgeon, not a butcher. We ought to have the sincerity and humility of a child.

Here is another thing about "gentleness." Sometimes when we are rejected for the gospel, we can take it personally and become defensive. Let our souls be gentle to the lost and submissive to our great God. Let us count it an honor if we indeed do suffer for Christ. We should never take persecution personally (cf Eph 6:11-12) but have a sincere and humble love for the lost regardless of whether they accept or reject our Lord.

Toward God

We are to evangelize the lost with "respect" or "reverence" toward God. That means we magnify the glory and greatness of God, and we should not be overcome by any fear of man in evangelism. People sometimes react negatively to the gospel. Let God be big and man be small in your heart. We need to remember that we are ambassadors, representatives of the Most High God. We must not be taken up with the fear of man. We need to magnify the Lord and see him as bigger than any rejection or persecution we may face by opening our mouths. In fearing God, we ought also show due respect and reverence for the people we are speaking to since they are made in God's image and are infinitely valuable as everlasting souls.

Have a Restful Conscience

1 Peter 3:16-17 | Having a good conscience, so that, when you are slandered, those who revile your good behavior in Christ may be put to shame. **17** For it is better to suffer for doing good, if that should be God's will, than for doing evil.

We must have a good conscience when we evangelize. We cannot trick our hearers into heaven. When Peter spoke of a "clear conscience," he's referring to the relationship of believers to God.[126] We live in the presence of God as Christians – his face shines upon us – so we cannot resort to anger, tricks, twisting or manipulation when we share the gospel. No one is going to get tricked into heaven. There is an integrity in

---

[126] Schreiner. *1 Peter*, 176.

the true Christian. He's not going to manipulate people. We must never do that.

For example, there are some Christians when they meet a Muslim, they will say "Allah" and the Trinity are the same. They are not the same. The one true and living God has revealed himself to us by his Son Jesus Christ. Christ is the exact nature and imprint of our loving Father. All other religions that see Christ as a mere man or creation are false. We cannot use syncretism to add to our pews. We must preach with a good conscience. We must at all costs preach the God revealed to us by divine revelation in the 66 books of the Christian Bible.

The Unrighteous' Shame is Eternal

1 Peter 3:16 | Having a good conscience, so that, when you are slandered, those who revile your good behavior in Christ may be put to shame.

If you share your faith, you will be shamed and slandered by the world. Now Peter says in 3:16, you need to be faithful to give the gospel even to those who are hostile and may slander Christians, remembering that "those who revile your good behavior in Christ may be put to shame" (3:16). Peter has been talking in 3:12 about the day when the "righteous" are rewarded, and "the face of the Lord is against those who do evil." This is judgment day, when those who do not trust in Christ will see how blessed all believers really have been.

Some unbelievers refuse to acknowledge the goodness of the lives of believers. On the last day, however, they will be put to shame by God himself and will be compelled to acknowledge that believers lived righteously.[127] On that final day, unbelievers will not wish they were in the dance club drunk out of their mind for just one more day. They will envy the followers of Christ and acknowledge that though they were not perfect, believers alone on the earth live the "good life." We live life the way God designed it!

The Righteous' Shame is Only Temporary

1 Peter 3:17 | For it is better to suffer for doing good, if that should be God's will, than for doing evil.

---

[127] Ibid.

We will be shamed in this world, but we must realize it is only temporary. When we are shamed and slandered for doing good, like spreading the gospel, then we should rejoice.

Christians ought never suffer the shame of a wrongdoer. The Christian will be shamed by the culture for doing God's will. For instance, we as Christians are to call sin what it is: sin. The culture is trying to make some sins like homosexuality and transgender confusion to be normal, and in the process, they are persecuting Christians for it. Christians who suffer for doing wrong greatly distract from the message of Christ. We need to stay accountable and encouraged in the local assembly so that we do not stray from Christ.

Have the Right Message

1 Peter 3:18 | Christ also suffered once for sins, the righteous for the unrighteous, that he might bring us to God, being put to death in the flesh but made alive in the spirit.

This verse gives one of the Bible's shortest, simplest, and richest summaries of the meaning of the cross of Jesus Christ.[128] We must have the right message and give people the reason of our hope – Christ redeems! We trust that as we give the "logos" or "reason" for Christ's death and resurrection (3:15), that God the Holy Spirit will open up a person's heart and mind. The logic behind the cross is that we are all wretched sinners, yet Christ loves us in our sin. He died for us, "the just for the unjust that he might bring us to God." In the giving of the gospel, the lost can be awakened from their slumber and be brought to new life in Christ.

Christ's Substitutional Death

1 Peter 3:18a | Christ also suffered once for sins, the righteous for the unrighteous, that he might bring us to God.

Verse 15 asks, what is the logic or the story behind the cross? What is the cross all about? Here we have it in verse 18. It explains penal substitution. Christ "once suffered for sins." It was a unique death. The "once" has the idea of unique. Peter up to this point is saying we all suffer and submit in many ways – as elect exiles in a fallen world, but

---

[128] Walls, *I & II Peter, I, II & III John, Jude*, 55.

Christ's suffering is unique. His death is substitutionary – "the righteous for the unrighteous that he might bring us to God." Jesus died to reach across the gulf between God and humanity. Taking our hand, he leads us across the territory of the enemy into the presence of God the Father. Jesus Christ opens the way and introduces us to God the Father. By removing sin as the cause of our separation from God, Jesus Christ provides access to God and makes us acceptable in his sight.[129]

People often say they are saved, and they don't know the gospel. They don't have a clear trust in the blood of Jesus. They don't understand his death and resurrection. Listen, Jesus died vicariously for us. That means, "in my place." I should receive hell, but he got hell for me. Anyone who trusts in him is completely forgiven. No sins. No condemnation.

Hell came to Calvary on the day Jesus died. He experienced all the dimensions of hell on the cross. The crucifixion of Jesus lasted for six agonizing hours. The trial and scourging of Jesus took place early in the day, and he was crucified at 9 o'clock in the morning. Many things happened during the next three hours. The crowd taunted him. Religious leaders mocked his claims. Thieves who were crucified beside him hurled abuse. Then, at midday, God stepped in. Darkness covered the whole land. This was not an eclipse. Jesus was crucified at Passover when there was a full moon, and besides, an eclipse does not last for three hours. The darkness at Calvary could only be explained by a direct intervention of God.

Jesus' suffering during these three awful hours of darkness is indescribable. Peter has already told us that Jesus "bore our sins in his body on the tree" (2:24). That is what was happening in the darkness. He carried the weight of the accumulated guilt and shame of the world. The wrath of God was poured out on him. He was cut off from the comfort and love of God the Father. Throughout this suffering he was in a conscious agony of body and soul, not only because of the physical pain, but the spiritual retribution he was receiving on our behalf. That is hell, and Jesus tasted every dimension of its pain on the cross. Jesus' descent into hell was not a disembodied visit for preaching between his death and resurrection. It was the heart of his suffering as he bore the

---

[129] Ibid., 56.

penalty of your sin on the cross. He entered hell so that you should never know what hell is like. Take a moment to pause and worship.

Christ's Glorious Resurrection

1 Peter 3:18b | Being put to death in the flesh but made alive in the spirit.

Jesus didn't stay dead. He was physically died, but through the Spirit of God, his physical body was made alive. "Made alive in the spirit" most naturally refers to his resurrection in which he rises to life in a new plane.[130] We are to give an answer for Jesus' physical, bodily resurrection from the grave.

BE READY TO CELEBRATE (3:19-22)

In 1 Peter 3:19ff, Peter now gives an example of someone who gave an answer in his day. He speaks of Noah. Now these verses may seem to be confusing at first, but if you take them in a simple way, they are deeply encouraging. Peter wants us to see that whenever we give a defense and an answer for our hope, Christ within us, the victory is already guaranteed. He gives us three examples of victory here.

Victory at Christ's Resurrection

1 Peter 3:19-20 | In which he went and proclaimed to the spirits in prison, **20** because they formerly did not obey, when God's patience waited in the days of Noah, while the ark was being prepared, in which a few, that is, eight persons, were brought safely through water.

Peter brings us to a day when it seemed impossible to defend the faith – in the days of Noah when the entire earth perished in their sins except eight people. And one of the first things Jesus did after his victorious death, it says is he "proclaimed [his victory] to the spirits in the days of Noah." Who were these spirits? Most theologians believe that these are fallen angels. The term "spirits" almost always refers to angelic beings.[131] Jude 1:6 tells us a little more about these fallen angelic

---

[130] Allen Black and Mark C. Black, *1 & 2 Peter*, The College Press NIV Commentary (Joplin, MO: College Press Pub., 1998), 1 Pe 3:18.

[131] *Cf* Mt 8:16; 10:1; 12:15; Mk 1:27; 3:11; 5:13; 6:7; Lk 4:36; 6:18; 7:21; 8:2; 10:20; 11:26; Acts 5:16; 8:7; 19:12–13; 1 Tim 4:1; Heb 1:14; 12:9; 1 Jn 4:1; Rev 16:13–14; cf. Heb 1:7.

beings. "And the angels who did not stay within their own position of authority, but left their proper dwelling, he has kept in eternal chains under gloomy darkness until the judgment of the great day" (Jude 1:6).

So get this point Peter is making. The fallen angels, even though they were chained, must have felt victorious in Noah's day. *"Ha! We've deceived the whole world,"* they must have said. But then at the cross, it seemed they had a greater victory and would finally go free. Some of these fallen demonic creatures that God chained in darkness must have thought they defeated the Son of God at the cross. But after Jesus' death on the cross "he went and proclaimed to the spirits in prison" –The hordes of hell thought they had won! I can just hear them. *"We killed the Son of God! The earth is now ours. We will soon be released. What? Who is this? The victorious Son of God?!!"* Jesus preached to the demons in hell announcing his victory. Death is dead. Hell is defeated. Love has won!

Victory in Noah's Day

What then was happening? Angels are supposed to be God's "ministering spirits" – but those chained in the darkness of the underworld were not ministering spirits. They were not helping the lost to come to Christ. They were chained there because "they formerly did not obey." I'm not completely sure what that means, but possibly in the days of Noah, God further restricted a group of fallen angels to chains or confinement in Hades.

Peter says, it was during this time that God has so much patience with the sinners of Noah's Day. Peter says: "God's patience waited in the days of Noah" (3:20). At this time Noah becomes "a herald of righteousness" (2 Pet 2:5, 9). God could have brought immediate judgment. But day after day for many decades, maybe up to a hundred years, Noah's family preached the truth and built the ark. Hebrews 11:7, "By faith Noah, being warned by God concerning events as yet unseen, in reverent fear constructed an ark for the saving of his household. By this he condemned the world and became an heir of the righteousness that comes by faith." Noah not only built the ark, but it seems he also preached.

Noah was not held back from giving an answer in his day. No one outside of his own family had faith enough to enter the ark. It may be the same in your experience. Be ready to see God work in small but mighty ways. He worked in Noah to save his own family. He'll work through you. Don't of course be discouraged by the day of small things. Only eight were saved on the ark.

Of all the characters in human history, God chose Noah as the model for our ministry. That is significant. Noah's generation was the most wicked in all of human history. Corruption and violence had multiplied, and God sent the Flood on them because He saw that the thoughts of that generation were "only evil all the time" (Gen 6:5). If you have found that some of the people around you are hard to reach with the gospel, then spare a thought for Noah. God called him to speak to the most resistant people who have ever lived (2 Pet 2:5).

Noah didn't see great results from his preaching. In fact, at the end of his entire life of ministry, only eight people were saved. That should teach us to be cautious about how we measure results. The important thing about Noah's ministry was that Christ spoke through him. This did not mean that vast crowds of people repented and believed. But they did hear the voice of Jesus. Ministry among highly resistant people isn't easy. What matters is not the number of people you lead to Christ, but your faithfulness to Christ in the place where He has set you. And if he has set you in a tough place, don't get discouraged by small results.[132]

Victory in Our Day

Through faith in Christ, we can have the victory that overcomes the world. The world wants answers, but nothing is more powerful than standing up for Christ publicly in baptism and declaring your faith in him.

> **1 Peter 3:21** | Baptism, which corresponds to this [*Noah's ark*], now saves you, not as a removal of dirt from the body but as an appeal to God for a good conscience, through the resurrection of Jesus Christ.

Noah's ark is a wonderful picture of Jesus Christ. God told Noah to enter the ark. It must have taken an act of faith for him to do this. The ark was on dry ground, and there was no sign of rain in the sky! But Noah believed God's promise and acted on it. He gathered his family and got into the ark. Then God closed the door, and the judgment he

---

[132] Colin S. Smith. *10 Keys to Unlock the Christian Life* (Chicago: Moody Publishers, 2010), 80.

had spoken about began. Rain fell from the heavens, and springs of water rose from the earth. The ark rose, carrying Noah and his family safely through the judgment and into a new world.

Here Peter says, you can be saved by getting into the true ark, Jesus. He refers to baptism. Not water baptism, but baptism into Christ. In Christ we die to our old life. Our old life is judged with him. But we come out of the water unscathed like Noah and his family. It's not water baptism we need but Spirit baptism – regeneration. This is what produces a "good conscience." Baptism is the sign of a person identifying fully with Jesus, and it is being "in Christ" that saves you.

Christ Victorious Over All!

1 Peter 3:22 | Jesus Christ, who has gone into heaven and is at the right hand of God, with angels, authorities, and powers having been subjected to him.

Christ is exalted in his ascension. The primary significance of Jesus' ascension to the right hand of God the Father is that his sacrifice for sin and sinners is accepted. No hurt or harm can come to the anyone who puts their trust in Jesus. Sin is defeated. Death is dead. The devil is bound and soon to be cast into the bottomless pit.

Peter makes the point that Satan and the demonic host are completely defeated. All the fallen angels and demonic authorities and powers are now subject to Christ. There is nothing holding back Christ from saving his people from their sin. So go proclaim the gospel. God give an answer for how God saved you. We are all called to do this. Jesus is exalted as Victor over all creation! Go preach the gospel to every creature.

Conclusion

What can we say to all this? In the end, we may suffer for our faith. We will speak for our faith. But we will most assuredly celebrate the amazing victory of our faith in Jesus. It's God who saves. It's Christ who can give eternal life to your loved ones and neighbors. Whether he saves only eight people, or eight hundred thousand people, salvation is of the Lord. Come to Jesus! If you are here without Christ, he is mighty to save. The day may be hard like Noah's day, but Jesus can easily save you. Christian, tell the world that Jesus saves! Be ready to give an answer for Jesus!

19 | 1 PETER 4:1-11
A SPIRITUALLY GIFTED LIFE

As each has received a gift, use it to serve one another, as good stewards of God's varied grace: whoever speaks, as one who speaks oracles of God; whoever serves, as one who serves by the strength that God supplies—in order that in everything God may be glorified through Jesus Christ. To him belong glory and dominion forever and ever. Amen.

1 PETER 4:10-11

Peter, the apostle to the Jews is writing from Rome. He's about to be imprisoned. The first great Gentile persecution of the church is on its way. Rome is burning as Peter writes this. The Roman emperor Nero is going to blame Christians.

Peter is going to tell us in 1 Peter 4 all about self-denial. Peter naturally was a man who did not deny self, but something powerful happened to him at Pentecost, and he lived the rest of his life empty of self and full of God. God wants to give us a life with his fullness, but that means we need be empty of self. Tradition tells us Peter and Paul preached together in Rome before they were put to death by Nero. Nero became emperor of Rome in 54 A.D. at age 16. He reigned until he was 30, death by suicide. He was a maniac of a young man. Things were fairly peaceful for Christians for the first ten years of Nero's reign, but he desperately wanted to tear down Rome and rebuild it in his name, it is said he had it burned down and then blamed it on the Christians. Christians as a result suffered great persecution. Peter's letters were completed after the fire of Rome which occurred in 64 A.D. The fire destroyed more than 70% of the city. As a consequence of this tragedy, and the widespread belief in Nero's complicity, the emperor became the brunt of intense criticism. Tacitus, a Roman historian tells us Christians were torn to death by dogs, others were crucified, still others were set on fire to illuminate the night. Nero would throw the children of Christians in bags with vipers. He would ride around the arena dressed as a charioteer in his chariot with Christians waiting in the middle of the arena for the lions to be released, when they would be torn to pieces.[133]

According to Josephus, the Jewish historian of the time, Peter was arrested two years after Nero's fire in September of the year 66 A.D. and rotted in the Mamertine prison for nine months. The Mamertine prison was a cruel place, where Peter was chained to the wall in shackles. He wasn't alone. He likely was imprisoned with the apostle Paul who was beheaded in January of 67 A.D.. In June of 67 A.D. Peter faces his own death.

Learning Self-Denial

Peter writes the epistles of 1 and 2 Peter in the midst of all this persecution. He likely wrote 1 Peter just before the persecution began, but suffering is clearly on the horizon. Rome is burning. Upheaval is beginning. There is a disdain for Christians. Peter in his chapter 4 teaches us the importance of self-denial and the crucified life. The whole point he makes in 1 Peter 4 is this: the crucified life is the abundant life. Do you believe that?

Self-denial became a way of life for the apostle so that at his death he asked to be crucified upside down because he was not worthy to die like his Lord. He addresses this idea of self-denial powerfully in our text in 1 Peter 4, that we will read in a moment. Yet Peter was not always a proponent of self-denial. When our Lord at Caesarea Philippi explained to Peter and the other disciples how he would "go to Jerusalem and suffer many things... and be killed, and on the third day be raised" (Mt 16:21), what did Peter do? He rebuked the Lord. That's what the Bible says. He rebuked deity! "Peter took him aside and began to rebuke him,

---

[133] Tacitus. *Annals* (XV.44).

saying, 'Far be it from you, Lord! This shall never happen to you'" (Mt 16:22). What did our Lord say to Peter? "Get behind me, Satan! You are a hindrance to me. For you are not setting your mind on the things of God, but on the things of man" (Mt 16:23).

Do you hear what Jesus says to Peter? He's got a problem "setting his mind on things of God." He's thinking in a worldly, selfish way. Jesus is thinking selflessly. Peter had to learn this lesson when our Lord was arrested in the Garden of Gethsemane. He did not want to deny self. This is not a natural thing for Peter or for anybody. Self-denial is the result of a revelation of the Holy Spirit. So Peter at Gethsemane thinks he's going to save the Savior. Think about that. He unsheathes his sword and cuts off the ear of Malchus the servant of the high priest.

And remember while Jesus was being mocked and beaten by the scribes and priests at the high priest's house, Peter was in the courtyard denying Jesus three times. He did not want to deny self, so he denied Jesus. I could give several more examples, Peter did not naturally gravitate toward self-denial. None of us do. Something happened to Peter.

Something profound happened to Peter. The Spirit of God changed Peter dramatically at Pentecost. Remember he had given up, but the Lord restored him. For the rest of his life, he is not looking to self. He's not filled with self anymore. He's filled with God. He's filled with the Spirit of Christ. Look at the boldness. He's thinking about others. This fullness of God is what should characterize every Christian. So Peter when he writes his first epistle, in chapter 4, he gives us the secret to self-denial.

> **1 Peter 4:1-11** | Since therefore Christ suffered in the flesh, arm yourselves with the same way of thinking, for whoever has suffered in the flesh has ceased from sin, **2** so as to live for the rest of the time in the flesh no longer for human passions but for the will of God. **3** For the time that is past suffices for doing what the Gentiles want to do, living in sensuality, passions, drunkenness, orgies, drinking parties, and lawless idolatry. **4** With respect to this they are surprised when you do not join them in the same flood of debauchery, and they malign you; **5** but they will give account to him who is ready to judge the living and the dead. **6** For this is why the gospel was preached even to those who are dead, that though judged in the flesh the way people are, they might live in the spirit the way God does. **7** The end of all things is at hand; therefore be self-controlled and sober-minded for the sake of

> your prayers. **⁸** Above all, keep loving one another earnestly, since love covers a multitude of sins. **⁹** Show hospitality to one another without grumbling. **¹⁰** As each has received a gift, use it to serve one another, as good stewards of God's varied grace: **¹¹** whoever speaks, as one who speaks oracles of God; whoever serves, as one who serves by the strength that God supplies—in order that in everything God may be glorified through Jesus Christ. To him belong glory and dominion forever and ever. Amen.

Peter says arm yourself with a crucifixion mindset, and you'll be done with sin. I want that. I need that. I need to be "crucified with Christ" so that I can have the fullness of God. That's not the normal response for most of humanity. Often suffering makes people bitter and hardened. But it's different for a Christian. A Christian is armed with a weapon Peter says. We are able to deny ourselves because of union with Christ. We are dead to the delights of the world when our mind is on Christ. The key thought in this passage is simple: self-denial is the pathway to fullness in God. Let me put it another way. Denying self is a small sacrifice for a full satisfying life of joy and usefulness for God. This is Peter's challenge to us. You can never be truly happy until you deny yourself and follow Christ. We see the Christian life in three ways in this passage: It's a crucified life, an abundant life, and a connected life.

WE LIVE A CRUCIFIED LIFE (4:1-6)

> **1 Peter 4:1-2** | Since therefore Christ suffered in the flesh, arm yourselves with the same way of thinking, for whoever has suffered in the flesh has ceased from sin, **²** so as to live for the rest of the time in the flesh no longer for human passions but for the will of God.

Definition of Self-Denial

Self-denial is "denying the self-life of sin by the power of the Spirit." The purpose of self-denial is that we may live the abundant life of the Spirit. That's why Peter says, if you are living the crucified life as Christ did, you have ceased from sin. You "no longer" live "for human passions, but for the will of God." This full life of joy and peace is the only life worth living. Hallelujah! The self-life brings misery. The Christ-life brings fullness of joy. It's a life worth living.

I bet if we had a testimony time right now, we could all confess the emptiness of the self-life. It's just not worth it. Sometimes it's the emptiness of this world's entertainment. It does not satisfy. Sometimes it's the ugliness of anger and getting our own way. Sometimes it's just forgetting God. Saints, that's no way to live! I want to live a life that has "ceased from sin." Of course, Peter doesn't mean sinless perfection. That's impossible while we are on this earth. Jesus says, "Whoever wants to be my disciple must deny himself and take up his cross daily and follow me" (Lk 9:23). That's what Peter is talking about here. As Christ suffered in the flesh (crucifixion) so we are to live the crucified life.

The Example of Jesus (4:1-2)

1 Peter 4:1a | Since therefore Christ suffered in the flesh, arm yourselves with the same way of thinking.

Wow, Peter looks at this as one of the greatest weapons of the Christian life: a person's mind. Paul says the same thing: "Be renewed in the spirit of your minds" (*cf* Eph 4:22-23).

Arm Yourself with Christ's Thinking

In 1 Peter 4, this word "arm yourself" is used in the NT to refer to "weapons" of spiritual warfare. "For the weapons of our warfare are not of the flesh but have divine power to destroy strongholds" (2 Cor 10:4). The word picture of the Christian as a soldier is common in the New Testament which constantly tells us we are soldiers in a spiritual battle. Commentator Kenneth Wuest writes,

> This word is used of a heavy-armed foot soldier who carried a pike and a large shield ... The Christian needs the heaviest armor he can get, to withstand the attacks of the enemy of his soul.[134]

Peter says to "arm yourself with the same thinking" as Christ. Peter's point is clear. Christ has not sent us into the world as vacationers on a self-guided tour of the playgrounds of this world, but as soldiers on a tour of duty in a battlefield. We are not called to kick back, relax, take in the scenery. We are in a fierce conflict on foreign soil. We need to arm ourselves with spiritual armor to withstand the temptations of

---

[134] Kenneth Wuest, *Wuest's Word Studies from the Greek New Testament for the English Reader* (Grand Rapids: Eerdmans, 1973), 2:110.

this world (*cf* Eph 6:10-18).¹³⁵ We are told in may places that this life is not a vacation, but a war. "Put on the whole armor of God, that you may be able to stand against the schemes of the devil" (Eph 6:11). Paul says, "No soldier gets entangled in civilian pursuits, since his aim is to please the one who enlisted him" (2 Tim 2:4). We need to die to the pursuits of this life. Our only ambition is Christ and him crucified. Paul said it this way: "I am crucified with Christ: nevertheless I live; yet not I, but Christ lives in me: and the life which I now live in the flesh I live by the faith of the Son of God, who loved me, and gave himself for me" (Gal 2:20). That's the life I want to live: the crucified life.

Arm Yourself with Christ's Freedom

1 Peter 4:1b | For whoever has suffered in the flesh has ceased from sin.

Freedom in Christ is a major way to protect yourself from sin. When a Christian suffers for doing God's will, he or she demonstrates that they have ceased from or are done with living in violation of God's will and are ready to do God's will even if it entails suffering.¹³⁶ The New Living Translation provides a useful paraphrase: "For if you are willing to suffer for Christ, you have decided to stop sinning." Jesus taught us that sin is slavery (Jn 8:34). We are no longer slaves to sin, but slaves to righteousness, where there is freedom (Rom 6:20-22). One key to this freedom is in Romans 6:14, "Sin will have no dominion over you, since you are not under law but under grace." It's the grace that we walk in during our suffering that keeps us strong to resist sin. No one ever stayed away from sin by "white-knuckling" it in the power of the flesh. Legalism never helped anyone resist sin. The grace of God's love is what satisfied us during suffering, so that we have no need to turn to sin, though we may at times be severely tempted through suffering. Plenty of people who suffer in the flesh get worse in their sins. But those who die to self as Christ died cease from sinning. Paul says, "I die daily" (1 Cor 15:31). Jesus says, "Whoever wants to be my disciple must deny himself and take up his cross daily and follow me" (Lk 9:23).

---

¹³⁵ Swindoll, *Insights on James and 1 & 2 Peter*, 212.
¹³⁶ A. Black, *1 & 2 Peter*, 1 Pe 4:1.

Arm Yourself with Christ's Focus

Focusing on the Father's will is another important way to protect yourself from sin. Peter says arm yourself with the Savior's way of thinking. All of Jesus' life he lived not for himself, but for his Father's will. Focusing on the Father's will gives us the power to suffer and deny self.

> **1 Peter 4:2** | So as to live for the rest of the time in the flesh no longer for human passions but for the will of God.

We don't live for human passions which always disappoints, but for the will of God, which always gives joy and satisfaction. The crucified life of self-denial, ironically, gives us the good life, the full life. If you deny yourself of your worldly passions, you will have a heart full for God and others. It's the only way to live. The Savior lived not "for human passions, but for the will of God." A focus on God's will is essential for a holy walk. Jesus armed himself with the purpose to do the will of the Father. Jesus said, "My food is to do the will of him who sent me and to accomplish his work" (Jn 4:34). Arm yourself with that thinking, that purpose for living.

Peter knew the Lord well. The Lord often stayed with Peter in his home in Capernaum. Jesus healed Peter's mother-in-law of a deathly fever there. One thing you do in a Jewish home is you always feed the guests. Jesus comes to Peter's home and there are no matzo balls! All he sees is a lady on a shelf in a ten-by-ten-foot room. I saw that room, part of several rooms in Peter's home. Jesus heals this woman and It's says immediately after she was healed, "she began to serve them." They had a great meal afterward! Matzo bread and matzo balls! In Capernaum where Peter lives, there is a synagogue 150 yards from his home. You can go there today. The foundation dates to the time of Peter. Mark 1 says Jesus was teaching in this very synagogue in Capernaum on the Sabbath when a demonic spirit interrupted him, and he healed the man. By nighttime, multitudes of people had been brought to Jesus. It says, "The whole city was gathered together" to Peter's door (Mk 1:33). So, Jesus, likely utterly exhausted, goes out early in the morning to a desolate place to meet with his Father. "And rising very early in the morning, while it was still dark, he departed and went out to a desolate place, and there he prayed" (Mk 1:35).

Our Lord lived a life of self-denial. It began everyday meeting with his Father. That's what God wants for us. He wants a life of fullness of God, which means we need be empty of self. How about you? Is your life full of self or full of God? There are just two choices on the shelf, serving God or serving self.

The Example of Your Past Life (4:3-5)

So we saw the example of Jesus. He lived a life wholly devoted to God, the crucified life. And the crucified life is the full life. We need to deny the emptiness of self so that we can have the fullness of God. You experienced this when you made an exodus from your past life. You used to live a life of emptiness and excess.

Self-denial is the mark that the Spirit of God dwells within you. If you have no power over sin, then God is not dwelling in you. This is a mark of conversion. If you love the world, the Bible tells us that you don't know the Father. "Do not love the world or the things in the world. If anyone loves the world, the love of the Father is not in him. 16 For all that is in the world—the lust of the flesh and the lust of the eyes and pride of life—is not from the Father but is from the world" (1 Jn 2:15-16).

Once Crazy for the World

> **1 Peter 4:3** | For the time that is past suffices for doing what the Gentiles want to do, living in sensuality, passions, drunkenness, orgies, drinking parties, and lawless idolatry.

Before our spiritual birthday in Christ, many of us lived out our former way of life—"sensuality, passions, drunkenness, orgies, drinking parties, and lawless idolatry" (4:3). We were crazy for all the world had to offer. Peter's list isn't exhaustive, but it paints an ugly picture of many believers' "B.C." years. When we consider that most people in the world still live in this "B.C." period, it shouldn't surprise us that they expect everybody to speak their foul language, follow their distorted mind-set and customs, and uphold their corrupt cultural values. When we don't conform, they notice.[137] When you are born again, you get a whole new way of living. You lose your friends and sometimes your family. But you have a whole new forever family.

---

[137] Swindoll, *Insights on James and 1 & 2 Peter*, 213.

Now Crazy for Jesus

1 Peter 4:4 | With respect to this they are surprised when you do not join them in the same flood of debauchery, and they malign you.

There is a radical change when we come to know Jesus. It's so radical that our friends now malign us. They think we are crazy. They can't understand. Your old friends, Peter says, are "surprised" at your new life, and they "malign you" (4:4). They think you are crazy. There's not only a war of wills among your family and friends, now there's a war of sanity. They often don't think you are just "different," they think you are "crazy." It says, "They are surprised ..." It's a word that's really quite a strong word. They will consider you absolutely bizarre, bonkers, out of your mind. As a result, you're going to have lots of abuse heaped on you. 1 Corinthians 2:14 says it all, "But the natural person does not receive the things of the Spirit of God: for they are foolishness to him: neither can he know them, because they are spiritually discerned." It takes a divine revelation from the Spirit to understand why you live the way you do.

Now Trusting in Jesus

1 Peter 4:5 | But they will give account to him who is ready to judge the living and the dead.

Those who slander and harass us as Christians will have to give an account to God for how they treat us when they meet him on judgment day. He is the judge of those who are currently living now and those who have already died. In other words, there is not escape. So the Christian doesn't have to fret about mistreatment and persecution. God is the judge. He will bring ultimate justice on Judgment Day.

The Example of the Martyrs (4:6)

Then, in verse 6, Peter gives an example of the martyrs who have died. This is the ultimate self-denial. Those who are now dead had the gospel preached to them, so that though the evil world judged them unworthy to live, they are now, after death, more alive than ever before.

1 Peter 4:6 | For this is why the gospel was preached even to those who are dead, that though judged in the flesh the way people are, they might live in the spirit the way God does.

Peter speaks directly to the awful fate of Christians who face death because of their faith. It seems that the great Nero persecution has begun. He speaks of those who are "now dead" and who have been "judged in the flesh." What's he talking about? The dead are those who had heard and believed the gospel but had died by the time he wrote.

Peter says "this is why the gospel was preached to the martyrs." This gospel is a powerful gospel. It allows you to die to the selfish part of you so that you are able to even give your life for Christ if necessary. Saints, that's the power of the crucified life.

When Christ was crucified, were his enemies successful? No, he rose on the third day! So we believers die to this world, and many die physically, but death doesn't kill us ultimately. When we die, we enter into the eternal life of the Spirit. If you are living for self as a pattern in your life, you are not living the Christian life. You need to die to self so that you can live.

WE LIVE AN ABUNDANT LIFE (4:7-9)

The Christian life is a full and abundant life. It's a life of serving God and others. That's what he says in 4:7-9. Peter now gives many examples of how Christians should live in light of our abundant life. We are no longer living for self but for God and others. Self-denial is important, because it frees you for fullness. Jesus says in John 10:10, "I have come that you may have life and have it abundantly."

> **1 Peter 4:7-9** | The end of all things is at hand; therefore be self-controlled and sober-minded for the sake of your prayers. ⁸ Above all, keep loving one another earnestly, since love covers a multitude of sins. ⁹ Show hospitality to one another without grumbling.

The Abundant Life of Prayer

> **1 Peter 4:7** | The end of all things is at hand; therefore be self-controlled and sober-minded for the sake of your prayers.

Peter begins to talk about prayer with a focus on the end of time. "The end of all things is at hand" (4:7a). What? He wrote this 2000 years ago. That doesn't seem like the end. Peter is referring to the last age before Jesus returns. We are living in it, and Jesus can return at any time. Christ's return is near. He can come at any time. "Therefore..." live a full life for God. Don't bother living for yourself. That's a waste. That's your old life. You can never live that way anymore. Live the full life in God. The crucified life is the full life. It's the abundant life. Peter now turns to the fullness of the life in God. He says we need to live the abundant life "for the sake of your prayers" (4:7b).

Prayer Requires Self Control

You will wake up with the weight of the world on your shoulders if your focus is not on the Lord. You've got to "be self-controlled," directing all your thoughts to the Lord. There are so many distractions, and we must intentionally put God first in our thinking and in all our ways if we are going to live a life of prayer (Mt 6:33; 7:7). We were not made to be slaves of this world, but to be free in the Spirit and in Christ. Self-control gives us boundaries so that we can give ourselves fully to the fellowship of Christ in prayer as we live the abundant life.

Prayer Requires Sobermindedness

Prayer also requires us to be "sober-minded" – "setting your affections on things above, not on things on the earth" (Col 3:1). The end is at hand, Peter says. We can't waste time on earthly endeavors. We are to be serious minded, thinking about eternity. This precludes fear of man and materialism and pleasure since everything that we see will soon burn up when Jesus comes again. The end is so near. Be sober with your thoughts and how you spend your time. This sobriety will free you to pray and fellowship with God as you ought, so you can have that abundant life.

The Abundant Life of Forgiveness

> **1 Peter 4:8** | Above all, keep loving one another earnestly, since love covers a multitude of sins.

Sometimes bitterness and difficult relationships can discourage us from living the abundant life. Peter then says, that in denying ourselves, we live an abundant life in another way. We are able to forgive those who sin against us.

It's easy to give up on relationships, even in the church. But Peter says we are to "keep loving one another" even though a brother or sister may consistently offend us. You'll never do this unless you are living the crucified life. You will abandon ship if you are a consumer Christian, living for what others or this church or that ministry can give you. Peter says, here's the test to see if you are living the crucified life: can you forgive people? Can you get along with them after they've offended you a "multitude" of times? Living a life of forgiveness is going to fill you with an abundant love that covers a multitude of sins and offences.

Of course, people are difficult. I can be difficult! I heard of the story of a family of porcupines that wanted to live together. While they were together they had warmth. They had courage. But they didn't live that way very long, because they kept sticking one another. So they decided to live separately. The problem with isolation came a life of coldness and loneliness. It left them open to the prey of wild animals. They realized this, so they decided to come together again. But it wasn't too long before they were offended with each other because everyone was sticking each other. So they decided to live separate. Until one day, cold and lonely and frightened, they decided to come together again. I could go on and on. But if you think about it, this is the story of the church.

As believers, we need each other. Jesus says our unity is the evidence to the world that Christ has come. Peter says, "Above all, keep loving one another earnestly, since love covers a multitude of sins" (4:8). What is love? Is it a feeling? Sometimes we feel love for one another. But love is not mainly a feeling. It is a commitment. "God so loved the world that he..." felt this overwhelming feeling of admiration for the world. Is that love? God didn't love the world for what the world could give him. That's consumer love. God loved the world for what he could give that vile bunch of sinners. That's covenant love. So love one another, not for what you get out of it, but for what you can give. That's agape love, covenant love.

This kind of love covers a multitude of sins. What's that mean? How many sins do you have? How many sins do you need forgiven? Mountains. Heaps. Oceans filled with sins. We are to forgive others the way God has forgiven us. You don't really know if you love someone, unless you've stayed with them enough where you have forgiven them multitudes of times. Have you forgiven? Are their broken relationships in the local assembly you attend? Are you loving your forever family and covering a multitude of sins?

The Abundant Life of Service

1 Peter 4:9 | Show hospitality to one another without grumbling.

Then Peter really pushes us hard as far as love goes. He says the abundant life is where we serve each other without complaining. We've all done it. *Having people over is too much work! Yes* it's a lot of work. *People drain me!* Sometimes they do. I'm sure I've drained plenty of people in my life. Peter says, don't just say you love people. Live the crucified life. Have people over. Don't just say you love people. Live life with them. That's the test to see if you are crucified with Christ. When is the last time you had people over to your home?

Maybe you as a man can have a group of men from the church over and just have a time of fellowship, the word, maybe some board games. What about you ladies having a ladies' night? Go bowling, or whatever ladies' do. Do something! Not shopping, ha! But do something together ladies. Encourage one another in the word and prayer. Fellowship together. Eat together. There is something about having a meal together that displays our love and unity.

Are you really living the abundant life? Then you'll be showing hospitality to the saints. Don't make excuses or start grumbling. That's the display of the crucified life. It's the abundant life!

WE LIVE A SHARED LIFE (4:10-11)

Finally, Peter ends by saying we live a shared life with entire body of Christ, and so we need to exercise our spiritual gifts in the realm of the local church.

> **1 Peter 4:10-11** | As each has received a gift, use it to serve one another, as good stewards of God's varied grace: [11] whoever speaks, as one who speaks oracles of God; whoever serves, as one who serves by the strength that God supplies—in order that in everything God may be glorified through Jesus Christ. To him belong glory and dominion forever and ever. Amen.

If you've been following, he says, the crucified life is the abundant life. And it is displayed in your prayers, that is your walk and worship with God, your walk with other Christians in their person life, and now we see in your walk in the local church, exercising your spiritual gifts.

A Spiritual Gift is Given to Every Believer

> **1 Peter 4:10** | As each has received a gift, use it to serve one another.

Who in the Body of Christ has a spiritual gift? Each one of us. No one gets "cheated" out of a spiritual gift! Every Christian has received at least one spiritual gift from God which he is responsible to use for the good of the church and for the glory of God. We are to be stewards of God's varied grace.

A Spiritual Gift is a Supernatural Ability

What is a spiritual gift? It is described here as a gift of God's grace God's "gift" or "varied grace" that is given to each believer. So a spiritual gift is a supernatural ability from God in our lives. We manage or steward these gifts. Christ's gift to us is his atonement and resurrection power that he gives to us. In most places in the Bible, the word grace means God's unmerited favor. But in some places, it means supernatural gifting and ability. Here it refers to ability. We have a special empowerment from God to edify the Body of Christ.

Every part in the body of Christ is necessary. There are thousands of pieces in a Boeing 747. Take off a wing! Take off the landing gear. Take out one of the engines. The truth is, just like in an airplane, in the Body of Christ, you need *all* the parts!!

A Spiritual Gift is a Stewardship

> **1 Peter 4:10** | As each has received a gift, use it to serve one another, as good stewards of God's varied grace.

Again in 1 Corinthians 12, Paul is talking about spiritual gifts, and he actually gives his own definition.

> To each is given the manifestation of the Spirit for the common good.
> — *1 Corinthians 12:7*

Paul defines spiritual gifts here as "the manifestation of the Spirit" that is to be exercised and used for the "common good." Since these gifts are in the context of the congregation, we can say that your spiritual gift is always for the "common good" and edification of the entire body. A spiritual gift is clearly a supernatural ability given by the Spirit of God that is also a stewardship to be used for the betterment of the body of Christ.

Let me be clear about spiritual gifts. A spiritual gift always ministers God's Spirit to someone else. You may be a good cook, but not have the gift of hospitality. You may be gifted in music, but there is a way to sing where it is a manifestation of the Spirit and a way in which it is just a performance. You may be a good mechanic, but a person with the gift of mercy and the gift of helps is going to fix someone's car in a way where it is a manifestation of the Spirit. Your spiritual gift is a supernatural ability that manifests the Spirit and builds up the body of Christ. Paul testifies to this and gives glory to God.

> But by the grace of God I am what I am, and his grace toward me was not in vain. On the contrary, I worked harder than any of them, though it was not I, but the grace of God that is with me.
> — *1 Corinthians 15:10*

It was the grace of God in Paul that worked in him to labor. The apostle Peter goes further and tells us not only that we have all received a gift as believers, but that every believer has a responsibility to use his gift as a stewardship from God. We are going to give an account to use our gift! A steward is not an owner. You are using something that belongs to someone else. Your spiritual gift belongs to God. You need to use it for him.

Spiritual Gifts Differ

> **1 Peter 4:10-11a** | As each has received a gift, use it to serve one another, as good stewards of God's varied grace: [11] whoever speaks, as one who speaks oracles of God; whoever serves, as one who serves by the strength that God supplies.

Peter says, there are two kinds of gifts: gifts of speaking and gifts of serving. If you speak, speak "as one who speaks oracles of God." Don't hold back. This is God's message. Don't edit it. Don't speak for people. Don't tickle their ears. Speak with authority because this is God's word. And if you have the gift of serving, then let God supply your strength. Serving God in ministry can be exhausting, so you need to depend on God's strength, living the abundant life.

A Spiritual Gift is to be God-Glorifying

Peter says the purpose of spiritual gifts is to bring honor and glory to God.

> **1 Peter 4:11b** | As each has received a gift...in order that in everything God may be glorified through Jesus Christ. To him belong glory and dominion forever and ever. Amen.

We are not called to use our spiritual gifts to build our own kingdom, but to bring glory and honor to God.

I think of Hophni and Phineas, the two sons of Eli. They used their spiritual office and gifting for themselves. God told them to burn all the fat off the sacrifices, but they disobeyed. They liked the savory pieces of meat. They disobeyed the Lord. It seems their father, who was high priest was aware of this, and the Bible says, "he was a very heavy man," so he might have been part of this. But God told Eli through the boy Samuel judgment was coming because, "his sons were blaspheming God, and he did not restrain them" (1 Sam 3:13). The tabernacle stayed at Shiloh for 369 years, until God brought judgment to Eli and his two sons. One day, the Philistines came in battle against Israel and burned the tabernacle down. That day Eli and his two sons, Hophni and Phineas died. That day Phineas' wife had a baby. As she was dying, "she named the child Ichabod, saying, 'The glory has departed from Israel!'" (1 Sam 4:21).

On the other hand, I think of Israel and why God chose them. He chose them because they were nothings. And today, in the church of Christ, God did not choose many mighty or wise, but he instead chose the foolish and weak to confound the mighty (1 Cor 1:26-27). Since we are nothing, anything they have is from God.

Conclusion

So, let me sum up this message. It's very simple: the life worth living is a crucified life; it's an abundant life; and it's a shared life where we build each other up. Let's live our lives and use our spiritual gifts for God's glory. "All glory and dominion belong to him forever and ever." Whether you are a teacher, then tremble at God's word and not at people. Speak the truth in love. Be filled with the Spirit when you speak. And if you are someone who serves, whether in music, setting up and tearing down for fellowship, washing dishes, serving in the nursery, being hospitable, praying or giving, do it with God's strength. On those days you feel so puny and without strength, let the joy of the Lord be your strength! Let's do it so that God may be glorified. He gets the glory because he has the control and dominion over our hearts and lives. Amen and amen.

20 | 1 PETER 4:12-19
WHY SUFFERING?

Beloved, do not be surprised at the fiery trial when it comes upon you to test you, as though something strange were happening to you. But rejoice insofar as you share Christ's sufferings, that you may also rejoice and be glad when his glory is revealed.

1 PETER 4:12-13

God tells us throughout the Bible that he is the Potter and we are the clay. Suffering is one way that God softens us and molds us to be a vessel he can use. I want to be used, don't you? Peter is writing to a hurting and persecuted people who desperately need to know God loves them.

An artist in Florence, Italy once asked the great Renaissance sculptor Michelangelo what he saw when he approached a huge block of marble. The famous sculptor stood back and looked at that big square block of white marble, rubbed his chin thoughtfully, and replied, "I see a beautiful form trapped inside and it is my responsibility to take my mallet and chisel and chip away until the figure is set free." I love that illustration because you can relate to it. Inside of us is a beautiful form, right? Colossians 1:27 says so. It speaks of the hidden figure inside of each believer longing to be "set free". It is "Christ in you, the hope of glory." It's within us, like a seed, like a possibility, like a potential; it's what you hope for: Christ in you glorified through your life, right? The idea is there and our Heavenly Father is a like a sculptor. He wants to form his Son in you. And so, he uses affliction like a hammer and trouble just like a chisel, and he chips and cuts away at us through trials to reveal Jesus' image in you and me. God chooses as his model his Son, Jesus Christ because Romans 8:29 says: "For those God foreknew he also predestined to be conformed to the likeness of his Son."

I don't need to tell you that you, and I have lot of hard marble in my life that needs to be chipped away before Christ can be seen in me. We all have that marble. That hammer hurts, doesn't it? Those trials, that chisel bites! After time, the rough form begins to take shape.

As Peter writes in AD 64, Rome is burning. The persecution has begun in some ways, but it is not in full force. Some have already died for Christ (4:6), and Peter is getting the church ready for suffering. The Roman government is about to try and obliterate Christianity. The Emperor Nero at 26 years of age wants Rome to burn down so he can rebuild it. Seventy percent of the city is in ashes. The once great city is smoldering as Peter writes. Nero blames the fire on the Christians. Rumor is spreading and the people's hatred is stirring against the followers of Jesus. Peter writes to warn them. Get ready. Suffering is coming. But the truth is, suffering is coming for all of us. Suffering is God's tool to conform us into the image of Christ.

> **1 Peter 4:12-19** | Beloved, do not be surprised at the fiery trial when it comes upon you to test you, as though something strange were happening to you. **13** But rejoice insofar as you share Christ's sufferings, that you may also rejoice and be glad when his glory is revealed. **14** If you are insulted for the name of Christ, you are blessed, because the Spirit of glory and of God rests upon you. **15** But let none of you suffer as a murderer or a thief or an evildoer or as a meddler. **16** Yet if anyone suffers as a Christian, let him not be ashamed, but let him glorify God in that name. **17** For it is time for judgment to begin at the household of God; and if it begins with us, what will be the outcome for those who do not obey the gospel of God? **18** And "If the righteous is scarcely saved, what will become of the ungodly and the sinner?" **19** Therefore let

those who suffer according to God's will entrust their souls to a faithful Creator while doing good.

Suffering is a fact of life for the Christian. C.S. Lewis of Narnia fame says this about suffering:

> God whispers to us in our pleasures, speaks in our conscience, but shouts in our pains: it is his megaphone to rouse a deaf world.[138]

Oh how deaf we are sometimes. Sometimes each of us in the church can be deaf. We are going to go through great pain in the Christian life. The Bible here tells us that Christians are undoubtedly called to suffer according to the will of God. This contradicts a lot of theology out there that negates any kind of suffering or trials for the Christian in the will of God. This passage is the death knell to the so-called "prosperity gospel." Christians are called to suffer in many ways. They are suffering today throughout the world. More Christians died in the last hundred years than in all the previous centuries combined. All over the world, Christians are suffering. Daily Christians are persecuted – in India, in all the Muslim countries, in Syria, Uganda, Nigeria, and in Sudan, over 2 million Christians have died over the last decade for Christ.

Here in 1 Peter 4, we have a call for believers to suffer "according to the will of God." Paul says, "that I may know him, and the fellowship of his suffering..." (Phil 3:10). Peter says that this suffering and evaluation will begin at the house of God. "It is time for judgment to begin at the house of God" (4:17). Suffering is sent from God for several reasons: purification (4:12), glorification (4:13), transformation (4:14), evaluation (4:15-18), and mobilization (4:19).

SUFFERING BRINGS REFINEMENT (4:12)

> **1 Peter 4:12** | Beloved, do not be surprised at the fiery trial when it comes upon you to test you, as though something strange were happening to you.

Refinement is for the Saints of God

Peter loves his brothers and sisters. He's wanting them to know that God loves them. They are beloved by him and by God. Suffering doesn't ever mean that God has stopped loving us. In fact, God is so

---

[138] C. S. Lewis. *The Problem of Pain, Collected Letters of C.S. Lewis* (San Francisco: HarperCollins, 92.

committed to conforming you to Christ's image, he allows suffering in your life. Remember Job's wife misunderstood the suffering Job was going through. She uttered the horrible words: "Curse God and die!" (Job 2:9). We must never be so near sighted. Though we go through suffering, God loves his children. He loves you.

Refinement Should Not be a Surprise

The believers to whom Peter was writing were surprised by their suffering. Peter says, "do not be surprised at the fiery trial when it comes upon you to test you, as though something strange were happening to you" (4:12). The Christians were not expecting to be treated so hatefully. You know how it is. We trust in Christ; our sins are forgiven. We are filled with "unspeakable joy, full of glory" (1 Pet 1:8). Now that we know true love in Christ, we don't expect people will hate us for it. But they do. God has called all of his children to enter into the crucible of suffering. Jesus says, "In the world you will have tribulation. But take heart; I have overcome the world" (Jn 16:33). Jesus also says, "If the world hates you, keep in mind that it hated me first" (Jn 15:18). "The servant is not greater than his master" (Jn 15:20). "All who live godly in Christ Jesus will suffer persecution" (2 Tim 3:12). All those who follow Christ must "count the cost" before we follow him. It's a high cost of suffering (Lk 14:28-32). "Something strange" is not happening to you if you are suffering as God's child. It's part of his plan.

Refinement is for Our Sanctification

The purpose of the "fiery ordeal" we are about to go through is purification. The "testing" Peter is talking about is the refining fire. Trials and suffering bring us into conformity to Christ's image (Rom 8:28-29). Job said, "He knows the way that I take; when he has tried me, I shall come out as gold" (Job 23:10). He wants to refine us like gold. He puts us in a furnace of suffering, like the furnace that melts down metal to purge it of impurities (*cf* Psa 66:10). Wise Solomon said: "The crucible is for silver, and the furnace is for gold, and the Lord tests hearts" (Pro 17:3). Don't be surprised by the suffering. Jesus wants to bring us into greater fellowship, greater communion and intimacy with him. It will be a fiery testing. It will begin with the people of God. Why is Jesus calling us to a place of suffering? Why must judgment begin at the house of God? Why? To try us. To put us to the test. God is trying us.

There is a sense of warning. There is a time of great trying and testing coming to the church worldwide. It's already begun.

In order for us to change we must be put to the test. At some point, our verbal commitment for Christ has to be put to the test. You say you love Jesus. Do you know what that means? It means he's the very center of your life. Some of you would not pass the test today. It's not enough to say you love Jesus. God promises trials to refine you and bring you to maturity in Christ.

God is not cruel. Remember Paul asked God to remove his "thorn in the flesh" three times. Do you recall Jesus' words to him? "My grace is sufficient for you, for my power is made perfect in weakness" (2 Cor 12:9a). Paul says, "Therefore I will boast all the more gladly of my weaknesses, so that the power of Christ may rest upon me. 10 For the sake of Christ, then, I am content with weaknesses, insults, hardships, persecutions, and calamities. For when I am weak, then I am strong" (2 Cor 12:9b-10).

If you know him, you will truly love him. Loving Jesus is costly. God will send trials and pain to test your faith. Can you love him still when all your earthly dreams come crashing down and he's all you have left? Is he enough? Is Jesus enough? In your suffering, God is purifying your motives. He's purifying your character. That's the number one thing God is after. He wants to purify your heart.

SUFFERING PREPARES US FOR GLORIFICATION (4:13)

Don't be surprised by the suffering and trials you are going through. Instead, rejoice! Jesus is preparing you for his Second Coming.

> **1 Peter 4:13** | But rejoice insofar as you share Christ's sufferings, that you may also rejoice and be glad when his glory is revealed.

We Share in Christ's Suffering Now

"Rejoice insofar as you share Christ's sufferings" (4:13a). The sweet Savior is with you. We must remember that he is a man of sorrows and acquainted with grief, according to Isaiah. We know him as the Lord of glory, the God of truth, the God-man with the Spirit of God and wisdom. But we are called to share in his sufferings and sorrows. Suffering brings his church into a new place of transformation. That's where transformation comes. Jesus has not come to simply save us from hell, but to transform us into his image. We are to enter into his sorrows. Yet he calls us to rejoice because we are not alone in our sorrows.

Suffering with Christ in Evangelism

We are sharing in Christ's sorrows! How is this possible? Paul clarifies this in Colossians 1:24, "Now I rejoice in my sufferings for your sake, and in my flesh I am filling up what is lacking in Christ's afflictions for the sake of his body, that is, the church." All that we do is in union with Christ, including our suffering. Filling up what is lacking in Christ's suffering has nothing to do with atoning for sin. Christ's death was unique in that he is the substitutionary atonement for our sins. No one can add to that. That would be blasphemous. The filling up of suffering that we as saints are now doing has to do with *evangelism*. Christ incarnated into the world of sinners without sinning. We too, are to be "Jesus with skin on." We are to go to any lengths in pursuing sinners.

Suffering with Christ in Our Union with Him

How else do we share in Christ's suffering? Remember when Paul was confronted by Christ? Jesus said, "Saul, Saul, why are you persecuting me?" (Acts 9:4). When people insult and persecute a believer, they are persecuting Christ. When we suffer, we need to remember that Christ is our head, and we are in union with Christ. Nothing can separate us from his love (Rom 8:38-39). In all our suffering he is with us. He will never leave or forsake us. I may lose everything in this life, but I will never lose Christ. No one can pluck me out of his almighty hand.

Suffering with Christ in Our Sanctification

All I have is Christ: rejoice! All the suffering the Christian goes through contributes to a transformation that matures us more and more into the image of Christ (2 Pet 3:18; Rom 8:29-30; Jas 1:2-3). Suffering humbles us and draws us closer to Christ. It demonstrates that when everything else in this world is stripped away, all is dung compared to knowing Christ (Phil 3:8-10). When great suffering comes, *all I have is Christ*. When great loss comes, *all I have is Christ*. When I'm persecuted for Christ's name, *all I have is Christ*. When severe depression comes, *all I have is Christ*. When confusion comes, *all I have is Christ*. Listen at the end of the day, if I lose everything, I have lost nothing, because *all I have, and all I need, and all I long for is Christ*!

We Will Rejoice with Christ Soon in Glory

Jesus is not only the man of sorrows. He is the King of glory! "Rejoice insofar as you share Christ's sufferings" (4:13a) – why? "that you may also rejoice and be glad when his glory is revealed" (4:13b). Jesus is not only the man of sorrows, he is the King of glory! Jesus is coming again! The Lord resumed the full exercise of his power and glory after he ascended to heaven, but he has not yet revealed it on earth for everyone to see. On that day, every knee will bow to Jesus. Every tongue will confess he is Lord! And when he comes again, we will be "caught up together with him in the air" (2 Thess 4:17). At that moment, we will be glad for all the suffering that brought us into closer relationship with him.

When you think of that glorious day, you realize that every insult is preparing you to see our precious Jesus. Every trial is getting you ready to see Jesus. Rejoice, because when you suffer, the Spirit rests upon you and prepares you for Jesus' final victory. He's coming again. Suffering is God's chisel, and he's molding you to be like Jesus. He's pushing you deeper and deeper into intimacy with Christ. Paul says, "I consider that the sufferings of this present time are not worth comparing with the glory that is to be revealed to us" (Rom 8:18).

SUFFERING BRINGS TRANSFORMATION (4:14)

Don't be surprised by the suffering and trials you are going through. Instead, rejoice! Jesus wants to bring us into greater fellowship, greater communion and intimacy with him. Affliction has the power to transform us. Can you testify with David? "It is good for me that I was afflicted, that I might learn your statutes" (Psa 119:71).

Transformed through Suffering

> **1 Peter 4:14a** | If you are insulted for the name of Christ, you are blessed.

Peter says "if" we are insulted for Christ, but we could also say "when" because persecution is inevitable if we are living a godly life.

> Indeed, all who desire to live a godly life in Christ Jesus will be persecuted. —*2 Timothy 3:12*

With a tea bag, hot water brings out what is inside. So it is with the Christian. Insults and trials and suffering bring out what is inside. Suffering therefore demonstrates the work of God's Spirit in the inner being. Peter says here that when we are persecuted for Christ's sake, we are blessed. He certainly is thinking of the words of Jesus in the Sermon on the Mount.

> Blessed are you when others revile you and persecute you and utter all kinds of evil against you falsely on my account. [12] Rejoice and be glad, for your reward is great in heaven, for so they persecuted the prophets who were before you. —Matthew 5:11-12

Jesus goes on to say that when we act our our identity in him in the "be-attitudes" we are salt and light. When God's Spirit rests upon you, you are a testimony to this lost world. You are salt and light. Your light shines and people have to give glory to our Father in heaven. God wants our lives to be a living example of Jesus' life. The apostle Paul said to his hearers: you are the Bible in action. You are a living "letter of Christ..." "known and read of all men" (2 Cor 3:2, 3).

You are a living letter testifying to the life and ministry and majesty of Jesus of Nazareth. Paul said this to those in Corinth. Live the life and majesty of Jesus! Shine his light! How? You suffer so differently than the world. We press into God when we suffer. We see the saints huddling around us when we suffer. We have the word pressed into us when we suffer. We are carried by the sufficient grace of God when we suffer. We suffer so differently. Peter says, "don't be surprised by the fiery trial that's about to try you." Jesus wants to bring you to a new place of fellowship with Jesus. How wonderful it is.

Transformed by the Spirit

> **1 Peter 4:14** | If you are insulted for the name of Christ, you are blessed, because the Spirit of glory and of God rests upon you.

There is a manifestation of the Spirit upon you when you suffer for Christ. The picture Peter uses is from the Old Testament when God's glory cloud rested on the tabernacle and temple. What a blessing that we are the temple of God's Spirit. There is no higher blessing.

Our suffering does not diminish our blessedness; suffering increases our blessing. How are we blessed? It's a present blessing, because the Spirit of glory and of God rests on you when you suffer. Let me clarify, you don't get more of the Spirit when you suffer. You have all of the Spirit already. But he manifests himself when you suffer.

We need to awaken to the fact that Jesus is more interested in transforming our character than anything else. When suffering occurs let us rejoice! We get an increase of influence from the Spirit. We grow deeper in intimacy with Christ through trials. We count it all joy (Jas 1:2-3).

SUFFERING BRINGS EVALUATION (4:15-18)

"To whom much is given, much will be required" (Lk 12:48). There is an evaluation that God brings through suffering. This is why Peter says, "it is time for judgment to begin at the household of God." That's where it began in the Old Testament. God used the Babylonians to purity his people. There is an evaluation of a Christian's life that God brings daily.

God Evaluates the Pattern of Our Lives

> **1 Peter 4:15** | But let none of you suffer as a murderer or a thief or an evildoer or as a meddler.

The idea is that God will evaluate his people in their suffering. Christ is here with us, and he's calling his people into a place of suffering. Why will there be this fiery trial? To evaluate you. To see what you are made of when the pressure is on. Are you a Christian? You will suffer according to the will of God – not "as a murderer or a thief or an evildoer or as a meddler" (4:15), but because your life is clean, and you love Jesus.

Christians live a new life. Murder and thievery were capital offenses in Rome. Believers practice righteousness, not evil. Meddling had the idea of getting too much involved in other people's business or getting carried away with the business civil politics. Keep your eyes fixed on God's kingdom. Don't get distracted. Our citizenship is in heaven. We live a life of fellowship with Christ, walking in righteousness. Evaluate your behavior. No true believer can live comfortable in sin. No true believer lives the life of any of these categories of sin. I need to get realigned at times. God brings suffering to realign me. In your suffering, God is evaluating the pattern of your life.

There is a radical change in the heart of a true Christian. The apostle John says in 1 John 3:9, "No one born of God makes a practice of sinning, for God's seed abides in him; and he cannot keep on sinning, because he has been born of God." In suffering, God is evaluating the pattern of your life. Is there a pattern of holiness? You can put on a show when life is easy, but when life is hard what you really are comes out. We are all like a tea bag. When we are in hot water, whatever is on the inside comes out! Suffering is a way where God evaluates the pattern of your life.

God Evaluates the Passion of Our Heart

> **1 Peter 4:16** | Yet if anyone suffers as a Christian, let him not be ashamed, but let him glorify God in that name.

"Christian" was first used as a derogatory term. Peter says, "glory in that name." Do you love the name of Jesus? Glory in that name! The world means it for an insult to you. Don't be afraid to identify with Jesus. Don't be afraid to walk the road that Jesus trod.[139] I hope your passion is to be identified with Jesus. He has a name that is exalted above all names. Though people insult you with that name, don't be ashamed, but rather "glorify God in that name." What an honor to suffer for the name of Jesus!

What an honor to suffer for the Lord! We should rejoice and glorify God in that name" (*cf* Mt 5:11-12). He has not forgotten us. Many prophets and preachers in the past have given their lives for him. Don't be ashamed to identify with Jesus. God uses these kinds of suffering to evaluate the passion of your heart.

God Evaluates the People of God

This divine evaluation begins with us, the household of God. We are the family of God. We have to be first to be judged. This is not a judgement of condemnation but evaluation, and it is for the people of God alone.

> **1 Peter 4:17-18** | For it is time for judgment to begin at the household of God; and if it begins with us, what will be the outcome for those who do not obey the gospel of God? **18** And "If the righteous is scarcely saved, what will become of the ungodly and the sinner?"

---

[139] Helm, *1 & 2 Peter and Jude*, 152.

As I said before "To whom much is given, much will be required" (Lk 12:48). God always begins his evaluation with his own family. What does it mean that "judgment begins at the house of God?"

It Means Believers are Marked

1 Peter 4:17a | For it is time for judgment to begin at the household of God.

This evaluation is for the household of God. We are marked as God's people. Peter is referencing Ezekiel 9 where God began to purify his saints at his very sanctuary in Jerusalem when God's glory departed from the temple. Before the glory of the Lord departs out of the Eastern Gate and onto the Mount of Olives, God marks every true believer in the city of Jerusalem. Anyone without the mark of God on them perished in the city of Jerusalem. Only God's remnant survived, and judgment was to begin at the house or temple of God (*cf* Jer 25:15-29). How serious God's judgment is! Those remaining were taken to Babylon for purification through suffering. Christ himself knows his own, and those who are not his he will say to them, "Depart from me you lawless people, I never knew you" (*cf* Mt 7:21-23). Christ knows his sheep and they follow him (Jn 10:27).

Amos 3:2 says that God will begin his evaluation where his name has been written. His name is written on Jerusalem (2 Chron 6:6). His name is also written on you. "To the one who overcomes... I will write on him the name of my God, and the name of the city of my God, the new Jerusalem, which comes down from my God out of heaven, and my own new name (Rev 3:12). God's name "El Shaddai" is literally written in the valleys of Jerusalem. The Hebrew letter "shin" looks like a W and these three valleys literally form God's initial, "El Shaddai." Psalm 91:1, "He who dwells in the shelter of the Most High will abide in the shadow of the Almighty [El Shaddai]."

True children of God suffer for Christ. We read in Romans 8 that we are children of God, and just as his Son suffered, we will suffer. "And if children, then heirs—heirs of God and fellow heirs with Christ, provided we suffer with him in order that we may also be glorified with him" (Rom 8:17). As we suffer well, we demonstrate that we truly are the household of God.

It Means Believers are Pruned

If you are one of God's true children, judgment, evaluation will begin with you. Jesus explains how true believers have areas of their life pruned and cut down so we can bear more fruit.

> I am the true vine, and my Father is the vinedresser. ² Every branch in me that does not bear fruit he takes away, and every branch that does bear fruit he prunes, that it may bear more fruit. ³ Already you are clean because of the word that I have spoken to you. ⁴ Abide in me, and I in you. As the branch cannot bear fruit by itself, unless it abides in the vine, neither can you, unless you abide in me. ⁵ I am the vine; you are the branches. Whoever abides in me and I in him, he it is that bears much fruit, for apart from me you can do nothing. ⁶ If anyone does not abide in me he is thrown away like a branch and withers; and the branches are gathered, thrown into the fire, and burned.
>
> —*John 15:1-6*

God is a good gardener. God will take care of his own garden. But if you are not part of his garden, you get thrown away and burned. If you are bearing some fruit in your life, God is always going to cut you back. Remember that. What happens if you are not bearing fruit? You are "thrown away" like a dead branch. You are "thrown into the fire and burned." True branches are pruned.

My favorite bush in my yard is our Purple Japanese Barberry bush. It was the first bush I planted in the front of our house when we purchased it in 2006. I was so proud of that bush because I bought it when it was so tiny. I watered it, tended it, and cared for it, and it became almost as tall as me. But after about twelve years, it started to die. There were more dead branches than living ones. I remembered Jesus promise to prune his people, and so I knew it was a good gardening principle. I cut that precious bush all the way back, almost to its roots. Just a few pitiful branches remained, so that I was just about convinced it wouldn't survive. But low and behold, the next year, it came back like a newborn bush. It was almost like it was "born again"! The next year it was even bigger. And the next year even bigger. Today it is a thriving bush once again. Like my precious bush, God cuts back his children so they can grow for the long term. He cuts out the dead areas of our lives. What areas is God cutting out of your life?

It Means Believers are Protected

This is not judgment in the sense of *condemnation*, but in *evaluation*. In Romans 8:30, the Bible promises we are "predestined to be conformed to the image of his Son." Paul says, I am "confident of this very thing, that he who has begun a good work in you will complete it until the day of Jesus Christ" (Phil 1:6). God evaluates our faith when we go through suffering. Who or what do you turn to when you suffer? Peter explains that the 'fiery ordeal', or 'refining fire', of verse 12 is really a fire of God's purification. "Whom the Lord loves he chastens" (Heb 12:6).

A fiery trial awaits us. The Old Testament saints suffered by being taken to Babylon. Their faith was tested. Think of Daniel and his three friends. They suffered. But they stood for the King. Not Nebuchadnezzar, but Jesus the King of kings! We too will be protected when we are persecuted by the world. The worst that can happen to us is death, which now has no sting thanks to Jesus.

It Means Unbelievers are Judged

1 Peter 4:17-18 | For it is time for judgment to begin at the household of God; and if it begins with us, what will be the outcome for those who do not obey the gospel of God?

The world is going to be judged in a different way. The saints get judged on earth in the sense of God's chastening. But the lost get judged for their sins. For believers, judgment is something good. It's something that purifies us. But for unbelievers, it's awful. There is an eternity in the lake of fire for anyone who will not obey the gospel to repent and believe. Every knee will bow and every tongue confess that Jesus is Lord. No one gets out of that. If you don't know Jesus, you will perish. You will be judged. "If anyone's name was not found written in the book of life, he was thrown into the lake of fire" (Rev 20:15).

1 Peter 4:17 | And "If the righteous is scarcely saved, what will become of the ungodly and the sinner?"

Peter reasons that if God's own children, whom he loves and cares for, cannot escape his discipline, then we can't begin to imagine what kind of punishment is in store for unbelievers who shake their fists at God![140]

Dear saints, let us reach the world. They will hate us. In some parts of the world you will lose your livelihood, your home, your belongings. You may even lose your own life. But what have you really lost if you die? "For me to live is Christ and to die is gain" (Phil 1:21). The world doesn't have your hope. We have been saved by the precious blood of Jesus. It took the blood of Jesus to save God's household, how much more impossible is it for ungodly sinners who have the great weight of their sins weighing them down to hell. What will become of them? Indeed, their fate is worse than anyone could ever imagine.

SUFFERING BRINGS MOBILIZATION (4:19)

What should be our response to suffering? Getting busy. Doing good. Serve God and others.

> **1 Peter 4:19** | Therefore let those who suffer according to God's will entrust their souls to a faithful Creator while doing good.

Those who trust God in suffering are used by God in magnificent mighty ways to bring the ultimate good of the gospel to others. Remember the persecuted believers in the book of Acts. They are hit hard with Jewish persecution, and they go everywhere spreading the good news of the gospel.

Mobilized by God's Will

Let's not forget, we are suffering "according to God's will." He works "all things after the counsel of his own will" (Eph 1:11). We can trust him. He is a faithful Creator. His mercies are new every morning. Let us say, "Great is Thy faithfulness" (Lam 3:22-23). He says, "I will never leave you nor forsake you" (Heb 13:5). Never, never, never, never. He will never in anyway leave you. You may not be able to see God, but he can see you. "The steps of a justified person are ordered and planned by the Lord, and He delights in his way. 24 Though he fall, he shall not be utterly cast down; For the Lord upholds *him with* His hand" (Psa 37:23-24). Trust God. He will carry you. Do not fear. He will lift you up. He is the "Sun of righteousness with healing in his wings" (Mal 4:2).

---

[140] Swindoll, *Insights on James and 1 & 2 Peter*, 231.

Mobilized To Do Good

Let's not forget, the purpose of suffering is to prepare you to do good. Your suffering is not in vain.

> **1 Peter 4:19** | Therefore let those who suffer according to God's will entrust their souls to a faithful Creator while doing good.

Paul in another place tells us the purpose of suffering is that God is growing our heart to do good. 2 Corinthians 1:3-4, "Blessed be the God and Father of our Lord Jesus Christ, the Father of mercies and God of all comfort, 4 who comforts us in all our affliction, so that we may be able to comfort those who are in any affliction, with the comfort with which we ourselves are comforted by God." You may wonder, "God why am I suffering so much." He's preparing you for a life of doing good. Get motivated. We are not victims. We are warriors. We are called to "put on the whole armor of God" and to "stand in Christ" (Eph 6:10ff). We are warriors in training. We are called in our suffering to learn from it and to do good.

Ultimately, God's brought suffering in your life according to his will so that you will learn to do good and trust him for the remarkable outcome. He is making us a people that harmonize our plans and our goals with the will of God. Confess to God and to the world that your life is entwined with the will of God.

Conclusion

God is the Potter; we are the clay. I've never been good at pottery. Maybe some of you are really good. But there is no one better at pottery than God. He's the Master Potter. We can trust him to make us vessels to do his will. Yes, it comes with much suffering, but his hands are gentle. One day, God will "wipe away all tears" from our eyes with those gentle hands (Rev 21:3-5). These trials will not last forever. Soon Jesus will come again and wipe away our tears. Even so come quickly Lord Jesus!

21 | 1 PETER 5:1-4
THE CALLING OF SHEPHERDS

> *I exhort the elders among you, as a fellow elder and a witness of the sufferings of Christ, as well as a partaker in the glory that is going to be revealed: shepherd the flock of God that is among you.*
> 1 PETER 5:1-2

Peter has us focus on the call of the pastor-shepherd. Being a pastor and an elder is a very high and holy calling. No one does this unless they are called by God to do it. The context of this charge to shepherd God's flock begins with a call to examine God's entire forever family.

> For it is time for judgment to begin at the household [family] of God.
> —*1 Peter 4:17*

Peter then considers his own self. "Lord, let judgment begin with me." This judgment of God's people can never be condemnation, for "there is now therefore no condemnation for those who are in Christ Jesus" (Rom 8:1) Judgment – not condemnation but examination – should always begin with leadership. The example and examination should always begin with leadership. Peter says, because judgment always begins with God's family, let's invite God's examination of us, and let's begin with the elders.

This discussion of pastoral leadership appears in the context of how Christians can endure the fiery ordeal of unjust treatment, trials, and tribulations in this life as they look with hope toward the next. We are in a nightmare period of darkness in our country, and we hope that it will pass. We need to stand together. We need to stand against the tyranny and the darkness. And by God's grace, we will.

Peter argues that strong, spiritual leadership is essential to thriving in this world. When leaders model holiness and hope to those sheep within their charge, the whole church will be able to look to the Chief Shepherd, who provides hope in hurtful times.[141]

> **1 Peter 5:1-4** | So I exhort the elders among you, as a fellow elder and a witness of the sufferings of Christ, as well as a partaker in the glory that is going to be revealed: **2** shepherd the flock of God that is among you, exercising oversight, not under compulsion, but willingly, as God would have you; not for shameful gain, but eagerly; **3** not domineering over those in your charge, but being examples to the flock. **4** And when the chief Shepherd appears, you will receive the unfading crown of glory.

By the way, everything that we see here concerning the Pastor really ought to be applied to any teacher or leader in the church! That means if God calls you or has already called you to be an elder (which is another word for pastor or shepherd), or if God has called you to be a leader, or a deacon, or a missionary, or a servant, or a Sunday School teacher, than you ought to listen to what I am about to say. There is a higher standard of judgment for leaders and teachers of the word.

> Not many of you should become teachers, my brothers, for you know that we who teach will be judged with greater strictness.
> —*James 3:1*

Notice Peter doesn't say he's a pope, which came much later, but he's humble. Peter says he is a "fellow elder." Peter is an apostle, but he's a humble person. He's a man who is growing and changing in Christ. He needs the presence of Christ to strengthen him. He's a weak

---

[141] Ibid., 235.

man in need of Christ's strength, like all of us. It wasn't Peter's idea to be a pastor and a shepherd and apostle. He was called by God. And remember, Peter failed miserably. Three times, Peter denied the Lord. But Jesus restored him. He asked Peter three similar questions.

Simon, son of John, do you love me more than these? —*John 21:15a*

Remember Peter had said, "Even if everyone else forsakes you Lord, I will never forsake you" (Mt 26:33). Peter failed. He denied the Lord three times. "Peter do you love me more than all the rest?" "Am I really number one in your life?" Peter three times says, "Yes, Lord, you know I love you." Remember Christ's restoration and threefold commission to Peter?

Feed my lambs. —John 21:15b

Tend my sheep. —John 21:16

Feed my sheep. —John 21:17

That's quite the calling. Let's remember that shepherds are not perfect. Far from it. None of the elders here come close to perfection. We are all growing and changing just like Peter. Peter often failed. I think that's why I am so encouraged by Peter. I relate with him. We are all imperfect shepherds, but we know the Perfect Shepherd. I'm so glad we can all say, "The Lord is my Shepherd." This passage in 1 Peter calls Jesus "our Chief Shepherd" (5:4). Aren't you glad Jesus is the "Good Shepherd" (Jn 10:10)?

Sheep are Dumb

The Bible isn't flattering us when it calls us a flock of sheep. You and I are sheep. We are Christ's sheep. Aren't you glad? Do you know what sheep are? *Dumb*! I don't mean to insult you; it's just the truth. You will never find sheep in the circus—ever! They're not jumping through hoops. They're not riding the elephants. Isaiah said, "All we like sheep have gone astray" (Isa 53:6). Sheep need guidance because we are human beings, and we are sinful. We are weak. We need Christ, our good Shepherd.

Sheep are Distracted

You never see sheep guiding a carriage (like a horse) in Chicago. That would be interesting. They are too weak. They are too distracted.

If there was a cliff, they'd lead you over it. They are quite distracted. But sheep will follow their Shepherd. Sheep need a Shepherd. Jesus is our Good Shepherd isn't he? We need a clear voice to follow.

> My sheep hear my voice, and I know them, and they follow me.
> — *John 10:27*

Sheep are Dirty

You know what else sheep are? They're dirty. Sheep are very dirty without a Good Shepherd to clean them up. Flies can nest in the sheep's wool and leave larvae. They can next and leave maggots in the sheep's wool. Sheep are dirty. All we like sheep have gone astray. We need a good shepherd to guide us and clean us up. He anoints our head with oil to keep the flies and bugs away. He cleans us with his living water. He sometimes sheers us and prunes us to keep us small and humble near him. Oh, I need the cleansing of my Savior.

Jesus Became a Sheep, a Lamb of God. And before you think that I'm just insulting you, because I'm not really insulting, because I'm one of those, too. I'm a lamb, too. Just remember that our Savior became the precious Lamb of God. He condescended and became like us. He knows how we are, and He became the Lamb of God.

Shepherds are called to care for the sheep in three ways: leaders must precede, feed, lead the flock and receive a crown for the flock. Leaders out there – ministry leaders, Titus 2 men and women, we should all strive to be disciple makers. Pastors, elders, deacons, mature men and women, who do we lead the congregation? We begin with getting to know the Shepherd. Peter knew the Shepherd in a precious way.

SHEPHERDS ARE CALLED TO PRECEDE THE FLOCK (5:1)

1 Peter 5:1 | So I exhort the elders among you, as a fellow elder and a witness of the sufferings of Christ, as well as a partaker in the glory that is going to be revealed.

Peter knew the Shepherd in a precious way. He was witness to his suffering and to his glory. He saw the Lord suffer and rise again from the dead. What amazing training for a pastor and elder. Peter was given the gift of Christ revealed to him. What a gift to worship Christ in that way. That's a gift, but it is absolutely necessary for every leader in the church.

Peter was blown away by witnessing the sufferings and glory of Christ. You can see he has quite the reason to worship Christ. Because of his walk with Christ, Peter addresses his fellow elders very humbly as a "fellow elder," not an exalted apostle. God promised he would give his church true shepherds who truly walk with God.

> And I will give you shepherds after my own heart, who will feed you with knowledge and understanding. —*Jeremiah 3:15*

God gives shepherds who experience and share an understanding of him. Peter had an intimate understanding of Christ – witness of his suffering and partaker of his glory. All shepherds need to have this understanding. Jonathan Edwards said that every home is like a little church and the father is the shepherd. We have so many shepherds here today! According to this passage we are all going to be held accountable. I want to be a shepherd after God's heart.

Precede the Flock in Suffering

1 Peter 5:1a | So I exhort the elders among you, as a fellow elder and a witness of the sufferings of Christ.

Peter was there when Christ sweat great drops of blood in the Garden of Gethsemane. He saw the Lord as he was being beaten the home of Caiaphas the high priest. Christ even met eyes with Peter through a window there after Peter had denied him. Peter scattered at the crucifixion "like a sheep without a shepherd," but perhaps he could see the Lord from a place of hiding. Peter witnessed Christ's sufferings.

The apostles were often called witnesses because they walked with Christ and were witnesses of his life and death and resurrection. Being an elder means that we are like all Christians "sharing in Christ's sufferings" (4:13). If you live a holy life, the world will hate you. There is a demonic opposition against all Christians who want to live holy in Christ. "All who live godly in Christ Jesus shall suffer persecution" (2 Tim 2:12). We're called to persevere through persecution and trials and disappointments and discouragements. "The joy of the Lord is my strength" (Neh 8:10). No matter what your suffering is on this earth, the joy we have in Christ is so much greater! And remember the words of Paul, "I consider that the sufferings of this present time are not worth comparing with the glory that is to be revealed to us" (Rom 8:18).

What do you turn to when you are suffering? Peter turned to worship. Look at what he says. He remembers the "sufferings of Christ." He's a witness to it! But he's also a "partaker of the glory" that will be revealed at the Second Coming!

Precede the Flock in Glory

> **1 Peter 5:1** | So I exhort the elders among you, as a fellow elder and a witness of the sufferings of Christ, as well as a partaker in the glory that is going to be revealed.

As Peter begins his exhortation to the church—he first turns to the office of the pastors and elders. He says something very precious. He says, "I've not only witnessed the sufferings of Christ," but I am "a partaker in the glory that is going to be revealed." You know the glory that we are going to experience when Jesus comes again? I've experienced it already.

The Glory of the Transfiguration

Peter says, "I was there when the Lord transfigured himself." Peter says, "I witnessed the glory that Christ had before the world began" up on that Mount of Transfiguration. Christ "led them up a high mountain by themselves. And he was transfigured before them, and his face shone like the sun, and his clothes became white as light" (Mt 17:1-2). I saw his glory! Christ for just a moment peeled back the robe of His humanity, and the Shekinah glory of His blinding divine presence was revealed. Peter was saying, *"You know that one day we will see Christ in all His glory? Well, I as an elder have experienced it already."*

The Glory of the Second Coming

The Pastor and elders and deacons are to be witnessing the glory of Christ. The Pastor is to shepherd the flock by being "a partaker of the glory that shall be revealed" (5:1). One day Christ's glory is going to be revealed to every person that has ever lived. Every soul that ever lived will finally understand Christ's glory. But Christians are those who partake of his glory now. We are "partakers of the divine nature" (2 Pet 1:4).

Many people have gifts, but they do not have the character that comes from walking with Christ. The Lord's people will rarely ascend to heights that the pastor has not scaled first. It is utterly vital that the pastor have a living dynamic loving walk with God, a man of fervent prayer. The pastor must be one who knows how to touch heaven and to cling to the Lord.

The pastor is one who must partake of the glory of Christ! He must succeed in his personal walk with God. In the book of Genesis, we read: Enoch walked with God (5:24), Noah walked with God (6:9). I want to know child of God do you walk with God? Your pastors and elders walk with God. And it is our highest joy to see you walking with him.

A leader must succeed in his walk with God. Any man that wants to lead God's church must precede in his own walk with God. To have power in preaching, he must constantly be before the Throne of Grace. He must succeed in devotion with his family. He has a family altar. He prays with his wife, prays with his children, prays with his forever family in Christ. He must be a man of continual prayer! The pastor must succeed in putting the word of God into practice! It's easy to defend what you believe. It's a whole 'nother story to live what you believe! The pastor if he is to preach powerfully, must live out the principles of God's word *before* he preaches them!

> Let us not love in word or talk but in deed and in truth.—1 John 3:18

In doing God's will the pastor desperately needs to be conscious of the power of God to change people. Pastors do not change people—God changes people!

SHEPHERDS ARE CALLED TO FEED THE FLOCK (5:2)

> **1 Peter 5:2-3** | Shepherd the flock of God that is among you, exercising oversight, not under compulsion, but willingly, as God would have you; not for shameful gain, but eagerly; **3** not domineering over those in your charge, but being examples to the flock.

Feed with Reverence

> **1 Peter 5:2a** | Shepherd the flock of God...

We are to shepherd God's flock. This is the flock of God! I love Psalm 23 that reminds us that God is the shepherd of his flock.

> The Lord is my shepherd; I shall not want. **2** He makes me lie down in green pastures. He leads me beside still waters. —*Psalm 23:1-2*

This is Christ's church. He gave his own blood for each of you.

> I will build my church, and the gates of hell shall not prevail against it. —*Matthew 16:18*

We have to be so careful to feed God's church, because Jesus obtained it with his own blood!

> Pay careful attention to yourselves and to all the flock, in which the Holy Spirit has made you overseers, to care for the church of God, which he obtained with his own blood. —*Acts 20:28*

Dear saint, your shepherds know that you are God's dear child first. You belong to him. We want to treat you with all the care and reverence as the adopted child of God that you are. You belong to God, sealed with his seal of ownership, the blessed Holy Spirit (Eph 1:13-14).

Feed with Substance

1 Peter 5:2-3 | Shepherd the flock of God…

The word "shepherd" can be translated "feed." Do you know that sheep are hungry? The elders must feed the flock with good doctrine (take heed to the doctrine). God has spoken. His word is authoritative. He knows what is best. He gives us the wisdom because he knows the way life should be lived to its fullest. We desperately need sound teaching.

> Keep a close watch on yourself and on the teaching. Persist in this, for by so doing you will save both yourself and your hearers.
> —*1 Timothy 4:16*

> Until I come, devote yourself to the public reading of Scripture, to exhortation, to teaching. —*1 Timothy 4:13*

> But as for you, teach what accords with sound doctrine. —*Titus 2:1*

There are some elders who would rather *dissect* the Bible rather than *digest* the Bible. If the pastor does not "taste and see that the Lord is good" he will have nothing but dry bones to give to others!

> Oh, taste and see that the Lord is good! Blessed is the man who takes refuge in him! —*Psalm 34:8*

> The blessed man's delight is in the law of the Lord, and on his law he meditates day and night. —*Psalm 1:2*

Feed with Balance

1 Peter 5:2b | Shepherd the flock of God that is among you, exercising oversight...

Preaching should be rich, expository, and practical! We are to "exercise oversight" over God's flock, viewing their lives, and applying the Bible in practical ways. People *do not* need entertainment in the pulpit; they need *food*. The man of God must be so God-saturated that he preaches out of the overflow. Preaching must emphasize the whole counsel of God. Paul said to the Ephesian elders that he taught a balanced diet of God's word.

> I did not shrink from declaring to you the whole counsel of God.
> —Acts 20:27

God's sheep need a *balanced* diet of the whole counsel of God. The sheep don't need the pastor's preferences or favorite parts of theology. It is best to preach through the Bible (lectuo continuo), book by book, chapter by chapter, verse by verse, line upon line, precept upon precept. Since you are God's flock, we can't just teach you what we want. We are to teach you the word of God, line upon line and precept upon precept. We are to feed you what God has already prepared for you, not psychology, or a social agenda, or some feel good stories. We are to feed you "the sincere milk of the word" (1 Pet 2:2). We are also to feed you the "solid food" (Heb 5:12) of sound doctrine.

Feed with Gladness

1 Peter 5:2c | Shepherd the flock of God that is among you, exercising oversight, not under compulsion, but willingly.

There is a joyful willingness in feeding the flock. This includes teaching in the pulpit and especially personal discipleship. We cannot be a disciple of Christ unless we are disciple makers. The work of a pastor is rigorous. If your eyes are not firmly fixed on Jesus, you will not last long. There should be a joy about ministry, not a compulsion. The pastor that serves just for the paycheck or just for the honor of the position won't last long in ministry. He will burn out. The true servant of God can say,

> The joy of the Lord is my strength. —Nehemiah 8:10

Get Out of Bed

Let me illustrate the negative side of this admonition with an amusing story. A young man fell sound asleep one Sunday morning when his mother burst in and said, "Wake up, son. You need to get out of bed *right now!*"

With his face buried in his pillow, he responded with a muffled voice, "Give me three good reasons why I should get out of this bed."

Engaging in a tug-of-war with his bedsheet, she said, "One: because it's Sunday and as Christians we always go to church on Sundays."

The man moaned.

"Two: because we have only forty minutes until church starts and you haven't even showered!"

The man tried to ignore his mother.

"Three: because you're the pastor and you need to be there!"

That's ministry under compulsion! While most pastors don't need their mothers to pull them out of bed on Sunday mornings, pulpits are often filled with preachers at the verge of ministry burnout, who can barely keep going. Maybe they went to Bible college and/or seminary and acquired the degree and skills for ministry, but their heart is no longer in it. [142]

There should be a great joy and willingness when it comes to feeding the flock. We are to study the word and proclaim it with gladness. There is a true joy in connecting with the sheep, because there is a deep love from the pastor. Sometimes a pastor is going to get a 3am phone call. That's when you know if he really loves shepherding. You can tell by how he answers the phone! Does he say "oh no" is there a real joy to serve the flock. I can say, no matter what time, day or night, it is my highest honor to shepherd the flock. I even get excited at the worst of times, because I believe God is a God of deliverance and "fullness of joy."

The shepherds are going to give an account, and so he must work hard! The truth of the matter is that ministry is hard work. There is not a place in ministry for the under motivated and the lazy. Much of the energy resident in any local church is in part the result of the leadership dynamic of its pastor. A shepherd is to lead by feeding the flock!

---

[142] Swindoll, *Insights on James and 1 & 2 Peter*, 237.

SHEPHERDS ARE CALLED TO LEAD THE FLOCK (5:2-3)

1 Peter 5:2-3 | Shepherd the flock of God that is among you, exercising oversight, not under compulsion, but willingly, as God would have you; not for shameful gain, but eagerly; **³** not domineering over those in your charge, but being examples to the flock.

Lead with Engagement

1 Peter 5:2a | Shepherd the flock of God that is among you, exercising oversight.

The term bishop, which means "overseer" is from the same word as is above "exercising oversight." This comes right out of the Old Testament. Paul's Hebrew mind was thinking of the word "watchman" in the Hebrew. In fact, the Hebrew nickname for a Christian in Israel is watchman. We are all called to watch over each other and watch out for the enemy.

What is this oversight? It means we are to engage in the lives of God's people. The pastor is not to be merely delivering homilies on Sundays and then isolated from the sheep the rest of the week. The shepherd should smell like the sheep. We are going to give an account for each of the souls connected to this church. Some of you are visiting. I am not accountable for you. You haven't willingly submitted yourself to this church. But I will give account for those who ask for oversight through church membership. We are called to lead God's precious flock by getting them ready for the day when we all meet Christ.

> Obey your leaders and submit to them, for they are keeping watch over your souls, as those who will have to give an account. Let them do this with joy and not with groaning, for that would be of no advantage to you. —*Hebrews 13:17*

Pastors and elders are to meet God's people where they are. In their homes, in their lives. We are to engage their problems. The Bible is God's sufficient word. It is everything we need to live a life of godliness. This means we oversee the flock and give guidance as to how to walk with God, how to read the Scriptures, and how to apply God's word to everyday life. The pastor is to exercise oversight. He is to live among the sheep. He is to keep a close watch upon himself and those who God has put under his charge. Or another sobering command to elders is Paul's exhortation to the Ephesian elders.

> Pay careful attention to yourselves and to all the flock, in which the Holy Spirit has made you overseers, to care for the church of God, which he obtained with his own blood. —*Acts 20:28*

You can hear the earnestness and the seriousness in those words: you elders shepherd the people "whom God purchased with his own blood." In other words, don't take this work lightly. Pastors are to be deeply involved in the life of the sheep.

Lead with Enthusiasm

> **1 Peter 5:2b** | Shepherd the flock of God that is among you, exercising oversight, not under compulsion, but willingly, as God would have you...

If an elder or pastor feels burned out and is not willingly and happily going about his duties to care for the flock, he should not be a leader in the church. I can testify that I have great joy when the people of God call me at any moment. I look at the phone, and I get excited. I know there may be a difficulty on the other end of the phone line. But I'm excited to see how God is going to work "this one" out. There should be a heavenly enthusiasm when it comes to the pastor and all the church in serving the Lord.

> Serve the Lord with gladness! Come into his presence with singing!
> —*Psalm 100:2*

There is no greater joy to a true shepherd, than serving God's people.

Lead with Effort

> **1 Peter 5:2c** | Shepherd the flock of God... not for shameful gain, but eagerly.

Eagerness implies effort. A pastor doesn't do it merely for a paycheck. That would be shameful gain. We do shepherd the flock whether or not we are paid, because we have submitted to God's calling. We love the sheep and want to be with them with great eagerness.

A leader and overseer is really an eager servant of the Lord Jesus Christ. Jesus came in the fashion of a slave, and the pastor should be a prototype of Jesus, conformed to his image. Our effort is not fleshly effort. Our power comes from the resurrection of Christ. Truly "the joy of the Lord is our strength" (Neh 8:10). That is, as we experience the deep love of God, we will have plenty of vigor and energy for the task at hand. In order to be a faithful pastor, we need to be following our Good Shepherd, being carried and loved by our Good Shepherd.

Lead as an Example

1 Peter 5:3 | Shepherd the flock of God ...not domineering over those in your charge, but being examples to the flock.

We are to have a family relationship with God's people, like a father setting the example. Pastors are to become sufficiently involved in the lives of the flock that they establish a godly pattern for the people to follow. An example is a prototype, a mold to be duplicated.

> Set the believers an example in speech, in conduct, in love, in faith, in purity. —*1 Timothy 4:12*

> Keep a close watch on yourself and on the teaching. Persist in this, for by so doing you will save both yourself and your hearers. —*1 Timothy 4:16*

Shepherds are to be a prototype of Christ. Every pastor should be able to say what Paul did to the Corinthians.

> Be imitators of me, as I am of Christ. —*1 Corinthians 11:1*

An Example, not a Control Freak

1 Peter 5:3 | Shepherd the flock of God ...not domineering over those in your charge.

Shepherds are not to command and domineer the flock. One thing that keeps pastors in check from being controlling and domineering is to have a plurality of elders. It is significant that Peter used the plural, elders. In reference to this ministry, the term always appears in the plural in the New Testament, affirming that the office was designed for a plurality of men.[143] There is a plurality of elders necessary in a healthy church. I can testify that the elders of our church have transformed my life. They have set the example of love, gentleness, tenderness, and courage. I can say the deacons have also embodied this. I am honored to serve with such humble men.

---

[143] MacArthur, *1 Peter*, 264.

SHEPHERDS RECIEVE A CROWN FOR THE FLOCK (5:4)

1 Peter 5:4 | And when the chief Shepherd appears, you will receive the unfading crown of glory.

The pastor will, like everyone else, appear before the throne of God on Judgment Day. We will all give an account. And so, his motive for all he does is first, to honor the chief Shepherd. We are going to give God's flock back to God. It's not my flock or your flock. This is the flock of God. He laid down his life for the sheep. You belong to Jesus. One day Jesus is coming back for his dear flock. He knows you all by name. He's written you down in his book, the book of Life.

The Chief Shepherd's Return

1 Peter 5:4a | And when the chief Shepherd appears...

Chief Shepherd is one of the most beautiful titles for the Savior in all of Scripture. The shepherd imagery for Messiah first appears in the Old Testament (Zech 13:7; *cf* Psa 23:1). We as pastors need to be careful how we treat the church, because Jesus is coming back for his bride! He's coming again. He could come at any time. I can't wait. How about you?

The Chief Shepherd's Accounting

Hebrews 13:17 is very convicting.

> Your leaders... are keeping watch over your souls, as those who will have to give an account. Let them do this with joy and not with groaning, for that would be of no advantage to you. —*Hebrews 13:17*

Or another sobering command to elders is found in Acts 20:28.

> Pay careful attention to yourselves and to all the flock, in which the Holy Spirit has made you overseers, to care for the church of God, which he obtained with his own blood. —*Acts 20:28*

Pastors and elders are going to give an account for the spiritual life of the congregation.

The Chief Shepherd's Crown

1 Peter 5:4 | And when the chief Shepherd appears, you will receive the unfading crown of glory.

Can you imagine? After all that Christ has done for us, when he returns, he's going to give us a reward: the unfading crown of glory. At the Second Coming shepherds will receive the unfading crown of glory. In the Greco-Roman world of Peter's day, perishable crowns rather than trophies were the awards for victory at athletic events (1 Cor 9:24-25). Temporal crowns would eventually rust, fade, or, if made from plants, die quickly. Peter was not looking forward merely to some unfading version of an earthly crown, but metaphorically to eternal glory, which can never fade.[144]

I believe we are all going to be like the elders in the book of Revelation who cast their crowns before the Lord. He is worthy, isn't he? Being a leader is such a high and holy calling. Paul said he had the daily care of all the churches. Christ's undershepherds face a daunting task, but faithful oversight brings eternal reward in the form of greater service and joy in the Lord's heaven: "His master said to him, 'Well done, good and faithful slave. You were faithful with a few things, I will put you in charge of many things; enter into the joy of your master'" (Mt 25:23).[145]

Conclusion

Pray for your pastors and elders. Friday night, we were at my son's football game. Throughout the game, I didn't know who was going to win. It was a close game. But in the second half, my son's team just took off. They intercepted the other team. They blocked a punt and returned it. And most of all, my son's team scored touchdowns. Lots of touchdowns. The coach on the sidelines kept telling his team: "Focus". The more they dialed in, the more they focused, the more they flawlessly executed their plays. Dear saint, your pastors are asking you to focus. Focus on Christ our Chief Shepherd. Look to him. He will never let you down. Victory is guaranteed.

---

[144] MacArthur, *1 Peter*, 270–271.
[145] Ibid.

22 | 1 PETER 5:5-7
GROWING IN SPIRITUAL MATURITY

God opposes the proud but gives grace to the humble. Humble yourselves, therefore, under the mighty hand of God so that at the proper time he may exalt you.
1 PETER 5:5-6

Pain is a blessing in disguise. Struggle and affliction are necessary in God's plan. Pain and struggle must run their course in order for proper growth to occur. I learned of the man who found a cocoon of the emperor butterfly. He took it home to watch it develop. One day a small opening appeared. He observed the caterpillar struggling for several hours to pass it's body pass a certain point – a very small opening. Finally, this well-intentioned scientist concluded there must be something wrong. So he took a pair of scissors, and snipped the remaining top of the cocoon. The moth emerged of course very easily. The body was large and swollen, it's wings small and shriveled. He expected in a few hours that the wings would spread out in natural beauty, but they didn't. Instead of having the natural ability to fly, the moth crawled around dragging around shriveled wings and a swollen body – without the ability to fly. Only later did the man understand that the constricting cocoon and the struggle was necessary to pass through, because the struggling through that constricting hole was God's way of passing fluid from the body into the wings – that the wings might be large and developed and the caterpillar be transformed into a butterfly able to fly with ease. God wants you to live a transformed life, and that only comes through struggle, pain, and difficulty. If we cut it off, we will be walking around with swollen fleshly habits in our life with shrunken spiritual wings, and no power to fly.

There is no need to fret or worry about the trials and difficulties in your life. God is using them to grow you for Christ. Are you ready for God to do his work of metamorphosis in your life? We are like big, fat caterpillars, but we are being transformed into beautiful butterflies. Let's fly saints. We are in the process of spiritual metamorphosis. We are to let examination and judgment to begin in our own lives as the family of God.

In 1:5:1-4, Peter says, let the judgment to begin with the elders. There needs to be a humility in leadership. There needs to be discernment in leadership. They've stood against the devil by the word of God, and they've resisted the devil successfully. There is a sense of humility among the elders. Then in 1 Peter 5:5-7, he there is an examination of the saints' spiritual growth.

> **1 Peter 5:5-7** | Likewise, you who are younger, be subject to the elders. Clothe yourselves, all of you, with humility toward one another, for "God opposes the proud but gives grace to the humble." **6** Humble yourselves, therefore, under the mighty hand of God so that at the proper time he may exalt you, **7** casting all your anxieties on him, because he cares for you.

We are to be growing in spiritual maturity. One of the great needs in the last days, and I believe we're living in the last of the last days, is to be mature, because if you're not mature, if you're immature, in perilous times you're going to find yourself folding up and caving in when you ought to be standing up for the Lord Jesus Christ. So I want to talk to you about how to hang tough when the going gets rough because I have an idea that the going is going to get quite rough. 1 Peter is really a handbook for survival, to teach you how to endure in desperate days. Christians are called to grow here in at least three ways: we are to grow in submission (5:5a), in humility (5:5b-6), and in serenity (5:7).

GROW IN ACCOUNTABILITY (5:5A)

> **1 Peter 5:5a** | Likewise, you who are younger, be subject to the elders.

The foundational attitude in the life of the saint must be submission, a relatively familiar theme already in this epistle. That means accountability in every area of life. In 2:13–20 and 3:1–7 Peter commanded believers to be submissive to employers, civil authorities, and within marriage. No less is required of those under the leadership of the divinely instituted office of elder in the most important entity on earth—Christ's own church.[146]

The Sweat of Accountability

Accountability is hard work. To "be subject" indicates a general willingness to support the elders' directions, except if they should ever direct one to sin.[147] How do we understand this idea of accountability? Plato said, "The unexamined life is not worth living."[148] Accountability brings a level of encouragement, fellowship, and comfort from those who have lived the Christian life and walked the path in front of us. Accountability also helps keep us motivated when we are discouraged and examines us to make sure we are not making excuses or being lazy. We all need accountability.

Humility and submission were the consistent marks of Jesus' character. If any young man had the right to put himself above his elders, it was Jesus of Nazareth. Yet the Bible is clear—he resisted taking the reins of leadership before God's appointed time came. Rather, he was quite content to simply "increase in wisdom and in stature and in favor with God and man" (Lk 2:52). As it was for the Son of God, so it is for every one of us. We are to be known for submission and humility.[149]

We are called to be accountable to elders. That is a tall order. But we can do it because the Chief Shepherd is watching over us. Wives are to submit to husbands, children to parents, and the spiritually less mature are to submit to the elders. This implies that the elders of the church are to be mature. This does not mean elders have to be 40 or 50. I was ordained as an elder and a pastor at 25. Timothy was young, and Paul urged him, "Let no one despise your youth" (1 Tim 4:12). Like a body, we need to submit to one another. Everyone in the flock of God

---

[146] MacArthur, *1 Peter*, 276.
[147] Grudem, *1 Peter*, 198–199.
[148] Plato, *The Apology* (Vancouver, Canada: Spartacus Books, 2020), 81.
[149] Helm, *1 & 2 Peter and Jude*, 164.

submits to Jesus (5:4). The flock submits to elders. Elders submit to elders.

The Scope of Accountability

Who is Peter addressing in verse 5? The term *neōteros* ("younger man") can mean several things. Our English prefix *"neo"* borrows from this term, which means "new" or "young." Its most common use in the New Testament is the most general—something new as opposed to old. It can also refer to a person of physically youthful age in contrast to somebody more mature. It's used once in reference to the "new" identity we have in Christ after salvation (Col 3:10). It may also generally refer to those under the authority of leaders—that is, servants, disciples, or assistants (Acts 5:6).

How does Peter use the term "younger" in 5:5? I think a key to understanding this use comes from Jesus' own words, no doubt recalled by Peter in this context. In the previous section on leaders, we saw the echoes of Jesus' warning about the Gentile method of leadership: "The kings of the Gentiles lord it over them … But it is not this way with you" (Lk 22:25–26a). This corresponds to Peter's call for leaders to reject "lording leadership" and to instead set an example of submissive servanthood (1 Pet 5:3). Similarly, Jesus continued: "But the one who is the greatest among you must become like the youngest [*neōteros*], and the leader like the servant" (Lk 22:26b). Thus, according to Jesus, the "greatest" in rank contrasted with the "youngest" in the same way a leader contrasts with a servant. Peter likely picks up on this contrast.[150] So when Peter says, "you younger, be subject to the elders," he's calling all believers by the nickname, "younger." No matter how great or small we are, we should all act like the younger person who would always be the servant. Peter is saying, "Have a servant's attitude when it comes to the elders. Submit to them."

The Supervisors of Accountability

The word *elders* (*presbyteroi*) in the New Testament can mean either 'older people' or 'those who have the office of elder', and the precise sense can only be determined from context. Therefore, some have thought that *the elders* in this verse must mean 'older people generally' in the church (so NIV: 'those who are older'), since Peter does not say,

---

[150] Swindoll, *Insights on James and 1 & 2 Peter*, 241.

'All of you be subject to the elders', but speaks directly to *you that are younger*. The contrast between *younger* and *elders*, it is said, indicates a contrast in age, not church office.

However, several considerations make it more likely that we should understand *elders* here, as in verse 1, to refer to those who have the office of "elder" within the church, not to older people generally. The first word of verse 5, "likewise," indicates that Peter is continuing the discussion begun in verses 1 to 4, just as "likewise" in 3:7 indicates the continuation of the discussion begun in 3:1–6. And since the subject in verses 1 to 4 is those who hold the office of "elder," verse 5 is to be seen as an instruction about relating to those who hold the office. Also, the command "be subject," implies submission to an authority, not just deference or respect, and older people generally did not have governing authority in churches, but those in the office of "elders" did.[151] One ancient commentator, Bishop Hilarius of what is today southern France, gives the sense of how the early believers would have heard Peter.

> By "young men" Peter means everyone who occupies a subordinate role in the church. But note that those who are superiors must also act humbly, for humility is what should be common to both.[152]

What Hilarius said makes sense since it also goes with what the author of Hebrews has said concerning the shepherds' duty.

> Obey your leaders and submit to them, for they are keeping watch over your souls, as those who will have to give an account. Let them do this with joy and not with groaning, for that would be of no advantage to you. [18] Pray for us, for we are sure that we have a clear conscience, desiring to act honorably in all things.   —Hebrews 13:17-18

We are to submit to the elders of a local church – but this does not mean I submit to elders of all churches at all times. That would be impossible. It says "submit to those who watch over you" (Heb 13:17; *cf* Acts 20:29-30). Elders are going to give an account. They care for your souls. So this is clearly referring to a local church at a certain location at a certain time in history. A specific council of elders is watching for your soul and going to give an account.

---

[151] Grudem, *1 Peter*, 199.

[152] Bishop Hilarius of Arles in Gerald Bray, *James, 1-2 Peter, 1-3 John, Jude*, Ancient Christian Commentary on Scripture NT 11 (Downers Grove, IL: InterVarsity Press, 2000), 123.

GROW IN HUMILITY (5:5B-6)

The Robe of Humility

1 Peter 5:5b | Clothe yourselves, all of you, with humility toward one another.

Peter says to the younger: it matters what you wear. You want to pay for the stuff where the seams bust and the rip and go out of style. What God offers is free but it costs. We are to "be clothed with" humility. The Greek word for "clothed" means "to gird oneself" or "to tie something on oneself," such as a work apron worn by servants. It describes the attitude of one who willingly serves, even in the lowliest of tasks (*cf* 1 Cor 4:1–5; 2 Cor 4:7; Phil 2:5–7). Perhaps even more so than today, humility was not an admired trait in the first-century pagan world. People saw it as a characteristic of weakness and cowardice, to be tolerated only in the involuntary submission of slaves.[153]

Humility means to wear the apron of a slave. Would you do that? Jesus did. Jesus washed His disciples' feet. He tied this apron around him, girded himself with a towel, with an apron, and got on his knees, and washed his disciples' feet. As Peter wrote this verse, he likely recalled Jesus' putting on the towel of a slave, teaching Peter about humility. Listen to our Lord as he teaches Peter: "Let the greatest among you become as the youngest, and the leader as one who serves... 27 I am among you as the one who serves" (Lk 22:26-27). Christ was content to wear humility as though it were a royal robe to grace the shoulders of a king (Phil 2:6–8).

Humility is something we wear. We put it on and tuck it in. We are to wear it around the house. We are to wear it in the marketplace, where we work, and where we worship. It is not an easy garment to put on, but it is most becoming.[154] Now, if Jesus could wash feet, don't you think you could work on a parking lot? If Jesus could wash feet, don't you think you could work in the nursery? Could our Lord greet people as they enter our church? How our Lord served. How are you serving?

---

[153] MacArthur, *1 Peter*, 277.
[154] Phillips, *Epistles of Peter*, 1 Pe 5:5b.

The Relevance of Humility

1 Peter 5:5c | For "God opposes the proud but gives grace to the humble." (*cf* Pro 3:34)

Is there anything more frightening to hear, but that God would oppose someone? This is the most serious matter one could imagine. I don't want to be that person whom God opposes. The only proper attitude in God's presence is humility. The prophet Isaiah stated the principle well.

> For thus says the One who is high and lifted up, who inhabits eternity, whose name is Holy: "I dwell in the high and holy place, and also with him who is of a contrite and lowly spirit, to revive the spirit of the lowly, and to revive the heart of the contrite." —*Isaiah 57:15; cf 66:2*

If you are not humble, if you don't have the spirit of a servant, not only will God not give you grace, but God will actually stand in your way. What we need in our church is some grown up, mature Christians who are more concerned about clothing themselves with humility than whatever the latest fashion is. If we don't gird our inner man first with that gentleness and humility, God will resist us. What could be more serious than that? God doesn't enjoy resisting us. His Son calls out to us.

> Come to me, all who labor and are heavy laden, and I will give you rest. ²⁹ Take my yoke upon you, and learn from me, for I am gentle and lowly in heart, and you will find rest for your souls. ³⁰ For my yoke is easy, and my burden is light. —*Matthew 11:28-30*

The Reward of Humility

1 Peter 5:6 | Humble yourselves, therefore, under the mighty hand of God so that at the proper time he may exalt you.

Peter says "therefore" because God's asked you to humble yourselves in all the varies realms of authority, you should indeed trust God, and you will not be disappointed. The Spirit of God is asking the Christian to realize that every area of authority is under the control of God, "under the mighty hand of God." Therefore, humbling oneself will involve bowing to God's wisdom, accepting the twists and turns of his providence, and entrusting all our concerns to him.

When we humble ourselves and submit to God in a spirit of meekness and surrender, God will lift us up. He will use us for his kingdom purposes. God wants to use his saints, but he will only use the humble. This special exaltation of his humble saints may mean an increased spiritual blessing of some kind. Perhaps it is deeper fellowship with himself. Or maybe a new stewardship or spiritual responsibility, reward, or honor. How God wants to make us more useful for his kingdom.

Peter says: humble yourselves. God will exalt you for his kingdom, but it may well mean personal disadvantage in this life. Don't worry if you are suffering in your submission and humility. God's promise is that *at the proper time he may exalt you*.[155] The early church father Chrysostom (c. 344 A.D.) says that Peter mentions this exaltation will happen in due time, because he is teaching them that they will have to wait until the next life for our ultimate exaltation.[156] There is coming a day when he will "be glorified in his saints, and to be marveled at among all who have believed" (2 Thess 1:10).

GROW IN SERENITY (5:7)

> **1 Peter 5:7** | Casting all your anxieties on him, because he cares for you.

There's a reason we are told, "Be still and know that I am God" (Psa 46:10). He cares for you. That's the centerpiece of the gospel: God's love. But instead, we worry, thinking it will actually do something for us.

The Damage of Sinful Worry

According to the dictionary, anxiety is "a feeling of worry, nervousness, unease, or even terror or fear – typically about an imminent event or something with an uncertain outcome." Anxiety can cripple you; it can steal your joy, zap your energy, and fill you with terror and dread. "What if" is a question we often ask ourselves. We want to control our uncertain future. We would feel much better if we had more control.

---

[155] Grudem, *1 Peter,* 201.
[156] John Chrysostom in J. A. Cramer, ed. *Catena in Epistolas Catholicas.* Oxford: Clarendon, 1840, 81.

But we don't. So we worry. Worry is a form of atheism. Atheism is forgetting God. When we worry and forget that God is in control and that he loves us, then we willfully remove ourselves from his embrace, his security, and his comfort. Don't be an "anxiety atheist." What can we do to rid ourselves of anxiety?

The Delight of God's Care

Realize there is a peace that comes with surrendering your anxieties and cares to God. He cares for you! He is the Chief Shepherd. He will leave the 99 and go after the wandering sheep (Mt 18:10-14). He loves you. Things in the mirror are closer than they appear. Can I say God is closer than he may appear in your life? Sometimes the cares in our life seem bigger than your God. But God is bigger than anything in your life. He's the biggest and closest.

If we go back to what Jesus warned, we will see that he tells us that worry is a worship issue. Worry is all about having competing treasures (Mt 6:19-21), competing eyes (Mt 6:22-23), or competing masters (Mt 6:24). In other words, worry is an idolatry indicator. Worry is wrong because it expresses heart idolatry. What do you sometimes tend to treasure more than the Lord? What you worry about is what you are worshipping.

Instead of having competing idols, you need to turn your focus on complete rest in Christ. Remember that understanding the love of Christ casts out all fear.

> There is no fear in love, but perfect love casts out fear. For fear has to do with punishment, and whoever fears has not been perfected in love. —*1 John 4:18*

Say no to fear, since there is no fear in receiving God's love. His love is based on the perfect work of Christ. It is finished. There is no condemnation now since we are in Christ. God washes away all your bad choices, all your sin and rebellion. He is that good. Let that love wash over you. We see this theme throughout the word of God.

> Cast your burden upon the Lord. —*Psalm 55:22*

> Do not worry about how or what you are to say. —*Matthew 10:19*

> Be anxious for nothing. —*Philippians 4:6*

Paul wrote these words while confined to a Roman prison. His circumstances may not have been pleasant, yet he penned these words. The circumstances of your life may appear unbearable, but there is hope because Christ is aware of what you're facing. He knows all about the bill due at the end of the month and your lack of money to pay it. He's already aware of the doctor's report that will mean you must face even more treatment. Wherever your prison happens to be, God is in it with you. Remember God's promises to you. He cares for you.

> You keep him in perfect peace whose mind is stayed on you, because he trusts in you. —*Isaiah 26:3*

> Do not be anxious about anything, but in everything by prayer and supplication with thanksgiving let your requests be made known to God. —*Philippians 4:6*

The great reformer Martin Luther once said: "Pray and let God worry." [157] I think he got it right. You see, worry is faith turned inside out. The word cast here speaks of a very deliberate act, a definite and deliberate, a decisive act. How many of you have a problem? How many of you have a care? How many have a, an anxiety? They come to all of us. You have, as a mature Christian, you have to resolutely cast that anxiety upon the Lord. That peaceful spirit is one of the great marks of maturity in your life.

When a mature believer walks into to a chaotic situation, he doesn't adopt the attitude of chaos, worry, fear, or anger. Any child can stop their feet or complain or cry in fear. No, the mature child of God walks into chaos and brings peace and calm to the situation. We are called to that peace of God that passes all understanding (Phil 4:7).

Conclusion

Dear child of God, you are called to maturity through three important marks: accountability, humility, and serenity.

We are living in the Babylon of this world. We are, as Peter describes us, "elect exiles." We are not at home. It's easy to get discouraged and stuck and paralyzed. It's easy for our Christian growth to be stunted, but we can grow in Babylon. We grow into maturity like the

---

[157] Martin Luther in Timothy J. Wingert, *The Pastoral Luther: Essays on Martin Luther's Practical Theology* (Minneapolis, MN: Fortress Press, 2017), 94.

palm trees in the desert. Palm trees are quite amazing trees. For starters, you can cut it, but you cannot kill it. The nutrients that most trees need to survive are found just below the bark, so when you cut them, they die, but not the palm tree. Its life comes from its heart, so it thrives even under attack. This reminds me of Psalm 92:12, "The righteous flourish like the palm tree and grow like the cedar in Lebanon."

Palm trees survive the dry times. If you are in Christ, you will survive those dry times. When you think about it, this whole world—apart from Christ—is a desert. But God can give his children the grace, the ability, to flourish—to grow, to be strong, to be fruitful, to be beautiful, even in a desert place. God can make "rivers in the desert" (Isa 43:19). They have an amazing root system that hits the water below. Palm trees bend but do not break. In Christ we can bloom in the desert.

Are you stuck, child of God? Are you not growing? Humble yourself before the Lord. Get some accountability. Let the peace and serenity of God grip your heart. That's the rich soil of growth for the Christian life.

23 | 1 PETER 5:8-14
GROWING IN SPIRITUAL WARFARE

Be sober-minded; be watchful. Your adversary the devil prowls around like a roaring lion, seeking someone to devour. Resist him, firm in your faith.

1 PETER 5:8-9

The book *Pilgrim's Progress* tells the story of Pilgrim who becomes Christian. He flees from the city of destruction. He sees the glories of heaven above him and the horrors of hell underneath him, and he sticks his fingers in his ears fleeing from the City of Destruction yelling, "Life! Life! Eternal life!" That's a picture of every one of us. [158]

Christian was on his way to the Celestial City, but before he got there he had to cross a path of two lions, one on either side. Their roar was fierce and vicious. He felt like they would tear him limb from limb. Thankfully, there was a friend named Watchful, and he cried out to Christian to have courage. Bunyan writes:

> He shouted, "Don't be afraid of the lions, for they are chained. They are placed there to test your faith at this point in your journey. They also show clearly those who have no faith. So stay in the middle of the path and you will not be harmed." Then I saw Christian go forward, though he still trembled with fear of the lions. He took care to follow

---

[158] John Bunyan, *Pilgrim's Progress* (Illustrated): Updated, Modern English. (Bunyan Updated Classics) (Abbotsford, WI: Aneko Press, 2020), 5.

the porter's directions and stayed to the middle of the path. The lions roared and snarled, but they did him no harm. He clapped his hands with joy and went on till he stood before the palace gate where the porter awaited him. [159]

We are at war with the devil, but because Christ has bound him on a chain, he can do us no harm, as long as we walk in the middle of the road, in obedience to the Lord.

Remember that famous video that shows President Franklin Roosevelt addressing Congress the day after the Japanese attack on Pearl Harbor in December of 1941? He described that day as "a day that will live in infamy." When the president made that statement, America was already at war. Roosevelt just needed a declaration of Congress to make it official. I am not a member of Congress or the president, but I have a declaration to make: You and I are at war! In fact, we are engaged right now in the mother of all battles. No war in history can compare with the battle you and I are fighting. It can be the cause of either your greatest joy as a Christian or your deepest pain. We read about this war in our text.

> **1 Peter 5:8-11** | Be sober-minded; be watchful. Your adversary the devil prowls around like a roaring lion, seeking someone to devour. [9] Resist him, firm in your faith, knowing that the same kinds of suffering are being experienced by your brotherhood throughout the world. [10] And after you have suffered a little while, the God of all grace, who has called you to his eternal glory in Christ, will himself restore, confirm, strengthen, and establish you. [11] To him be the dominion forever and ever. Amen.

Peter is using the language of war. We have an adversary. But we are on the winning side. The war Peter is talking about is the spiritual warfare that you became a part of the day you received Jesus Christ as your Savior. This war affects every area of your life. There is no way you can avoid the conflict. There is no bunker or foxhole you can crawl into that will shield you from the effects of this cosmic battle between the forces of God and the forces of Satan. You may not even know you're at war. A lot of Christians don't. But other people can see the results of the battle in those people's lives because they have become casualties of spiritual warfare.

---

[159] Ibid., 52.

Some Christians are emotional casualties of spiritual warfare. They are discouraged, depressed, downtrodden, and defeated. Others are marital and family casualties. Divorce, conflict, and abuse are some of the "battle scars" these believers bear. Still others have been wounded morally in the battle. They cannot control their passions, or they make poor moral choices. For some Christians, the wounds have been inflicted on their finances. They are losing the financial battle because they are losing the spiritual battle. It's not just a matter of how they use their credit cards.

Since we are all at war, and since there is so much at stake both here on earth and in eternity, we'd better find out what spiritual warfare is all about and how to fight the battle successfully. Don't let your weaknesses be a gateway to Satan's control. Remember what Jesus says to Paul, "My grace is sufficient for you, for my power is made perfect in weakness." Therefore I will boast all the more gladly of my weaknesses, so that the power of Christ may rest upon me. 10 For the sake of Christ, then, I am content with weaknesses, insults, hardships, persecutions, and calamities. For when I am weak, then I am strong" (2 Cor 12:9-11). God wants us to understand that it is his will for every Christian to live in victory against the devil. How do we do that?

BE READY FOR THE FIGHT (5:8-9)

Be Sober-minded

1 Peter 5:8a | Be sober-minded.

With all the pain and suffering of life, it's easy to check out or be distracted. Peter says, you have to take this seriously. Now, we're to cast our burdens upon the Lord, but to be carefree doesn't mean to be careless. Peter is deadly serious about what he has to say. We are to remember that this has been a war since the beginning. God created hell not for you, but for the devil and his angels. Yet all who follow Satan will end up in hell. That's serious. That's why Peter says, "Be soberminded." This life has serious consequences.

Notice what he says, "...your adversary the devil...." Did you know you have an adversary? He doesn't merely say *the* adversary. "... *your* adversary..." Satan has a personal vendetta against you now because you are God's child. Be serious. Be sober. We cast our cares on Jesus, but we are not careless. We are serious about the battle. Don't be uncaring.

Peter says in 1 Peter 1:13, "Prepare your minds for action, and being sober-minded, set your hope fully on the grace that will be brought to you at the revelation of Jesus Christ." He says literally, "Gird up the loins of your mind." Roll up the garment of your mind so you don't get it caught on anything. The work of the new life is mind renewal. We are to put off the old life, the former way of thinking and put on the new life and be "renewed in the spirit of your mind." This makes sense because Ezekiel says we have the old stubborn heart of stone removed and a new tender heart with the Spirit of God given to us. We now have a lot of work to remove and replace our thinking.

Be Watchful

1 Peter 5:8b | Be watchful. Your adversary the devil prowls around like a roaring lion, seeking someone to devour.

Paul says in 2 Cor 2:11 that we should "not be outwitted by Satan; for we are not ignorant of his designs." We already know the enemy's battle plans. He doesn't just want to hurt you temporarily. He wants to destroy you eternally. Don't be ignorant of your enemy. You have an enemy. You'd better recognize him. He has plans to sabotage your life The dynamite is in place, the fuse is laid, and the match is struck.

Satan is a Hidden Lion

Satan is raging and roaring as Peter says in 1 Peter 5:8, "your adversary the devil, as a roaring lion, walks about, seeking whom he may devour." But don't think you are going to see him directly. He works through people, culture, what's popular. He works through philosophy. The devil is a roaring lion, but he's always undercover.

Paul tells us it's a real war, but it's a spiritual and invisible war. Ephesians 6:12–13, "For we do not wrestle against flesh and blood, but against the rulers, against the authorities, against the cosmic powers over this present darkness, against the spiritual forces of evil in the heavenly places. 13 Therefore take up the whole armor of God, that you may be able to withstand in the evil day, and having done all, to stand firm."

There is an unseen war. In Daniel 10, we see that the demons are territorial. The demonic principality (governor) of Persia and Greece are mentioned. But God says to Daniel "O man greatly loved" (Dan 10:19), I have sent the archangel Michael to be by your side. God has sent to us angels as "ministering spirits" to help the saints. We can't see them, and sometimes in our hospitality we "minister to angels unawares."

Satan is a Hungry Lion

He is "seeking whom he may devour" (5:8b). This is way you need to be "sober-minded." Be "watchful." How do you do that? Remember Satan is a hungry lion. Joaquim Fragoso and I were talking and he told me that when he and Christine bring their kids to the zoo, the lion is always tired and lazy. Have you ever noticed that? Why are the lions at the zoo so lazy? Because they are *well fed*.

Satan is not that way. He's hungry. He's being starved because he is a defeated enemy. He knows his time is short. His strategy is to take you down with him. You are now free from this enemy. He had you in his grip when you were lost, but "the reason the Son of God appeared was to destroy the works of the devil" (1 Jn 3:8).

Satan is a Hateful Lion

He is "seeking whom he may devour" (5:8b). He's not looking to wound you. He's looking to take you out permanently. He "knows his time is short" (Rev 12:12). He wants to destroy you. Christians no longer belong to Satan, but they certainly can be harassed and demonized by the enemy.

The enemy is territorial. He's roaming about the earth looking for an opportunity. Now not everyone is harassed by Satan himself. Peter is using a literary device called synecdoche – naming part of something for the whole. There is a whole host of demons. When we refer to demonic activity as "Satan," we are not just talking about the father of lies, but about any demonic activity. "The whole world lies in the power of the evil one" (Jn 5:19b). There is "the prince of the power of the air, the spirit that now works in the children of disobedience" (Eph 2:2). Remember that "the god of this world has blinded the minds of them which believe not" (2 Cor 4:4).

Satan is hateful. He's the accuser of the brothers and sisters. He is hateful. He'll do anything to stop us. He wants to prevent us from going forward for the kingdom of God. Paul says to the Thessalonians, "We wanted very much to come to you, and I, Paul, tried again and again, but Satan prevented us" (1 Thess 2:18).

Be Firm

1 Peter 5:9a | Resist him, firm in your faith.

You can't just coast in the Christian life. You have to be proactive. Put on the whole armor of God. Be ready to fight.

Engage in the Fight

Paul says, "I have fought the good fight..." The idea of resisting is fighting. Paul explains in Ephesians 6 that we have a war chest filled with armor. We're going to need to put on the full armor of God. We are to fight against the wicked one. How? You can't do it. You are no match for him. Resist Satan, "firm in your faith." It's your faith in Christ that will "quench the fiery arrows of the devil." Paul says, "the weapons of our warfare are not carnal, but mighty through God to the pulling down of strong holds" (2 Cor 10:4, KJV).

You were a rebel against God, taken captive by the wicked one. You were behind the prison bars and you could not free yourself. Your prison was impenetrable. You cannot escape. You're doomed – because when the enemy comes in, at the very end, he's going to finish you off. He has legal right to destroy you, and he relishes moment your final destruction comes. In comes your Intercessor, your Advocate – your Warrior. And he stands between you and your accuser. And he takes the hit that was rightfully yours. He takes the blow that was intended for you. This is an extraordinary reality, that Jesus Christ was turned to a pulp for you. God's very word, his very expression took on human form and God in human flesh – he died for you! Over your prison cell, it has always said "condemned" – "separated eternally from God" – "Guilty!" But suddenly it switches. In a moment everything changes. It now says, "Justified" – "Forgiven" – "No Condemnation" – "Redeemed"! We need to be engaged in the fight. The enemy can be overcome by prayer. Jesus said, "This kind comes out only through prayer" (Mk 9:29).

Engage with Faith

Satan wants you to panic. God wants you to rest and "be firm." 1 Peter 5:9, "Resist him, firm in your faith..." James says: "Resist the devil and he will flee from you." Our enemy is a defeated foe. 1 John 4:4 says we are fighting from a point of victory. He says, "greater is He who is in you than he who is in the world." We don't stand in our own power to resist Satan. We are "firm" in our faith in Christ.

REMAIN FOCUSED (5:9)

Focus on Christ, Not Satan

1 Peter 5:9a | Resist him, firm in your faith.

We can't be distracted by the harassment and confusion of Satan. Fix your eyes on Jesus who is "the founder and perfecter of our faith" (Heb 12:2). One day a father and his little boy were watching the lions at the zoo when a lion let out a deafening roar. The terrified boy screamed and ran off, begging his father to run too. But his father told him to come back because the lion wouldn't hurt him. "Son," the father said, "don't look at the lion. Look at the cage." As long as we focus on the Person and power of Christ, we won't have to worry about Satan's roar. Keep your eyes on the Lord, and you will be relieved. The cage that's around Satan are God's hands. God will never let that lion lose on you. He'll only hurt you if you make your way near to him and stick your arm in the cage. Satan is a defeated foe. He's bound by Jesus (Mt 12:29). Just don't give in to his temptations and schemes.

Focus on Christ, Not Your Suffering

1 Peter 5:9 | Resist him, firm in your faith.

Satan wants to isolate you and make you think you are the only one going through this type of suffering. The enemy has many tools in his tool house, but he likes to use suffering to bring discouragement, bitterness, chaos, and confusion. God always brings perfect peace. Satan can roar but he cannot defeat you. You belong to the Lion of the tribe of Judah. Often, we get so hurt in life that we can't see the Lord. We need to stay focused. Be like Peter in the storm. He focused on Jesus and began walking on water. That's what God wants for us. We need to live above the circumstances of our lives, focused on Jesus. In a moment, Jesus can command the wind and the waves: "Peace be still."

Focus on Christ, not Your Sin

1 Peter 5:9 | Resist him, firm in your faith.

You've got to resist Satan, because he is the accuser of the brothers and sisters in Christ. That's his main work. Ephesians 4 gives us insight into Satan's devices. Any sin you give way to will open the door for the devil. "Be angry and do not sin; do not let the sun go down on your anger, 27 and give no opportunity to the devil" (Eph 4:26-27).

All life is war. From the cradle to the grave, we fight. Before the new birth, we were held captive by the devil. Now we must "stand against the schemes of the devil." Though Christ has delivered the death blow to the powers of darkness, they are not yet fully destroyed. At the end of Paul's life, he said "I have fought a good fight."

Fight with Christ's Weapons

1 Peter 5:9 | Resist him, firm in your faith.

Before we consider Christ's weapons, let's recognize the enemy's weapons: chaos, discouragement, confusion, fear, anger, distraction, worldliness, escape, etc. How do we resist the devil? We can't wage war according to our own understanding or our limited power. "For though we walk in the flesh, we are not waging war according to the flesh. 4 For the weapons of our warfare are not of the flesh but have divine power to destroy strongholds" (2 Cor 10:3–4). Our spiritual armor equips us to live by faith in Christ. God's weapons are means of grace, such as prayer, the Scriptures, worship, prayer, fellowship, and godly living.

Paul gets specific and instructs us: "Put on the whole armor of God, that you may be able to stand against the schemes of the devil. 12 For we do not wrestle against flesh and blood, but against the rulers, against the authorities, against the cosmic powers over this present darkness, against the spiritual forces of evil in the heavenly places." Now just outside of the very near presence of God is a war chest. God says, "My children will not lose. Give me your body – your whole being, and I will come in and make it my own. Your hands, your feet, your mouth, will be my hands, feet, and mouth. And I will take out your heart of stone and make it a heart of flesh and I will give you my burdens to bear and you will speak my words and go forth in my power and you will be my instrument!" Now go into that war chest and put on the whole armor of God. Put on the belt of truth, the breastplate of righteousness, the boots of peace, the shield of faith, the helmet of salvation, the sword of the Spirit (God's word), and the walkie-talkie of prayer.

We don't stand in our own power. Paul says in Eph 6:13-14, "Therefore take up the whole armor of God, that you may be able to withstand in the evil day, and having done all, to stand firm. Stand therefore." We are to stand in Christ. If you go in your own power you will fail. "Not by might, nor by power but by my Spirit says the Lord" (Zech 4:6).

Fight Side by Side with Christ's Forever Family

> **1 Peter 5:9b** | Knowing that the same kinds of suffering are being experienced by your brotherhood throughout the world.

The ravages that Satan is still able to unleash upon this planet are part of the "mystery of iniquity" (2 Thess 2:7). These will not be abolished completely until the second coming of Christ and the final incarceration of Satan in the lake of fire (Rev 20:10). Satan, through the malice of Nero, was bringing terrible afflictions upon the church.

This fight wasn't just happening in one town or another, but "throughout the world." We are God's forever family. We are together, fighting side by side. We need each other in the suffering that comes from this war. We need to line up together with our shields of faith and take on the enemy. Perhaps Peter had seen Roman soldiers going through their battle drills. In one maneuver, the troops would stand shoulder to shoulder, their large, octagonal shields locked together to form a solid wall of steel. This maneuver enabled them to bear the brunt of all of the attacking force of the enemy. Peter urges his readers to lock shields with believers all over the world to use their spiritual weapons and resist the foe. [160]

REST IN GOD'S FAVOR (5:10-11)

1 Peter 5:10-11, "And after you have suffered a little while, the God of all grace, who has called you to his eternal glory in Christ, will himself restore, confirm, strengthen, and establish you. 11 To him be the dominion forever and ever. Amen."

---

[160] Phillips, *Epistles of Peter*, 1 Pe 5:9.

The Lord is with you in Suffering

> **1 Peter 5:10** | And after you have suffered a little while, the God of all grace, who has called you to his eternal glory in Christ, will himself restore, confirm, strengthen, and establish you.

We are going to suffer for "a little while." Suffering rightly reacted to will just toughen you and will stabilize you. And a, a mature person can stand in tough times. That's the way you get mature. No pain, no gain. There is so much suffering during this short life, be we must remember the words of Paul: "I consider that the sufferings of this present time are not worth comparing with the glory that is to be revealed to us" (Rom 8:18). Suffering is a huge tool God uses in our life to draw us nearer to him. C.S. Lewis said, "Pain is God's megaphone to rouse a deaf world." Suffering is never pointless for a Christian. God always has a plan for it. The Christian is called to "wait on the Lord" through the pain and suffering. The Lord told Paul, "My grace is sufficient for you, for my power is made perfect in weakness" (2 Cor 12:9a). Our response ought to be the same as Paul's, "Therefore I will boast all the more gladly about my weaknesses, so that Christ's power may rest on me. 10 That is why, for Christ's sake, I delight in weaknesses, in insults, in hardships, in persecutions, in difficulties. For when I am weak, then I am strong" (2 Cor 12:9b-10).

The Lord is with you in Sanctification

> **1 Peter 5:10b** | The God of all grace, who has called you to his eternal glory in Christ, will himself restore, confirm, strengthen, and establish you.

Your sanctification is promised! Paul said that God would bring about a complete sanctification of believer. "Now may the God of peace himself sanctify you completely, and may your whole spirit and soul and body be kept blameless at the coming of our Lord Jesus Christ. 24 He who calls you is faithful; he will surely do it" (1 Thess. 5:23-24). Jude tells us that he is able to keep us from falling away and surrendering to the enemy. "Now to him who is able to keep you from stumbling and to present you blameless before the presence of his glory with great joy, to the only God, our Savior, through Jesus Christ our Lord, be glory, majesty, dominion, and authority, before all time and now and forever.

Amen (Jude 24-25). Paul says that God will complete his work of sanctification in you. "And I am sure of this, that he who began a good work in you will bring it to completion at the day of Jesus Christ" (Phil. 1:6).

The Lord is with you in His Sovereignty

1 Peter 5:11 | To him be the dominion forever and ever. Amen.

Little David, before he was king knew this. Here is this giant Goliath cursing David and his God. But David replies, "You come to me with a sword and with a spear and with a javelin, but I come to you in the name of the Lord of hosts, the God of the armies of Israel, whom you have defied. This day the Lord will deliver you into my hand, and I will strike you down and cut off your head. And I will give the dead bodies of the host of the Philistines this day to the birds of the air and to the wild beasts of the earth, that all the earth may know that there is a God in Israel, and that all this assembly may know that the Lord saves not with sword and spear. For the battle is the Lord's, and he will give you into our hand" (1 Sam 17:46-47). Do you understand that your battle is not your battle. The battle is the Lord's! We are resting in the sovereign one who has all dominion. Jesus is described in the prophets as the one who is going to crush all other kingdoms. John says he is "King of kings and Lord of lords." He calls Jesus "the Alpha and the Omega, the Beginning and the End, the Almighty" (Rev 1:8). Wow. He's sovereign over your enemy, and one day God is going to cast the enemy into a lake of fire and sulfur, prepared for the devil and his angels.

REJOICE IN GOD'S FAMILY (5:12-14)

Examples of Spiritual Growth

As we conclude, I want to look at the end of the chapter where we have three examples of spiritual growth: Silas, John Mark, and the church in Rome.

Silas, the Faithful Brother

1 Peter 5:12 | By Silvanus, a faithful brother as I regard him, I have written briefly to you, exhorting and declaring that this is the true grace of God. Stand firm in it.

Silvanus (better known as Silas) was Peter (and Paul's) faithful companion and brother in the Lord. He was faithful to help Peter write to the churches of Asia Minor. In other words, Paul dictated the letter, but Silas transcribed it. This is a major reason the Greek of the first epistle of Peter is much more refined than the second epistle.

What did Silas and Peter exhort and declare to the churches? That God's grace is sufficient in suffering. We are to "stand firm" in it, even though we are living in Babylon, a metaphor for Rome, representing the hostile world that every Christian faces (5:13).

The Chosen Church at Babylon (Rome)

1 Peter 5:13a | She who is at Babylon, who is likewise chosen, sends you greetings.

Peter speaks of the female who is at Babylon who is chosen. Who is this? It is the church at Rome. She sends "greetings" to the church in Asia Minor. Peter here returns to his theme that we as Christians are elect exiles. Babylon is the nickname for any city a Christian resides, and it refers back to Israel's Babylonian exile, where they were taken away to a strange land for seventy years.

In mentioning this theme, Peter is going back to his opening greeting to the "elect exiles" scattered around the Roman empire. We too are in exile in regard to our relationship with this world, but in regard to God, we are chosen and loved.

Peter closes the letter by giving greetings from the Christians in a metaphorical Babylon, referencing Rome where Peter would later die by being crucified upside down. The message is that we are not at home here on earth. We are in exile. He says those Christians in Babylon are "chosen." So Peter begins and ends with the theme of election. We may be rejected by the world, but we are chosen and cherished. Before we could ever choose God, he chose us. Before we could love him, he loved us (1 Jn 4:4). We choose God because he chose us. The doctrine of election should not divide Christians, it should bring us to worship the Lord, since salvation from beginning to end is all of grace. If it were up to us, no one in the history of the world would have ever sought God. God sought us. I was lost, not looking for God, but he was looking for me. He opened my eyes and I believed. I was immediately uncomfortable in this sin cursed world. I am an exile living in spiritual Babylon, elect and esteemed.

Peter's "Son" John Mark

1 Peter 5:13 | She who is at Babylon... sends you greetings, and so does Mark, my son.

Mark is then mentioned. He's called Peter's "son." This is referring to John Mark (5:13), the author of the second gospel, also considered to be Peter's gospel. It was John Mark who was with Peter listening to him and transcribing for him this gospel narrative that presents our Lord as a servant. This is important because in Rome estimates of slaves in the empire are as high as 50%.

Examples of Saintly Love

1 Peter 5:14a | Greet one another with the kiss of love.

A Kiss of Love. There is affection to be shown by a "kiss of love" (5:14). What is this kiss? It's different in every culture, but it is a sign that we treat each other as family. We are elect exiles, so we love to be together, greeting each other, fellowshipping with each other in our native language (praise and prayer), with our forever family.

1 Peter 5:14b | Peace to all of you who are in Christ.

Peace to All. The epistle closes with "Peace to all of you who are in Christ" (5:14b). This is what we can have if we are in Christ. Though there is suffering, slavery, spiritual warfare, there is peace in the storm. There is rest in the righteousness of Christ. This is the hope of 1 Peter. Part of that peace comes as we think about the spiritual growth that takes place in all believers as they grow in love for one another. We are all to be "conformed to the image of God's dear Son" (Rom 8:30).

Conclusion

Here we conclude the book of First Peter. This was a book of shining as lights in the midst of darkness, in the midst of suffering. Consider God's protection of Jim Elliot, missionary who was put to death by the people he came to reach. Elizabeth Elliot's brother Dave Howard used to be a member of our church. It is said the tribesman that killed Jim Elliot and the other missionaries saw angels who surrounded those missionaries when they died. Jim Elliot and those missionaries died preaching the gospel to those who put him to death. The Auca Whoudani Indians who killed him, said at the death of the five missionaries, the curtains were thrown back and they saw a host of angels and heard singing. God's protection did not mean that he was immortal. It meant he was immortal until God was finished with him. Don't fear the enemy! Fear the Lord and rest in his victory in this spiritual war. We are on the winning side!

You may obtain this and many other fine resources made available by Proclaim Publishers by contacting us:

Web:
proclaimpublishers.com

Email:
contact@proclaimpublishers.com

Postal Mail:
Proclaim Publishers
PO Box 2082
Wenatchee, WA 98807

SOLI DEO GLORIA

www.ingramcontent.com/pod-product-compliance
Lightning Source LLC
Chambersburg PA
CBHW031428160426
43195CB00010BB/655